DOCUMENTS OF THE BAPTISMAL LITURGY

TEF Study Guides

This series was first sponsored and subsidized by the Theological Education Fund in response to requests from Africa, Asia, the Caribbean, and the Pacific. The books are prepared by and in consultation with theological teachers in those areas. Special attention is given to problems of interpretation and application arising there as well as in the west, and to the particular needs of students using English as a second language.

General Editor: Daphne Terry

ALREADY PUBLISHED

1. A Guide to the Parables
2. A Guide to St Mark's Gospel
3. A Guide to the Book of Genesis
4. A Guide to the Book of Amos
5. Church History 1: The First Advance
6. A Guide to Psalms
7. Old Testament Introduction 1: History of Israel
8. Church History 2: Setback and Recovery
9. Applied Theology 1: 'Go . . . and make disciples'
10. Old Testament Introduction 2: The Books of the Old Testament
11. A Guide to Romans
12. A Guide to Religions
13. A Guide to Exodus
14. Church History 3: New Movements
15. Old Testament Introduction 3: Theology of the Old Testament
17. A Guide to 1 Corinthians

IN PREPARATION

A Guide to Isaiah 1–39
A Guide to Isaiah 40–66
Church History 4: The Church Worldwide
Applied Theology 2: 'Feed my Sheep'
Applied Theology 3: 'Be good at managing'
A Guide to Revelation

DOCUMENTS
OF THE
BAPTISMAL LITURGY

E. C. WHITAKER

Vicar of Plumpton, Penrith
Honorary Canon of Carlisle

LONDON

SPCK

First published in 1960
Second edition revised and supplemented 1970
First published in paperback in 1977
SPCK
Holy Trinity Church
Marylebone Road,
London NW1 4DU
Reprinted 1979

© E.C. Whitaker, 1960, 1970

Originally published as Alcuin Club Collections No. 42

Made and printed in Great Britain by
Hollen Street Press Ltd., Slough, Berks

ISBN 0 281 02983 0

Contents

Foreword

The opportunity of preparing a second edition of this book has enabled me to improve the original in a number of ways. The omission of Cyprian was a serious mistake which I can now make good. It has been possible to enlarge some other sections of the book, notably those on Tertullian and St John Chrysostom, and to make slight improvements to the introductions to some of the documents. The addition of the Sarum rite should help to make the volume more useful to students. An attempt to improve the pedestrian quality of much of my translation would have been too large a task, but a number of the more serious errors of translation in the first edition have been corrected in this, and I can only hope that none are left.

I am grateful to Canon J. D. C. Fisher for the opportunity to make use of his translation of the Sarum rite. This has been reproduced as it stands in his book *Christian Initiation: Baptism in the Medieval West*. Finally, I am glad of this occasion to set on record my gratitude to Canon Bernard Wigan for much help and advice in this and other matters over the many years since we were students together.

E. C. WHITAKER

Acknowledgements

Translations have been borrowed from the following sources with the kind permission of their publishers.

PUBLISHED BY S.P.C.K.
The Apostolic Tradition of Hippolytus, ed. Dom. Gregory Dix.
The Lectures of St Cyril of Jerusalem, ed. F. L. Cross.
The Pilgrimage of Etheria, ed. M. L. McClure and C. L. Feltoe.
Bishop Sarapion's Prayer Book, ed. J. Wordsworth.
Coptic Offices, ed. R. M. Woolley.
St Ambrose on the Sacraments and on the Mysteries, ed. J. H. Srawley.
Tertullian's Homily on Baptism, ed. E. Evans.
Christian Initiation: Baptism in the Medieval West, by J. D. C. Fisher.

PUBLISHED BY THE CLARENDON PRESS, OXFORD
Didascalia Apostolorum, ed. R. H. Connolly.
Rituale Armenorum, ed. F. C. Conybeare and A. J. Maclean.
The Apocryphal New Testament, ed. M. R. James.

PUBLISHED BY THE CAMBRIDGE UNIVERSITY PRESS
The Liturgical Homilies of Narsai, ed. R. H. Connolly.

PUBLISHED BY W. HEFFER AND SON, LTD, CAMBRIDGE
Woodbrooke Studies, by A. Mingana.

PUBLISHED BY PARKER AND SON, OXFORD
The Works of Dionysius the Areopagite, trans. J. Parker.

PUBLISHED BY LONGMANS, GREEN AND CO. LTD
St John Chrysostom: Baptismal Instructions, ed. P. W. Harkins.

Cross-References

Liturgical formularies which are common to certain Latin documents. are noted by a system of marginal cross-references, to which the key is as follows:

LO The *Liber Ordinum.*
A The Ambrosian Manual.
G The Gelasian Sacramentary.
B The Bobbio Missal.
S The Stowe Missal.
O The *Ordo Romanus XI.*
Goth The *Missale Gothicum.*

Introductory Essay

THE SACRAMENT OF CHRISTIAN INITIATION

Tertullian first in his *Treatise concerning Baptism*, and then Hippolytus in *The Apostolic Tradition*, provide the two earliest full accounts which we possess of Christian initiation. Since *The Apostolic Tradition* is a quasi-liturgical document, it is no matter for surprise if the information which it supplies is fuller and more detailed than what we gain from Tertullian's treatise; even so the two documents reveal a rather different procedure in the ordering of the sacrament. According to each of them the renunciation of Satan is a preliminary, but in Tertullian's account it is performed in the water, whereas it took place *before* entering the water in that of Hippolytus. When the candidate entered the water, he was questioned in the triple interrogation on the faith out of which the Apostles' Creed was later to grow, and to each question he answered: I believe. After each response the deacon laid his hand on the candidate's head and baptized him in the water. We note that no form of words is provided other than the credal interrogation and its responses. This was to be the way in the Western Church for some years. The formula which is familiar to us today was only introduced into the West from the Syrian Church gradually over the centuries.[1] Until then the interrogation and its responses may properly be described as the baptismal formula of the Western Church, and by its close integration with the baptismal washing it was made clear that his faith is the most important characteristic of the Christian, and that his faith assumes concrete form in baptism.

[1] See *The Journal of Ecclesiastical History*, vol. XVI (1965) pp. 1-12, article, E. C. Whitaker, "The History of the Baptismal Formula"; also *The Church Quarterly Review* (1960), article, E. C. Whitaker, "The Baptismal Formula in the Syrian Rite", pp. 346-52.

It is necessary now to take careful note of what happened when the candidates came up from the baptismal water.

1. While still wet and unclothed they were anointed "with holy oil in the Name of Jesus Christ".
2. Once dried and dressed they were ready to appear before the bishop and the congregation of the faithful.
3. The bishop laid his hand on them and said a prayer. We may infer both from the length of this prayer and its contents that this laying on of the hand was not performed on each candidate separately but over all of them together with the hand extended over them as the prayer was said.
4. Each candidate then appeared individually before the bishop, who poured oil on his head or forehead (Hippolytus is not specific), laid his hand in the oil, and said: I anoint thee with holy oil in God the Father Almighty and Christ Jesus and the Holy Ghost.
5. The bishop sealed each candidate individually, that is to say he made the sign of the cross on his forehead, most probably in the oil.

Tertullian's account of the matter is not so precise and perhaps not quite the same. We may gather from his description that the candidate's whole body was anointed when he rose from the water, he then dressed and appeared before the bishop who laid his hands upon his head in the form of a cross, either in oil specially poured out or in what remained from the previous anointing.

In each of these accounts we may discern three separate actions following the baptismal washing: they are the imposition of the hand, the anointing, and the sign of the cross. J. Ysebaert has persuasively argued[1] that these should not be regarded as three distinct rites but as one "complicated liturgical act". He points to the high probability that the baptismal bath was normally and naturally followed by an anointing of the body. Dr L. L. Mitchell has set out some of the evidence from which we learn that oil was commonly associated with the bath in the pagan and secular world of ancient times, just as naturally as soap is today.[2] There is evidence in the Bible that it was not different in the Jewish world.[3] Ysebaert shows also that from New Testament

---

[1] J. Ysebaert, *Greek Baptismal Terminology* (Nijmegen 1962), pp. 264, 289f.
[2] L. L. Mitchell, *Baptismal Anointing* (London 1966), pp. 25f.
[3] Ruth 3.3; Exod. 40.12f; Judith 10.3; Susannah v.17; Luke 7.38; Matt. 6.17.

times a formal anointing was frequently associated with an imposition of hands and *vice versa*. It would not therefore be surprising if from the beginning Christian baptism was accompanied by an anointing with which an imposition of the hand might readily be associated; and we should expect to find that the sign of the cross soon made its way into the complex in one way or another. The effect of Ysebaert's argument is thus to show that if there is a difference in detail between the practice described by Tertullian and that advocated by Hippolytus; if some later documents appear to connect the gift of the Spirit with the imposition of the hand, and others with the anointing; if some areas have retained only one post-baptismal anointing although others have two; then the differences arise from differences in the way in which one basic and complex act has developed and disintegrated in response to circumstances.

The Church in the East developed its institutions in a milieu quite different from the Hellenized West, and this fact applies in full measure to the rites of Christian initiation. Although historians are accustomed to write of east Syrian and west Syrian rites, the basic rite of initiation which underlies both is attested by the documents of the Syrian rite, some of them ante-Nicene, which are set out below. We have had occasion already to refer to one notable difference between East and West as it concerns the baptismal formula. The formula which is universally used throughout the Church today, and which seems to be attested in St Matthew's Gospel (28. 19), was used from the first in Syria in a variety of similar forms, and only by degrees replaced the interrogation on the faith which, as we have seen, provided the Western Church with its baptismal formula in the earlier centuries. This difference is not unimportant in itself and accounts for some of the differences in the way in which the Eastern and Western rites developed. More important still is the absence in the Syrian rite of any post-baptismal anointing. Basically the rite consisted of an anointing, the baptismal washing, and the celebration of the Eucharist. The evidence of all the early documents of the Syrian rite is that nothing intervened between the baptismal washing and the celebration of the Eucharist. It is not certain that a post-baptismal anointing or imposition of the hand is attested by Theodore of Mopsuestia[1] (p.50). And when a post-baptismal anointing does appear in the Syrian documents, as in

---

[1] See L. L. Mitchell, op.cit., p.41; also article, Dom B. Botte, "Le Baptême dans l'Eglise Syrienne", p. 144 [*L'Orient Syrien*, vol. 1 (1956)].

the *Catecheses* of St Cyril of Jerusalem (p.30) or *The Apostolic Constitutions* (pp.32, 34), there are good reasons to suppose that it is a novel importation from the West.[1] The question then arises: Did the Syrian Church observe only one sign, of water, in Christian initiation, while the Western Church had the two signs of water and oil? Did the Syrian Church believe that the gift of the Spirit together with all the other effects of initiation into the Church was conveyed in the solitary act of the baptismal washing? Or, to put the matter crudely, what has become of confirmation in the Syrian rite? Many answers have been returned to these questions.

1. T. Thompson first stated the opinion that the pre-baptismal anointing of the Syrian rite "is really the unction of confirmation".[2] His principal argument is that this is "clear from the language of the homilies of Narsai". In fact, however, if the reader will turn to the homilies he may find this far from clear. The homilies of Narsai are written in rhapsodic language which does not always allow precise interpretation, but they seem to point more readily to the possibility that the gift of the Holy Spirit was conveyed in and by the water of baptism; and Narsai's account of the anointing before baptism suggests that its purpose was healing and the expulsion of the devil—in a word, it was an exorcism.[3]

More recently E. C. Ratcliff has adduced different evidence[4] to reach the same conclusion as Thompson. The *Acts of Judas Thomas* include a number of *epicleses* for the blessing of the oil, and Ratcliff quotes one sentence from them as evidence that the oil was to convey the gift of the Spirit. The sentence runs: "Come, holy Name of the Messiah . . . come, messenger of reconciliation: and communicate with the minds of these youths; come, Spirit of holiness, and purify their reins and their hearts" (p.14). Against this it might well be argued that if the purpose of the Spirit's coming was purification, this is by no means what we understand by confirmation. And if we examine the

---

[1] L. L. Mitchell, op.cit., p. 45; E. C. Ratcliff, article, "The Old Syrian Baptismal Tradition", p. 32 (*Studies in Church History*, ed. G. J. Cuming, vol. II).

[2] T. Thompson, *The Offices of Baptism and Confirmation* (Cambridge 1914), p. 31.

[3] For a discussion of Thompson's arguments see Fr H. B. Green C.R., article, "The Significance of the Pre-Baptismal Seal in St John Chrysostom [*Studia Patristica*, vol. VI (1962), pp. 84-90]; also E. C. Whitaker, article, "Unction in the Syrian Baptismal Rite" [*Church Quarterly Review* (1961), pp. 176-87].

[4] Op.cit., *passim*.

epicleses as a whole we may think that they regard the oil in the same way as Narsai did. Its purpose seems to be healing and the expulsion of the devil. In fact these *epicleses* led F. J. Dölger to the conclusion that the pre-baptismal anointing of the Syrian rite was an exorcism.[1]

A second document cited by Ratcliff is c.16 of the *Didascalia* (p.13), of which he says: "The Didascaliast compares the pre-baptismal anointing with that of the priests and kings in Israel, expecting his readers to recall those passages of the Old Testament in which the spiritual effect of the anointing is described." In these words Ratcliff associates the anointing before baptism with the gift of the Holy Spirit. But it is not necessary to suppose that the comparison which the Didascaliast makes between the unction of the Church in baptism and the unction of the old Israel is necessarily on the level of their inward meaning and effect. It may equally well be on the external level and relate simply to the outward and visible aspects of the rite. To say that the Church's anointing is like the anointing of the Old Testament is not necessarily to say that the spiritual effect of each anointing is the same. An instructive parallel to this passage in the *Didascalia* is to be found in an Egyptian source known as *The Statutes of the Apostles*.[2] It contains a prayer which runs as follows:

God, my Lord Almighty, the Father of our Lord and Saviour Jesus Christ, stretch out thine hand invisible upon the fruit of this olive with which thou anointedst the Priests and Prophets; and thou hast given power to it with thine own hand, that for those who shall be anointed therewith it may be for healing and safety and benefit in all diseases and sicknesses, and for extermination of every Satanic adversary; make an unction by thine own grace, really for them for whom it is given, the Holy Spirit, through the name and through the power of our Lord Jesus Christ.

The oil to which this prayer refers is plainly for exorcism; but it is nevertheless described as the oil with which priests and prophets were anointed. In the light of this prayer it seems impossible to assume that because the *Didascalia* compares the anointing before baptism with the anointing of priests and kings, the anointing before baptism was understood as a vehicle for the gift of the Holy Spirit.

Ratcliff's thesis is further weakened by his failure to take any serious

---

[1] F. J. Dölger, *Der Exorcismus in altchristlichen Taufritual* (Paderborn 1909), pp. 10, 12; see also pp. 137f.

[2] G. W. Horner, *The Statutes of the Apostles* (London 1904), p. 163.

note of a number of sources of evidence. Thus the *Didache* provides for baptism in water and says nothing about any other rite in initiation. If we take this fact at its face value, it appears to imply that initiation is complete in the water, and that the gift of the Holy Spirit is conveyed in water baptism. The *Didache* therefore calls for explanation, but Ratcliff is silent. Similarly the *Instructions* of St John Chrysostom seem to make clear what is hinted by Narsai and in the *Acts of Judas Thomas*. Chrysostom's account of the pre-baptismal anointing affords no room at all for the view that it conveyed the Holy Spirit; but it evidently has much in common with exorcism (p.40). Chrysostom says very clearly that the Holy Spirit is conveyed to the candidate as he stands in the water (p.40). But Ratcliff does not discuss this evidence. There is another important and damaging passage in the *Apostolic Constitutions* which Ratcliff has ignored; we shall return to it later.

2. Another attempt to find confirmation in the Syrian rite is based on the *Instructions* of St John Chrysostom. In the course of these addresses Chrysostom speaks of the moment when the candidate is standing in the water and says: "It is at this moment that through the words and hands of the priest the Holy Spirit descends on you" (p.40). This sentence appears to identify the gift of the Holy Spirit specifically with the imposition of hands in baptism, and from this it has been inferred by Ysebaert[1] and J. Lecuyer[2] that the two sacraments of baptism and confirmation were combined in one act. By this means they seek to escape from the unwelcome conclusion that the gift of the Holy Spirit is conveyed in the sacrament of baptism in water. But in fact Chrysostom is not as specific as the one sentence which we have quoted above may suggest. There are other passages in the *Instructions* which are relevant to the matter. They are set out in the text below and have been well summarized by T. M. Finn in the following words:

> The Holy Spirit is, so to speak, omnipresent in the baptismal action: with His presence and action He sanctifies the water, the bishop, the bishop's hand, the words, and the candidate himself, transforming him into a new creature. The imposition of the hand is the sign *par excellence* which testifies to the presence, action, and

[1] Op.cit. pp. 376-9.
[2] J. Lecuyer, article, "San Juan Crisostomo y la Confirmacion" [*Orbis Catholicus*, (Barcelona 1958), pp. 385-7].

gift of the Holy Spirit in the whole of the baptismal action.[1]

It is true that the Syrian Church paid particular attention to the imposition of the hand at the moment of baptism, and we find frequent references to it (pp.22, 49). In the context of baptism by submersion it was almost a practical necessity, and is thus attested in the Western *Apostolic Tradition* (p.5); in the Syrian rite it continued to have a specific mention in the later liturgical books, even when the candidates were infants and baptized in a font. But, since the imposition of the hand in baptism in the Syrian rite was a part of the total action of baptism and inseparable from it, it does not seem very meaningful to identify it specifically with confirmation. It provides no escape from the conclusion that according to Chrysostom the gift of the Holy Spirit in Christian initiation is conveyed in baptism rather than at any other moment or in any other way.

3. In his approach to the earlier documents of the Syrian rite, Ysebaert appears to start from the assumption that anointing followed baptism in New Testament times and that this practice was followed universally. He does not entertain the possibility that custom may have varied, or that the post-baptismal anointing did not arise or continue so naturally or so surely in some parts of the world as it did in others. Accordingly he assumes that, if the Syrian rite as we find it in the surviving early documents has no post-baptismal anointing, this can only be because it has disappeared. The only evidence he finds to support this theory is his interpretation[2] of c.16 of the *Didascalia*. According to the common assumption, this passage implies the same rite as is attested by most other Syrian works of the period, in which the pre-baptismal anointing is started by the bishop with the imposition of the hand and completed in the case of female candidates by a deaconess who anointed the whole body; baptism follows and completes the rite. Ysebaert's interpretation requires that we pay particular attention to the first phrase in the extract below (p.12), "In the first place (*Primo*)" and regard the word "afterwards (*postea*) "which comes later in the passage as its correlative. *Primo* means before baptism, *postea* means after baptism, and thus the whole passage may be read in

---

[1] T. M. Finn, c.s.p., *The Liturgy of Baptism in thē Baptismal Instructions of St John Chrysostom* (Washington, D.C. 1967), p. 180.

[2] Op.cit., pp. 312, 360f.

such a way that it is seen to preserve the traces of a stage when there were two anointings in the rite, one before and the other after baptism. The words "as we have already said (*sicut praediximus*)" mean that the same holds good for the second anointing as for the first. Modesty was the determining factor in the development by which the second anointing disappeared. In the case of female candidates modesty required that both of these anointings should be conducted under cover of the water. Two anointings performed under these circumstances would easily become fused into one, with the consequence that the Syrian rite lost the tradition of a post-baptismal anointing.

It is unfortunate that we do not possess the original Greek text of the *Didascalia*, and that most people must approach the existing Syriac translation through the medium either of Funk's Latin or Connolly's English translation from the Syriac. Nevertheless, we may say that as an interpretation of the texts available Ysebaert's argument seems very strained. And it suffers from a number of other defects. If the water was to serve the purpose of modesty, it must have had some appreciable depth; the anointing had to be a thorough one, as is clear from many sources, and we may find it hard to imagine how a thorough anointing could be conducted under such circumstances. Again, it seems unreasonable to assume that the baptism of women should be determinative in so important a matter, and that an ancient tradition of a post-baptismal anointing should be lost to the male on account of the female candidates. In any case, even if a thorough post-baptismal anointing was not found practicable, and if the matter was really supposed to have any importance, as, for instance, to convey the gift of the Spirit, there could have been no difficulty in preserving at least an anointing of the forehead after baptism.

4. One other solution has been proposed for the problem with which the Syrian rite presents us, and that is that the pre-baptismal unction was an exorcism and that the rite had no confirmation. The principal evidence to support this conclusion has already been briefly indicated in the previous paragraphs, and the matter is well summed up by Fr Green in the words: "The accurate description of Antiochene practice (and by implication that of the Syrian tradition in general) is not that it has a rite of confirmation in an unusual place, but that it lacked it altogether."[1] We have taken note of some desperate expedients

[1] Op.cit., p. 90.

which have been adopted to avoid this conclusion, and we have seen that they are not very convincing. It remains to examine one passage from the *Apostolic Constitutions* which is worth quoting in full.

But thou shalt first anoint the person with holy oil, and afterward baptize him with water, and finally shalt seal him with the chrism; that the anointing with oil may be a participation of the Holy Spirit, and the water a symbol of the death, and the chrism a seal of the covenants. But if there be neither oil nor chrism, the water is sufficient both for the anointing, and for the seal, and for the confession of him that is dead (pp.31-2).

Commenting on this passage, which he does not quote, Ratcliff says: "The Constitutor has made it abundantly clear, in his comments upon his editing of *Didascalia* XVI and *Didache* VII, that he holds the Holy Spirit to be given in the pre-baptismal oil."[1] But this is a very limited interpretation of the passage and quite ignores its second part. In this the Constitutor makes it abundantly clear that there is no cause for concern if oil and chrism are not available, for then the water is sufficient for all purposes; so long as the baptism in water is performed, the whole effect and benefit of Christian initiation will be conveyed to the candidate, and this must include the gift of the Holy Spirit.

We may observe that the teaching of this passage in the *Apostolic Constitutions* seems to be implicit in our original premiss, that the origin of confirmation is to be found in the oil which accompanied the baptismal bath. If the various meanings and implications of Christian baptism were distributed as seemed appropriate between the water and the oil and any other associated ceremonies, it is not surprising if the gift of the Holy Spirit was early associated with the oil in some quarters. The association lay ready to hand in the Old Testament. But equally it is not surprising if in other quarters the identification of the oil with the Spirit was not made, or only sometimes made, or as in the *Apostolic Constitutions* was not regarded as important. "The water is sufficient" because it is primary, and the full meaning of initiation was thus seen to reside in it: the oil was an adventitious and optional addition. The practice of assigning one part of the total meaning of Christian initiation to one part of the rite and another strand in the meaning to another part of the rite was reasonable and acceptable, so long as the original complex of rites retained its integrity and coherence. But what if some parts of the complex should lapse? To this question

[1] Op.cit., p. 35.

the Syrian Church had a clear answer: "The water is sufficient."

There is no evidence to prove the theory that confirmation originated in a development within the early Church by which the oil at the baptismal bath came to share the sacramental associations of the water, any more than there is evidence to prove the theory that confirmation originated in the institution of our Lord. It is precisely because of the lack of any clear evidence on the point that we may think the former explanation the more probable, since it arises naturally from the circumstances of baptism. It has this further advantage, that it explains the variety of sign and form which characterized the post-baptismal ceremonies of the Church. This is what we should expect in a rite which has developed from such informal origins as we suggest. We deal, however, not with speculation and theory but with fact and evidence when we conclude that the Syrian Church in the early centuries did not have any rite separate and distinguishable from baptism such as we might call confirmation. It is certainly true to say that over the course of the centuries the Eastern Church added to its baptismal rite a second sign, a post-baptismal anointing which theologians have been content to regard as confirmation, and which has enabled some writers to turn a blind eye to the awkward and inconvenient facts of the earlier rite. Nevertheless, in view of the evidence which we have briefly summarized and the documents which are set out in this book, there seems no reason to doubt that by a tradition no less real and apostolic than that which we have received in the West the early Syrian Church had no second sign, no rite of confirmation, in their forms of Christian initiation: for them the water was sufficient.

1. *The Ante-Nicene Church*

THE DIDACHE

Text: Prof. Lietzmann, in *Kleine Texte*, Vol. 5, Bonn, 1923.

The date of this work and its place of origin have been the subject of controversy in the past, and in spite of its primitive appearance it has been argued that it may be as late as the fourth century. Today there is a growing consensus of opinion that it comes to us from Syria and that its date is *c*.100, and possibly earlier. For a summary of the discussion, see F. L. Cross, *The Early Christian Fathers*, 1960.

7. And as touching baptism, thus baptize ye: when ye have first recited all these things [i.e. the precepts regarding the ways of life and death, in the previous chapters], baptize in the Name of the Father and of the Son and of the Holy Spirit, in running water. But if thou hast not running water, baptize in other water; and if thou canst not in cold, then in warm. And if thou hast not either, pour forth water thrice upon the head, in the Name of the Father and Son and Holy Spirit. And before baptism, let the baptizer and him that is to be baptized and such others as are able first fast; but thou shalt bid him that is to be baptized fast one or two [days?] before.

9. But let no one eat or drink of your eucharist but such as have been baptized in the name of the Lord.

THE FIRST APOLOGY OF JUSTIN MARTYR

Text: Prof. Lietzmann, in *Kleine Texte*, Vol. 5, Bonn, 1923.

This defence of the Christian faith was made by St Justin in Rome in about A.D. 160, and is addressed to the Emperor Antoninus Pius. It includes the following accounts of baptism. They are tantalizingly vague, but more exact accounts were not necessary to Justin's purpose. This may explain why they include no mention of confirmation. See E. C. Ratcliff, "Justin Martyr and Confirmation", in *Theology*, April 1948.

61. I shall now lay before you the manner in which we dedicated ourselves to God when we were made new through Christ: for should I omit this, I might seem to err in this account. As many as are persuaded and believe that these things which we teach and describe are true, and undertake to live accordingly, are taught to pray and ask God, while fasting, for the forgiveness of their sins: and we pray and fast with them. Then they are led by us to a place where there is water, and they are reborn after the manner of rebirth by which we also were reborn: for they are then washed [or, wash themselves] in the water in the Name of the Father and Lord God of all things, and of our Saviour Jesus Christ, and of the Holy Spirit . . .

. . . over him that now chooses to be reborn and repents of his sins is named the Father and Lord God of all things. This Name only is called upon by him that leads to the washing him that is to be washed: for no one can speak the Name of God, who is ineffable: and anyone who might boldly claim to do so is quite mad. This washing is called enlightenment, because those that are experiencing these things have their minds enlightened. And he that is being enlightened is washed [or, washes himself] in the Name of Jesus Christ who was crucified under Pontius Pilate, and in the Name of the Holy Spirit, which through the prophets foretold all things concerning Jesus.

65. After we have thus washed him that is persuaded and declares his assent, we lead him to those who are called brethren, where they are assembled, and make common prayer fervently for ourselves, for him that has been enlightened, and for all men everywhere, that, embracing the truth, we may be found in our lives good and obedient citizens, and also attain to everlasting salvation.

[An account of the Eucharist follows.]

THE APOSTOLIC TRADITION OF HIPPOLYTUS

The *Apostolic Tradition* was written in Greek by Hippolytus in Rome, c.A.D. 215 No text of the original survives. However, it is widely believed that this is the work which underlies a number of documents from Syria and Egypt, notably *The Egyptian Church Order* in several dialects of Egypt, *The Canons of Hippolytus*, *The Testament of our Lord*, and passages in the *Apostolic Constitutions*. All these works clearly rest upon a common original, and attempts to discern the original from these later recensions have been made by Dom B. Botte, in *La Tradition Apostolique* (Westphalen, 1963), and by Dom Gregory Dix, in

The Treatise on the Apostolic Tradition (S.P.C.K., 1968), from which the following text has been taken.

It has been commonly assumed that the *Apostolic Tradition* reflects the Roman liturgical tradition, possibly varied by the imagination or the prejudices of Hippolytus himself. However, the possibility cannot now be excluded that if any liturgical tradition is reflected in the work it is not necessarily that of Rome. See J. M. Hanssens, *La Liturgie d'Hippolyte* (Rome, 1959). But see also Professor Henry Chadwick's introduction to the second edition of Dom Gregory's edition of the *Apostolic Tradition* (S.P.C.K., 1968).

It should be noted that Dom Gregory placed great reliance on a fragmentary fifth-century Latin translation of the *Apostolic Tradition*, which may not reflect the practice of the second or third century as accurately as he supposed. This affects c.XXI, 14 onwards to the end of our extract.

XVI

1. Those who come forward for the first time to hear the word shall first be brought to the teachers at the house before all the people [of God] come in.

2. And let them be examined as to the reason why they have come forward to the faith. And those who bring them shall bear witness for them whether they are able to hear.

3. Let their life and manner of living be enquired into, whether he is a slave or free.

[Sections 4–24 consist of regulations determining the conditions under which men or women might be admitted to instruction, according to the manner of their past lives and their readiness to forsake evil ways and forbidden occupations.]

XVII

1. Let a catechumen be instructed for three years.

2. But if a man be earnest and persevere well in the matter, let him be received, because it is not the time that is judged, but the conduct.

Whole thing is to do with discerning H.S.

XVIII

1. Each time the teacher finishes his instruction let the catechumens pray by themselves apart from the faithful.

3. But after the prayer is finished the catechumens shall not give the kiss of peace, for their kiss is not yet pure.   *ie not a Christ kiss*

XIX

1. After the prayer let the teacher lay hands upon them and pray and dismiss them. Whether the teacher be an ecclesiastic or a layman let him do the same.

B

2. If anyone being a catechumen should be apprehended for the Name, let him not be anxious about undergoing martyrdom. For if he suffer violence and be put to death before baptism, he shall be justified having been baptized in his own blood.

Final stage of catecumenate.

XX

1. And when they are chosen who are set apart to receive baptism let their life be examined, whether they lived piously while catechumens, whether they "honoured the widows", whether they visited the sick, whether they have fulfilled every good work.

2. If those who bring them bear witness to them that they have done thus, then let them hear the gospel. *ie sponsors (god parents)*

3. Moreover, from the day they are chosen, let a hand be laid on them and let them be exorcized daily. And when the day draws near on which they are to be baptized, let the bishop himself exorcize each one of them, that he may be certain that he is purified. *Easter Day*

4. But if there is one who is not purified let him be put on one side because he did not hear the word of instruction with faith. For the strange spirit remained with him.

5. And let those who are to be baptized be instructed to wash and cleanse themselves on the fifth day of the week [i.e., Thursday]. *Maunday*

6. And if any woman be menstruous she shall be put aside and baptized another day. *Per Leviticus.*

7. Those who are to receive baptism shall fast on the Preparation [Friday] and on the Sabbath [Saturday]. And on the Sabbath the bishop shall assemble those who are to be baptized in one place, and shall bid them all to pray and bow the knee.

8. And laying his hand on them he shall exorcise every evil spirit to flee away from them and never to return to them henceforward. And when he has finished exorcizing, let him breathe on their faces and seal their foreheads and ears and noses and then let him raise them up. *prev*

9. And they shall spend all the night in vigil, reading the scriptures to them and instructing them.

10. Moreover those who are to be baptized shall not bring any other vessel, save that which each will bring with him for the eucharist. For it is right for every one to bring his oblation then.

XXI

1. And at the hour when the cock crows they shall first [of all] pray over the water.

2. When they come to the water, let the water be pure and flowing.

3. And they shall put off their clothes.

4. And they shall baptize the little children first. And if they can answer for themselves, let them answer. But if they cannot, let their parents answer or someone from their family.

5. And next they shall baptize the grown men; and last the women, who shall have loosed their hair and laid aside their gold ornaments. Let no one go down to the water having any alien object with them.

6. And at the time determined for baptizing, the bishop shall give thanks over the oil and put it into a vessel and it is called the Oil of Thanksgiving.

7. And he shall take other oil and exorcise over it, and it is called the Oil of Exorcism.

8. And let a deacon carry the Oil of Exorcism and stand on the left hand. And another deacon shall take the Oil of Thanksgiving and stand on the right hand.

9. And when the presbyter takes hold of each one of those who are to be baptized, let him bid him renounce saying:

I renounce thee, Satan, and all thy service and all thy works.

10. And when he has said this let him anoint with the Oil of Exorcism, saying:

Let all evil spirits depart far from thee.

11. Then after these things let him give over to the presbyter who stands at the water. And let them stand in the water naked. And let a deacon likewise go down with him into the water.

12. And when he goes down to the water, let him who baptizes lay hand on him saying thus:

Dost thou believe in God the Father Almighty?

13. And he who is being baptized shall say:
I believe.

14. Let him forthwith baptize [baptizet: *probably*, let him dip. *So also 16 and 18*] him once, having his hand laid upon his head.

15. And after [this] let him say:

Dost thou believe in Christ Jesus, the Son of God,
Who was born of Holy Spirit and the Virgin Mary,
Who was crucified in the days of Pontius Pilate,
And died,
And rose the third day living from the dead

And ascended into the heavens,
And sat down at the right hand of the Father,
And will come to judge the living and the dead?

16. And when he says: I believe, let him baptize him the second time.

17. And again let him say:

Dost thou believe in the Holy Spirit in the Holy Church,
And the resurrection of the flesh?

18. And he who is being baptized shall say: I believe. And so let him baptize him the third time.

19. And afterwards when he comes up he shall be anointed with the Oil of Thanksgiving saying:

I anoint thee with holy oil in the Name of Jesus Christ.

20. And so each one drying himself they shall now put on their clothes, and after this let them be together in the assembly.

tunica alba (now worn by clergy)

XXII

1. And the bishop shall lay his hand upon them invoking and saying:

O Lord God, who didst count these worthy of deserving the forgiveness of sins by the laver of regeneration, make them worthy to be filled with thy Holy Spirit and send upon them thy grace, that they may serve thee according to thy will; to thee is the glory, to the Father and to the Son with the Holy Ghost in the holy Church, both now and ever and world without end. Amen.

2. After this pouring the consecrated oil and laying his hand on his head, he shall say:

I anoint thee with holy oil in God the Father Almighty and Christ Jesus and the Holy Ghost.

3. And sealing him on the forehead, he shall give him the kiss of peace and say: *with sign of the +*

The Lord be with you.

And he who has been sealed shall say:

And with thy spirit.

4. And so shall he do to each one severally.

5. Thenceforward they shall pray together with all the people. But they shall not previously pray with the faithful before they have undergone all these things.

6. And after the prayers, let them give the kiss of peace.

XXIII

[This section describes the Eucharist which followed baptism. A mixture of milk and honey, and a chalice of water were offered, as well as the bread and wine. The Bread was administered first, followed by the water, the milk and honey, and the Eucharistic Cup, in that order. It has been suggested that the compound of milk and honey referred to here and elsewhere is a last trace of the meal in which the Eucharist originated and from which it was soon detached.]

TERTULLIAN

Tertullian was a member of the Church in North Africa. Converted to the faith in about 195, he defected to the Montanist sect in about 213. Of the works which are here quoted, *De Corona* and *Adversus Praxean* belong to the Montanist, the others to the Catholic period of his life.

With the exception of a passage from *De Spectaculis*, which is translated from *C.S.E.L.*, Vol. 20, the translations below are those of Dr Ernest Evans in *Tertullian's Homily on Baptism* (S.P.C.K., 1964). This edition of *De Baptismo* includes the Latin text and translation, valuable notes on the text and contents, and a useful essay on the baptism service as Tertullian knew it.

1. DE BAPTISMO, c. 2

Because with such complete simplicity, without display, without any unusual equipment, and (not least) without anything to pay, a man is sent down into the water, is washed to the accompaniment of very few words, and comes up little or no cleaner than he was, his attainment to eternity is regarded as beyond belief.

2. DE BAPTISMO, c. 4

Therefore, in consequence of that ancient original privilege, all waters, when God is invoked, acquire the sacred significance of conveying sanctity: for at once the Spirit comes down from heaven and stays upon the waters, sanctifying them from within himself, and when thus sanctified they absorb the power of sanctifying . . . Thus when the waters have in some sense acquired healing power by an angel's intervention, the spirit is in those waters corporally washed, while the flesh is in those same waters spiritually cleansed.

3. De Baptismo, c. 7

After that we come up from the washing and are anointed with the blessed unction, following that ancient practice by which, ever since Aaron was anointed by Moses, there was a custom of anointing them for priesthood with oil out of a horn. That is why [the high priest] is called a christ, from "chrism" which is [the Greek for] "anointing": and from this also our Lord obtained his title, though it had become a spiritual anointing, in that he was anointed with the Spirit by God the Father.

4. De Baptismo, c. 8

Next follows the imposition of the hand in benediction, inviting and welcoming the Holy Spirit . . . But this too is involved in that ancient sacred act in which Jacob blessed his grandsons, Joseph's sons, Ephraim and Manasseh, by placing his hands interchanged upon their heads, turned transversely upon themselves in such a manner as to make the shape of Christ, and at that early date to prefigure the blessing that was to be in Christ.

5. De Baptismo, c. 13

For there has been imposed a law of baptizing, and its form prescribed: *Go*, he says, *teach the nations, baptising them in the Name of the Father and the Son and the Holy Ghost* [Matt. 28.19].

6. De Baptismo, c. 17

It remains for me to advise you of the rules to be observed in giving and receiving baptism. The supreme right of giving it belongs to the high priest, which is the bishop: after him, to the presbyters and deacons, yet not without commission from the bishop, on account of the Church's dignity: for when this is safe, peace is safe. Except for that, even laymen have the right.

7. De Baptismo, c. 18

It follows that deferment of baptism is more profitable, in accordance with each person's character and attitude, and even age: and especially so as regards children. For what need is there, if there really is no need, for even their sponsors to be brought into peril, seeing they may possibly themselves fail of their promises by death, or be deceived by the subsequent development of an evil disposition? It is true our Lord says, *Forbid them not to come to me* [Matt. 19.14]. So let them come when they are growing up, when they are learning, when they are being taught what they are coming to: let them be made Christians when they have become competent to know Christ. Why should innocent infancy come with haste to the remission of sins? Shall we take less cautious action in this than we take in worldly matters? Shall one who is not trusted with earthly property be entrusted with heavenly? Let them first learn how to ask for salvation, so that you may be seen to have given to one that asketh. With no less reason ought the unmarried also to be delayed until they either marry or are firmly established in continence.

8. DE BAPTISMO, c. 19

The Passover provides the day of most solemnity for baptism, for then was accomplished our Lord's passion, and into it we are baptized ... After that, Pentecost is a most auspicious period for arranging baptisms, for during it our Lord's resurrection was several times made known among the disciples, and the grace of the Holy Spirit first given ... For all that, every day is a Lord's day: any hour, any season, is suitable for baptism. If there is a difference of solemnity, it makes no difference to the grace.

9. DE BAPTISMO, c. 20

Those who are at the point of entering upon baptism ought to pray, with frequent prayers, fastings, bendings of the knee, and all-night vigils, along with the confession of all their sins, so as to make a copy of the baptism of John.

10. DE SPECTACULIS, c. 4

When we have entered the water, we make profession of the Christian faith in the words of its rule: we bear public testimony that we have renounced the devil, his retinue, and his works.

11. ADVERSUS PRAXEAN, c. 26

For not once only, but thrice are we baptized into each of the three persons at each of the several names.

12. DE CORONA, c. 3

In short, to begin with baptism, when on the point of coming to the water we then and there, as also somewhat earlier in church under the bishop's control [*sub antistitis manu*] affirm that we renounce the devil and his pomp and his angels. After this we are thrice immersed, while we answer interrogations rather more extensive than our Lord has prescribed in the gospel. Made welcome then [into the assembly] we partake of a compound of milk and honey, and from that day for a whole week we abstain from our daily bath.

13. DE RESURRECTIONE CARNIS, c. 8

The flesh is washed that the soul may be made spotless: the flesh is anointed that the soul may be consecrated: the flesh is signed [with the cross] that the soul too may be protected: the flesh is overshadowed by the imposition of the hand that the soul also may be illumined by the Spirit: the flesh feeds on the Body and Blood of Christ so that the soul as well may be replete with God.

CYPRIAN

Among the letters of Cyprian, there are a few which supply information about the baptismal rites as he knew them. They belong to a brief series of letters concerned with the controversy about the rebaptism of heretics, and their date is about 256. It should be noted that one of the letters (75) is written not by Cyprian but to Cyprian by Firmilian, Bishop of Caesarea in Cappadocia.

The following translation is made from the text of the *Corpus Scriptorum Ecclesiasticorum Latinorum*, Vol. 3, Pt. 2, ed. G. Hartel. Note that these letters are slightly differently numbered in the edition of Migne, *Patrologia Latina*, Vol. 4.

A valuable study of some of these extracts has been made by Dr J. N. D. Kelly, *Early Christian Creeds*, pp. 56ff.

LETTER 69, TO MAGNUS

7. If anyone objects and says that Novatian holds by the same law as the catholic church, baptizes with the same symbol as we, acknowledges the same God the Father, the same son Christ, the same Holy Spirit, and therefore that he is able to assume the authority to baptize, since he does not seem to differ from us in the baptismal interrogation: anyone with this objection should know straight away that we and the schismatics do not share the same law of the symbol or the same interrogation. For when they say "Dost thou believe in the remission of sins and eternal life through the church?" they lie in their interrogation, since they have no church.

12. My dear son, you have asked my opinion about those who attain

to the grace of God at a time of infirmity or weakness, whether they ought to be had for Christians since they were not fully washed with the saving water but sprinkled [only] . . . My own humble opinion is that the divine benefits cannot be reduced or weakened and cannot fall short, when they are received with full and entire faith on the part of him that gives and him that receives . . . (13) And in so far as there are some people who give the name *clinicus* and not Christian to men who have attained to the grace of Christ in the saving water and with the acknowledged faith, I do not know from what source they get this name.

Letter 70, to Januarius

1. . . . It is required then that the water should first be cleansed and sanctified by the priest, that it may wash away by its baptism the sins of the man that is baptized . . .

2. But moreover the very interrogation which is put in baptism is a witness of the truth. For when we say, "Dost thou believe in eternal life and remission of sins through the holy church?" we mean that remission of sins is not granted except in the church . . . It is also necessary that he who is baptized should be anointed: so that having received the chrism, that is the anointing, he may be the anointed of God and have in him the grace of Christ. Further, it is the Eucharist whence the baptized are anointed with the oil sanctified on the altar. But he cannot sanctify the creature of oil who has neither an altar nor a church.

Letter 73, to Jubaianus

6. . . . If a man, relying on a degenerate faith, can be baptized outside the church and gain remission of sins, then relying on the same faith he can gain the Holy Spirit also and there is no need for him to come [to the church] for the imposition of the hand so that he may gain the Holy Spirit and be signed.

9. . . . They who are baptized in the church are brought to the prelates of the church, and by our prayers and by the imposition of the hand obtain the Holy Spirit, and are perfected with the Lord's seal [*signaculo dominico*].

Letter 74, to Pompeius

5. If they attribute the efficacy of baptism to the majesty of the name,

so that anyone who is baptized in the name of Jesus Christ, wherever it may take place and however it may be performed, is held to be renewed and sanctified, why is not the hand also laid on him after baptism in the name of the same Christ so that he may receive the Holy Spirit, why does not the same majesty of the same name avail in the imposition of the hand which avails, as they maintain, in the sanctification of baptism?

LETTER 75, FIRMILIAN TO CYPRIAN

10. . . . That woman dared also to baptize many, making use of the usual and lawful words of interrogation, that nothing might seem to be different from the ecclesiastical rule. (11) what then shall we say about baptism of this kind, in which the most wicked demon baptizes through a woman? Do Stephen and his associates approve of this also, especially since it lacked neither the symbol of the Trinity nor the legitimate and ecclesiastical interrogatory?

DIDASCALIA APOSTOLORUM

The *Didascalia Apostolorum* was originally written in Greek, in Syria in the third century, probably the earlier half of the century. The Greek original has been lost. The following extracts have been taken from Dom R. H. Connolly's edition and translation of the Syriac version in *Didascalia Apostolorum* (Oxford, 1929.)

CHAPTER 9

. . . the bishop, through whom the Lord gave you the Holy Spirit, and through whom you have learned the word and have known God, and through whom you have been known of God, and through whom you were sealed, and through whom you became sons of the light, and through whom the Lord in baptism, by the imposition of the hand of the bishop, bore witness to each one of you and uttered his holy voice, saying: *Thou art my son: I this day have begotten thee.*

CHAPTER 16

ON THE APPOINTMENT OF DEACONS AND DEACONESSES

. . . In the first place, when women go down into the water, those who go down into the water ought to be anointed by a deaconess with the oil of anointing: and where there is no woman at hand, and especially no deaconess, he who baptizes must of necessity anoint her who is being baptized. But where there is a woman, and especially a deaconess, it is not fitting that women should be seen by men: but with the imposition of the hand do thou anoint the head only. As of old the priests and kings were anointed in Israel, do thou in like manner, with the imposition of the hand, anoint the head of those who receive baptism, whether of men or women: and afterwards—whether thou thyself baptize, or thou command the deacons or presbyters to baptize —let a woman deacon, as we have already said, anoint the women. But let a man pronounce over them the invocation of the divine Names in the water.

THE ACTS OF JUDAS THOMAS

Syriac text and translation: W. Wright, *Apocryphal Acts of the Apostles*, London, 1871.

Greek text: Lipsius and Bonnet, *Acta Apostolorum Apocrypha*, Vol. 2, 2nd part, Leipzig, 1891.

English translation from the Greek: M. R. James, *The Apocryphal New Testament*, Oxford, 1924.

See particularly A. F. J. Klijn, *The Acts of Judas Thomas*, Leiden, 1962. This includes Wright's translation, with full introduction and notes.

According to Klijn, *The Acts of Thomas* was first written in Syriac probably at Edessa, in the beginning of the third century. Since copyists and translators were bound by no duty of fidelity to their original, the Greek version is sufficiently different from the Syriac to require a separate presentation.

THE SYRIAC VERSION
[THE BAPTISM OF GUNDAPHORUS]

And they begged of him that they might receive the sign, and said to him: "Our souls are turned to God to receive the sign for we have heard that all the sheep of that God whom thou preachest are known to him by the sign." Judas saith to them: "I too rejoice, and I ask of you to partake of the Eucharist and of the blessing of this Messiah whom I preach." And the king gave orders that the bath should be closed for seven days, and that no man should bathe in it. And when the seven days were done, on the eighth day they three entered into the bath by

night that Judas might baptize them. And many lamps were lighted
in the bath.

And when they had entered into the bath-house, Judas went in
before them. And our Lord appeared unto them, and said to them:
"Peace be with you, my brethren." And they heard the voice only,
but the form they did not see, whose it was, for till now they had not
been baptized. And Judas went up and stood upon the edge of the
cistern, and poured oil upon their heads, and said: "Come, holy name
of the Messiah; come, power of grace, which art from on high: come,
perfect mercy; come, exalted gift; come, sharer of the blessing; come,
revealer of hidden mysteries; come, mother of seven houses, whose
rest was in the eighth house; come, messenger of reconciliation, and
communicate with the minds of these youths; come Spirit of holiness,
and purify their reins and their hearts." And he baptized them in the
Name of the Father and of the Son and of the Spirit of holiness. And
when they had come up out of the water, a youth appeared to them,
and he was holding a lighted taper; and the light of the lamps became
pale through its light. And when they had gone forth, he became
invisible to them; and the Apostle said: "We were not even able to
bear Thy light, because it is too great for our vision." And when it
dawned and was morning, he broke the Eucharist.

[THE BAPTISM OF A WOMAN WHO HAD BEEN POSSESSED BY A DEVIL AND HEALED]

And the woman begged of him and saith to him: "Apostle of the
Most High, give me the seal of my Lord, that the enemy may not again
come back upon me." And he went to a river which was close by
there, and baptized her in the Name of the Father and the Son and the
Spirit of holiness: and many were baptized with her. And the Apostle
ordered his deacon to make ready the Eucharist.

[THE BAPTISM OF MYGDONIA]

Mygdonia saith to her nurse Narkia: "Many flagons are of no use to
me, but a mingled draught in a cup, and one whole loaf, and a little
oil, even if [it be] in a lamp, bring unto me."

And when Narkia had brought them, Mygdonia uncovered her
head, and was standing before the holy Apostle. And he took the oil,
and cast [it] on her head, and said: "Holy oil, which wast given to us
for unction, and hidden mystery of the Cross, which is seen through it
—thou, the straightener of crooked limbs, thou, our Lord Jesus, life

and health and remission of sins—let thy power come and abide upon this oil, and let thy holiness dwell in it." And he cast it upon the head of Mygdonia, and said: "Heal her of her old wounds, and wash away from her her sores, and strengthen her weakness." And when he had cast the oil on her head, he told her nurse to anoint her, and to put a cloth round her loins; and he fetched the basin of their conduit. And Judas went up and stood over it, and baptized Mygdonia in the Name of the Father and the Son and the Spirit of holiness. And when she had come out and put on her clothes, he fetched and brake the Eucharist.

[THE BAPTISM OF SIFUR]

And Sifur the general said to him: "I and my daughter and my wife will henceforth live purely, in one mind and in one love; and we beg that we may receive the sign [of baptism] from thy hands." . . .

And he [Judas] began to speak of baptism, and said: "This is the baptism of the remission of sins; this is the bringer forth of new men; this is the restorer of understandings, and the mingler of soul and body, and the establisher of the new man in the Trinity, and which becometh a participation in the remission of sins. Glory to thee, thou hidden power of baptism. Glory to thee, thou hidden power, that dost communicate with us in baptism. Glory to thee, thou power that art visible in baptism. Glory to you, ye new creatures, who are renewed through baptism, who draw nigh to it in love." And when he had said these things, he cast oil upon their heads and said: "Glory to thee, thou beloved fruit. Glory to thee, thou name of the Messiah. Glory to thee, thou hidden power that dwellest in the Messiah." And he spake, and they brought a large vat, and he baptized them in the Name of the Father and the Son and the Spirit of holiness.

And when they were baptized and had put on their clothes, he brought bread and wine.

[THE BAPTISM OF VIZAN AND CERTAIN WOMEN]

And when he had prayed thus, he said to Mygdonia: "My daughter, strip thy sisters." And she stripped them, and put girdles on them, and brought them near to him. And Vizan came near first. And Judas took oil, and glorified [God] over it, and said: "Fair fruit, thou art worthy to be glowing with the word of holiness, that men may put thee on and conquer through thee their enemies, when they have been cleansed from their former works—yea, Lord, come, abide upon this oil, as thou didst abide upon the tree, and they who crucified thee were not able to bear thy word. Let thy gift come, which thou didst breathe upon thy enemies, and they went backwards and fell on their faces, and let it abide upon this oil, over which we name thy name." And he cast it upon the head of Vizan, and then upon the heads of these [others], and said: "In thy name, Jesus the Messiah, let it be to these persons for the remission of offences and sins, and for the destruction of the enemy, and for the healing of their souls and bodies." And he commanded Mygdonia to anoint them, and he himself anointed Vizan. And after he had anointed them, he made them go down into the water in the Name of the Father and the Son and the Spirit of holiness. And after they had been baptized and were come up, he brought bread and the mingled cup.

THE GREEK VERSION

[THE BAPTISM OF GUNDAPHORUS]

And they besought him that they also might henceforth receive the seal of the word, saying unto him: "Seeing that our souls are at leisure and eager toward God, give thou us the seal; for we have heard thee say that the God whom thou preachest knoweth his own sheep by his seal." And the Apostle said unto them: "I also rejoice and entreat you to receive this seal, and to partake with me in this Eucharist and blessing of the Lord, and to be made perfect therein. For this is the Lord and God of all, even Jesus Christ, whom I preach, and he is the father of truth, in whom I have taught you to believe." And he commanded them to bring oil, that they might receive the seal by the oil. They brought the oil therefore, and lighted many lamps; for it was night.

And the Apostle arose and sealed them. And the Lord was revealed unto them by a voice, saying: "Peace be unto you, brethren." And they heard his voice only, but his likeness they saw not, for they had not yet received the added sealing of the seal. And the Apostle took the oil and poured it upon their heads and anointed and chrismed them, and began to say:

"Come, thou holy Name of the Christ that is above every name.
Come, thou power of the Most High, and the compassion that is perfect.
Come, gift of the Most High.
Come, compassionate mother.

Come, communion of the male.

Come, she that revealeth the hidden mysteries.

Come, mother of the seven houses, that thy rest may be in the eighth house.

Come, elder of the five members, mind, thought, reflection, consideration, reason; communicate with these young men.

Come, Holy Spirit, and cleanse their reins and their heart, and give them the added seal, in the Name of the Father, and Son, and Holy Ghost."

And when they were sealed, there appeared unto them a youth holding a lighted torch, so that their lamps became dim at the approach of the light thereof. And he went forth and was no more seen of them. And the Apostle said unto the Lord: "Thy light, O Lord, is not to be contained by us, and we are not able to bear it, for it is too great for our sight."

And when the dawn came and it was morning, he brake bread and made them partakers of the Eucharist of the Christ.

[THE BAPTISM OF A WOMAN WHO HAD BEEN POSSESSED BY A DEVIL AND HEALED]

And the woman besought him, saying: "O Apostle of the Most High, give me the seal, that that enemy return not again unto me." Then he caused her to come near unto him, and laid his hands upon her and sealed her in the Name of the Father and the Son and the Holy Ghost; and many others also were sealed with her. And the Apostle bade his minister to set forth a table.

[THE BAPTISM OF MYGDONIA]

But she saith to the nurse: "Flagons I desire not, nor the many loaves: but this only, bring wine mingled with water, and one loaf, and oil." And when Narcia had brought these things, Mygdonia stood before the Apostle with her head bare: and he took the oil and poured it on her head, saying: "Thou holy oil given unto us for sanctification, secret mystery whereby the cross was shown unto us, thou art the straightener of the crooked limbs, thou art the humbler [softener] of hard things, thou art it that showeth the hidden treasures, thou art the sprout of goodness; let thy power come, let it be established upon thy servant Mygdonia; and heal thou her by this freedom." And when the oil was poured upon her, he bade her nurse unclothe her and gird a linen cloth about her: and there was there a fountain of water upon which the Apostle went up, and baptized Mygdonia in the Name of the Father and the Son and the Holy Ghost. And when she was baptized and clad, he brake bread and took a cup of water and made her a partaker in the body of Christ and the cup of the Son of God, and said: "Thou hast received thy seal, get for thyself eternal life." And immediately there was heard a voice from above saying: "Amen".

[THE BAPTISM OF SIPHOR]

And Siphor said: "I and my wife and daughter will dwell henceforth in holiness, and in chastity, and in one affection. I beseech thee that we may receive of thee the seal, and become worshippers of the true God and numbered among his sheep and lambs."

And he [Judas] began to say concerning baptism: "This baptism is remission of sins: this bringeth forth again light that is shed about us: this bringeth to birth the new man: this mingleth the spirit [with the body], raiseth up in threefoldwise a new man, and maketh him partaker of the remission of sins. Glory be to thee, hidden one, that art communicated in baptism. Glory to thee, the unseen power that is in baptism. Glory to thee, renewal, whereby are renewed they that are baptized and with affection take hold upon thee."

And having thus said, he poured oil over their heads, and said: "Glory be to thee the love of compassion [bowels]. Glory to thee, name of Christ. Glory to thee, power established in Christ." And he commanded a vessel to be brought, and baptized them in the Name of the Father and the Son and the Holy Ghost. And when they were baptized and clad, he set bread on the table, and blessed it.

[THE BAPTISM OF IUZANES (VIZAN) AND CERTAIN WOMEN]

Having thus prayed over them, the Apostle said unto Mygdonia: "Unclothe thy sisters." And she took off their clothes and girded them with girdles and brought them: but Iuzanes had first gone before, and they came after him: and the Apostle took oil in a cup of silver and spake thus over it: "Fruit more beautiful than all other fruits, unto which none other whatsoever may be compared: altogether merciful: fervent with the force of the word: power of the tree which men putting upon them overcome their adversaries: crowner of the conquerors: help and joy of the sick: that didst announce unto men their salvation, that showest light to them that are in darkness: whose leaf is bitter, but in thy most sweet fruit thou art fair; that art rough to the sight but soft to the taste: seeming to be weak, but in the greatness of thy strength able to bear the power that beholdeth all things." Having thus said [*a corrupt word follows*]: "Jesu, let his victorious might come and be established in this oil, like as it was established in the tree [wood] that was its kin, even his might at that time, whereof they that crucified thee could not endure the word: let the gift also come whereby breathing upon his [thine] enemies thou didst cause them to go backward and fall headlong, and let it rest upon this oil, whereupon we invoke thy holy Name." And having thus said, he poured it first upon the head of Iuzanes and then upon the women's heads, saying: "In thy Name, O Jesu Christ, let it be unto these souls for remission of sins and for turning back of the adversary, and for salvation of their souls." And he commanded Mygdonia to anoint them, but he himself anointed Iuzanes. And having anointed them, he led them down into the water in the Name of the Father and the Son and the Holy Ghost.

And when they were come up, he took bread and a cup, and blessed it.

THE ACTS OF XANTHIPPE
AND POLYXENA

Text: ed. M. R. James, in *Texts and Studies*, Vol. 2, part 3, Cambridge, 1893. Dr James shows that the date of this work must be about A.D. 250.

2. And while they were saying these things, his mistress Xanthippe, hearing these words and having learnt the teaching about Paul, said: "What is the name of that physician, and what cure is there to heal such sickness?" The servant replied: "The invocation of a new name, and the unction of oil, and the laver of water. By this treatment I have seen many incurable people restored to health."

13. . . . But she [Xanthippe] rising up from the ground said to him: "Master, why do you leave me desolate? Even now, hasten to seal me, that, though death overtake me, I may go to him that is merciful and kind." (14) Straightway then Paul took her by the hand, led her into the house of Philotheus, and baptized her in the Name of the Father and of the Son and of the Holy Ghost. Then he took bread and gave thanks and gave it to her, saying: "Let this be to thee for the remission of sins and the renewal of thy soul."

21. Probus rose early and went to Paul. He found him baptizing many people in the name of the life-originating Triad and said: "If I am worthy to receive baptism, my Lord Paul, lo, the hour is come." Paul replied: "See, my son, the water is ready for the cleansing of those that come to Christ." Straightway then, eagerly stripping off his clothes, Paul holding his hand, he leaped into the water, crying: "Jesus Christ, Son of God and God eternal, may all my sin be done away in this water." And Paul said: "We baptize thee in the Name of the Father and of the Son and of the Holy Ghost." And then he made him partake of the Eucharist of Christ.

2. *Syria*

THE HISTORY OF JOHN THE SON OF ZEBEDEE

Syriac text and translation: W. Wright, *Apocryphal Acts of the Apostles*, London, 1871.

Dr Wright says that this Syriac document is evidently a translation from Greek, and that its date must be about the middle of the fourth century. Dom Connolly, on the other hand, writing in the *Journal of Theological Studies*, Vol. 8, argues that Syriac must have been the original language, and puts the date "not much later than the end of the fourth century". The exordium of the book says: "This history was composed by Eusebius of Caesarea concerning St John who found it in a Greek book, and it was translated into Syriac, when he had learned concerning his way of life, etc."

[THE BAPTISM OF TYRANNUS, THE PROCURATOR OF EPHESUS]

And the holy man commanded the procurator that he should have a place made in one of the corners of the theatre; and the stone-cutters came, and set to work in that very hour, and made a place like a cistern, and the water came and the cistern was filled. And it was spacious on every side, twelve cubits in length and twelve cubits in breadth, and it was two and a half cubits deep.[1]

And the holy man besought the procurator to command and let fine, scented oil come, seventy pints. And he commanded, and it came, and a vat was filled with it. And the holy man drew nigh and kneeled down, and looked up to heaven, and cried out in the midst of the theatre: "Holy is the Father and the Son and the Spirit of holiness for ever. Amen." And the whole assembly answered, "Amen". Then John made the sign of the Cross over the oil, and said with a loud voice: "Glory be to the Father and to the Son and to the Spirit of holiness for ever. Amen." And again the third time he said: "Holy is the Father and the Son and the Spirit of holiness. Amen." And straightway fire

[1] A cubit is about 22 inches.

21

blazed forth over the oil, and the oil did not take fire, for two angels had their wings spread over the oil and were crying, "Holy, holy, holy, Lord Almighty".

And the people, when they saw these things, were afraid with a great fear, and fell on their faces, and were worshipping to the East. And when the oil was consecrated, then the holy man drew near to the water, and signed it, and said: "In the Name of the Father and of the Son and of the Spirit of holiness, for ever. Amen." And the whole people cried, "Amen". And straightway these two angels came and hovered over the water, and were crying, "Holy, holy holy, Father and Son and Spirit of holiness", after him. And St John cried after them, "Amen".

And John answered and said to the whole assembly, "Arise in the power of God". And they all arose with fear, and their hands were stretched out to heaven, and they were crying out, saying: "Great is the mystery. We believe in the Father and the Son and the Spirit of holiness." And it was about the eighth hour of the night. Then the procurator drew near, and fell on his face before John, and said to him: "What is it necessary for us to do?" And St John said to him: "Strip off thy garments from thee." And when he had stripped, the holy man drew nigh, and took oil in his hand, and made him a cross on his forehead, and anointed his whole body, and brought him nigh to the cistern, and said to him: "Descend, my brother, who art become a new firstling, which enters in at the head of the flock into the fold of the owner of the sheep. Descend, my brother, for the lambs are looking at thee, and running that they may go down, and become white, and get a new fair fleece, instead of that which is rent by ravening wolves." The procurator says: "What must I say, and then descend?" John says to him: "According as thou hast seen and found true and believed." And the crowd was silent, as if there was not a man there, that they might see what the procurator and John would say. And the procurator stretched out his hands to heaven, and cried out, weeping and saying: "I believe in the Father and in the Son, and in the Spirit of holiness"; and he leaped down into the font. Then the holy man drew near, and placed his hand on the head of the procurator, and dipped him once, crying out, "In the Name of the Father"; and the second time, "In the Name of the Son"; and the third time, "In the Name of the Spirit of holiness". And when he had come up out of the water, then he clothed him in white garments, and gave to him the kiss of peace, and said to him: "Peace be unto thee, thou new

bride-groom, who hadst grown old and effete in sin, and lo, to-day
art become a youth, and thy name has been written in heaven."

[THE BAPTISM OF THE PRIESTS OF ARTEMIS]

And when the font was prepared, the procurator commanded and
oil was brought. Then St John arose, and prayed, and said: "Glory to
thee, Father and Son and Spirit of holiness, for ever. Amen." And they
answered after him, "Amen". And he said: "Lord God Almighty,
let thy Spirit of holiness come, and rest and dwell upon the oil and
upon the water; and let them be bathed and purified from uncleanness; and let them receive the Spirit of holiness through baptism; and
henceforth let them call thee "Our Father who art in Heaven". Yea,
Lord, sanctify this water with thy voice, which resounded over the
Jordan and pointed out our Lord Jesus as with the finger, saying, "This
is my beloved Son, in whom I am well pleased, hear ye him". Thou
art here who wast on the Jordan. Yea, I beseech thee, Lord, manifest
thyself here before this assemblage who have believed on thee with
simplicity, and let the nations of the earth hear that the city of Ephesus
was the first to receive thy gospel before all cities, and became a
second sister to Urhai [Edessa] of the Parthians." And in that hour fire
blazed forth over the oil, and the wings of the angels were spread forth
over the oil; and the whole assemblage was crying out, men and
women and children, "Holy, holy, holy, Lord Almighty, of whose
praises heaven and earth are full". And straightway the vision was
taken away.

And the priests fell down on their faces and wept. And St John drew
nigh and raised them up, and they said: "We believe in the Name of
the Father and the Son and the Spirit of holiness, and we will never
know aught else." And John drew near, and washed them clean of the
soot [which they wore in token of grief], and anointed them with oil,
and baptized them in the Name of the Father and the Son and the
Spirit of holiness, for the forgiveness of debts and the pardon of sins.
And St John said to the procurator: "Command that they go and
fetch fine white bread and wine."

ST CYRIL OF JERUSALEM

Text: F. L. Cross, *St Cyril of Jerusalem's Lectures on the Christian Sacraments*,
S.P.C.K., 1951. The translation of the fifth Catechetical lecture is that of Dean
Church: for the Procatechesis and Mystagogical Catecheses, Dean Church's

translation has been used as a basis, but amended to conform with Dr Cross's Greek text.

The only literary remains of St Cyril, Bishop of Jerusalem, consist of his Catechetical lectures, and if they are correctly attributed to him, then their date is probably early in his lengthy and disturbed episcopate, about A.D. 350. The theory has, however, been advanced that they are the work of his successor John, in which case they must be dated some forty years later. They consist of a Procatechesis, delivered at the beginning of the Lenten course, eighteen Catechetical lectures delivered during Lent, and five Mystagogical Catecheses for Easter Week. It is the last series of these lectures which treats particularly of the baptismal rites, since until the candidates were baptized the *disciplina arcani* would restrain St Cyril from speaking of the rites of baptism to the uninitiated. It is possible that this latter series is incomplete, since in the course of the Catechetical lectures (18, 33) the writer promises six, and not five as we have them.

The rite described by St Cyril is not the typical rite of the Syrian Church. It appears that St Cyril has imported certain features from the West, e.g. the credal interrogations at baptism, and the post-baptismal anointing. See E. C. Ratcliff, *The Old Syrian Baptismal Tradition* (*Studies in Church History*, Vol. 2, p. 19, ed. G. J. Cuming, London, 1965); L. L. Mitchell, *Baptismal Anointing*, p. 45 (London, 1966, Alcuin Club Collections No. 48).

THE PROCATECHESIS

1. Already there is on you the savour of blessedness, O ye who are being enlightened: already are you gathering spiritual flowers, to weave heavenly crowns withal: already hath the fragrance of the Holy Ghost refreshed you: already are ye at the entrance-hall of the King's house: may you be brought into it by the King! For now the blossoms of the trees appear: may but the fruit likewise be perfected! Thus far, your names have been given in, and the roll-call made for service; there are the torches of the bridal train, and the longings after heavenly citizenship, and a good purpose, and a hope attendant; for he cannot lie who hath said, *To them that love God, all things work together for good* [Rom. 8.28]. God is indeed lavish in his benefits: yet he looks for each man's honest resolve: so the Apostle subjoins, *To those who are called according to purpose* [Rom. 8.28]. Honesty of purpose makes thee *called*: for though the body be here, yet if the mind be away, it avails nothing.

*   *   *

4. For we, the ministers of Christ, have admitted every man, and holding as it were the place of doorkeepers, have left the door un-

fastened. Thou hast been free then to enter with a soul bemired with sins, and a defiled purpose. Entered thou hast: thou hast passed, thou hast been enrolled. Seest thou these venerable arrangements of the Church? Viewest thou her order and discipline, the reading of the Scriptures, the presence of the religious, the course of teaching? Let then the place affect thee, let the sight sober thee. Depart in good time now, and enter to-morrow in better. If avarice has been the fashion of thy soul, put on another, and then come in: put off, I pray thee, fornication and uncleanness, and put on the most bright robe of soberness. This charge I give thee, before Jesus the spouse of souls come in, and see their fashion. Thou art allowed a distant day; thou hast a penitence of forty; thou has full time to put off, and to wash thee, to put on, and to enter in. But if thou abide in thy evil purpose, he who speaks is blameless, but thou must not look for grace: for though the water shall receive thee, the Spirit will not accept thee. Whoso is conscious of a wound, let him take the salve: whoso has fallen, let him rise; let there be no Simon [Magus] among you, no hypocrisy, no idle curiosity about the matter.

* * *

9. Let thy feet hasten to the catechizings, receive with earnestness the exorcisms; for whether thou art breathed upon, or exorcized, the Ordinance is to thee salvation. It is as though thou hadst gold unwrought and alloyed, blended with various substances, with brass, and tin, and iron, and lead: we seek to have the gold pure, but it cannot be cleansed from foreign substances without fire. Even so, without exorcisms, the soul cannot be cleansed; and they are divine, collected from the divine scriptures. Thy face is veiled, that thy mind may be henceforth at leisure; lest a roving eye cause a roving heart. But though thine eyes be veiled, thine ears are not hindered receiving what is saving. For as the goldsmith, conveying the blast upon the fire through delicate instruments, and as it were breathing on the gold which is hid in the hollow of the forge, stimulates the flame it acts upon, and so obtains what he is seeking; so also, exorcizers, infusing fear by a divine breath, and setting the soul on fire in the crucible of the body, make the evil spirit flee, who is our enemy, and salvation and hope of eternal life abide: and henceforth the soul, cleansed from its sins, hath salvation. Let us then, brethren, abide in hope, surrendering ourselves and hoping: so may the God of all, seeing our purpose, cleanse us from sins, and impart to us good hopes of our estate, and

grant us saving penitence! He who calls is God, and thou art the person called.

*　　　*　　　*

12. Now when the catechizing has taken place, should a catechumen ask what the teachers have said, tell nothing to a stranger; for we deliver to thee a mystery, even the hope of the life to come: keep the mystery for him who pays thee. Let no man say to thee, What harm, if I also know it? So the sick ask for wine: but if it be unseasonably given them, it occasions delirium, and two evils follow; the sick man dies, and the physician gets an ill name. Thus it is with the catechumen also if he should hear from the believer: the catechumen is made delirious, for not understanding what he has heard, he finds fault with it, and scoffs at it, and the believer bears the name of a betrayer. But now thou art standing on the frontiers; see thou let out nothing; not that the things spoken do not deserve telling, but the ear that hears does not deserve receiving. Thou thyself wast once a catechumen, and then I told thee not what was coming. When thou hast by practice reached the height of what is taught thee, then wilt thou understand that the catechumens are unworthy to hear them.

*　　　*　　　*

15. I will behold each man's earnestness; each woman's reverence. Let your mind be refined as by fire unto reverence, let your soul be forged as metal. Let the stubbornness of unbelief feel the anvil, let the superfluous scales drop off as of iron, and what is pure remain: let the rust be rubbed off, and the true metal be left. May God at length show you that night, that darkness which shows like day, concerning which it is said, *The darkness shall not be darkened from thee, and the night shall be light as the day* [Ps. 139.12, LXX]. At that time to each man and woman among you may the gate of paradise be opened; may you then enjoy the fragrant waters which bear Christ: may you then receive Christ's name and the efficacious power of divine things. Even now, I beseech you, lift up the eye of your understanding; imagine the angelic choirs, and God the Lord of all sitting, and his only-begotten Son sitting with him on the right hand, and the Spirit with them present, and thrones and dominions doing service, and each man and woman among you receiving salvation. Even now let your ears ring with the sound, when after your salvation the angels shall chant over you, *Blessed are they whose iniquities have been forgiven* [Ps. 32.1]; when

like stars of the Church you shall enter into it, bright in the outward man and radiant in your souls.

CATECHETICAL LECTURE NO. 5

12. But take thou and hold that faith only as a learner and in profession, which is by the Church delivered to thee, and is established from all Scripture. For since all cannot read the Scripture, but some as being unlearned, others by business, are hindered from the knowledge of them; in order that the soul may not perish for lack of instruction, in the articles which are few we comprehend the whole doctrine of the faith. This I wish you to remember even in the very phrase, and to rehearse it with all diligence among yourselves, not writing it upon paper but by memory graving it on your heart as on a monument: being watchful during your exercise, lest haply some of the Catechumens hear the things delivered to you. . . . Behold, therefore, brethren, and *hold the traditions* [2 Thess. 2.15] which ye now receive, and *write them on the table of your hearts* [Prov. 7.3]. .

[The Nicene Creed follows here in some MSS.]

13. This keep with godly fear, lest haply any of you being puffed up be spoiled by the enemy.

MYSTAGOGICAL CATECHESIS 1

The reading is from the first catholic epistle of Peter, from Be sober, be vigilant [1 Peter 5.8] *to the end of the epistle.*

1. I long ago desired, true born and dearly beloved children of the Church, to discourse to you concerning these spiritual and heavenly mysteries; but knowing well that seeing is far more persuasive than hearing, I waited till this season; that finding you more open to the influence of my words from this your experience, I might take and lead you to the brighter and more fragrant meadow of this present paradise; especially as ye have been made fit to receive the more sacred mysteries, having been accounted worthy of divine and life-giving baptism. It remaining therefore to dress for you a board of more perfect instruction, let us now teach you exactly about these things, that ye may know the deep meaning to you-ward of what was done on that evening of your baptism.

2. First ye entered into the outer hall of the baptistry, and there

facing towards the west ye heard the command to stretch out your hand, and as in the presence of Satan ye renounced him . . .

4. However, thou art bidden with arm outstretched to say to him as though actually present, *I renounce thee, Satan.* I wish to say wherefore ye stand facing to the west; for it is necessary. Since the west is the region of sensible darkness, and he being darkness has his dominion in darkness, ye therefore looking with a symbolical meaning towards the west, renounce that dark and gloomy potentate . . .

5. Then in the second sentence thou art told to say, *and all thy works.* Now . . .

6. Then thou sayest, *and all thy pomp.* Now . . .

8. And after this thou sayest, *and all thy service* . . . The watching of birds, divination, omens, or amulets, or charms written on leaves, sorceries or other evil arts, and all such things, are services to the devil; therefore shun them. For if, after the Renunciation of Satan and the Adherence to Christ thou fall under their influence, thou shalt find the tyrant more bitter in his temptations . . .

9. When therefore thou renouncest Satan, treading under foot all covenant with him, and breaking that ancient league with hell, there is opened to thee the paradise of God, which he planted towards the east, whence for his transgression our first father was exiled; and symbolical of this was thy turning from the west to the east, the place of light. Then wast thou told to say, *I believe in the Father and in the Son and in the Holy Ghost and in one Baptism of repentance.* Of which things we spoke at length in the former lectures, as God's grace allowed us.

10. Therefore, guarded by these considerations, be sober. *For our adversary the devil,* as was just now read, *as a roaring lion, walketh about, seeking whom he may devour* [1 Pet. 5.8]. In former times, death was mighty and devoured; but at the holy laver of regeneration God has *wiped away every tear from off all faces* [Rev. 7.17; Isa. 25.8]. For thou shalt no more mourn, now that thou hast put off the old man; but thou shalt keep holy-day, clothed in the garment of salvation, even Jesus Christ.

11. And these things were done in the outer chamber. But if God will, when in the succeeding expositions of the mysteries we have entered into the Holy of Holies, we shall then know the symbolical meaning of what is there accomplished. Now to God the Father, with the Son and the Holy Ghost, be glory and power and majesty, for ever and ever. Amen.

MYSTAGOGICAL CATECHESIS 2

The reading is from the epistle to the Romans, from Know ye not that so many of us as were baptized into Christ Jesus were baptized into his death *to* for ye are not under the law, but under grace [Rom. 6.3-14].

1. These introductions into the mysteries day by day and these new instructions, which are the announcements of new truths, are profitable to us; and most of all to you, who have been renewed from oldness to newness. Therefore, as is necessary, I will lay before you the sequel of yesterday's lecture, that ye may learn of what those things, which were done by you in the inner chamber, were the emblems.

2. As soon therefore as ye entered in, ye put off your garment; and this was an image of *putting off the old man with his deeds* [Col. 3.9]. Having stripped yourselves, ye were naked; in this also imitating Christ, who hung naked on the Cross, and in his nakedness *spoiled principalities and powers and openly triumphed over them* [Col. 2.15] on the tree . . .

3. Then, when ye were stripped, ye were anointed with exorcized oil, from the very hairs of your head to your feet, and were made partakers of the good olive tree, Jesus Christ . . .

4. After these things ye were led to the holy pool of divine baptism, as Christ was carried from the Cross to the Sepulchre which is before our eyes. And each of you was asked, whether he believed in the Name of the Father and of the Son and of the Holy Ghost, and ye made that saving confession, and descended three times [Greek: *triton*] into the water, and ascended again, here also covertly pointing by a figure at the three days burial of Christ . . .

MYSTAGOGICAL CATECHESIS 3

The reading is from the first catholic epistle of John, from And ye have an unction from God, and know all things *to* that we may not be ashamed before him at his coming [1 John 2.20-8].

1. Having been *baptized into Christ* and having *put on Christ* [Gal. 3.27], ye have been made conformable to the Son of God; for God, having *predestinated us to the adoption of sons* [Eph. 1.5], made us *share the fashion of Christ's glorious body* [Phil. 3.21]. Being made therefore *partakers of Christ* [Heb. 3.15], ye are properly called Christs, and of you God said *Touch not my Christs* [i.e., anointed ones: Ps. 105.15]. Now ye were made Christs by receiving the emblem of the Holy Ghost;

and all things were done upon you in representational fashion, because ye take the part of Christ. He also bathed himself in the river Jordan, and having imparted of the fragrance of his Godhead to the waters he came up from them: and the Holy Ghost in substance rested upon him, like resting upon like. In the same manner to you also, after ye had come up from the pool of the sacred streams, was given the unction, the emblem of that wherewith Christ was anointed; and this is the Holy Ghost . . .

4. And ye were first anointed on your forehead . . . Then on your ears . . . Then on your nostrils . . . Then on your breast . . .

5. When ye are counted worthy of this holy chrism, ye are called Christians, verifying also the name by your new birth. For before you were vouchsafed this grace, ye had properly no right to this title, but were advancing on your way towards being Christians.

THE APOSTOLIC CONSTITUTIONS

Text: F. X. Funk, *Didascalia et Constitutiones Apostolorum*, Paderborn, 1905.

The basis of this translation is that of the Library of Ante-Nicene Fathers, which, however, has been amended to conform with Funk's Greek text.

The date of this anonymous work is about 375. It is related to the class of literature known as the Church orders. It will be noted that the rite in book 3, chapters 16ff, is based upon the *Didascalia*, that in book 7, chapter 22, upon the *Didache*, while that of book 7, chapters 39ff, has no known connections.

BOOK 3

CHAPTER 16

2. For we stand in need of a woman, a deaconess, for many necessities; and first in the baptism of women, the deacon shall anoint only their foreheads with the holy oil, and after this the deaconess shall anoint them: for there is no necessity that the women shall be seen by men; 3. but in the laying on of hands the bishop shall anoint her head only as the priests and kings were formerly anointed, not because those who are now being baptized are being ordained priests, but as being Christians, or anointed, from Christ the Anointed, *a royal priesthood, and an holy nation* [1 Pet. 2.9], *the Church of God, the pillar and ground* [1 Tim. 3.15] of the marriage chamber, *who in time past were not a people* [1 Pet. 2.10], but now are beloved and chosen. 4. Thou therefore, O bishop, according to that type, shalt anoint the head of those that are being baptized, whether men or women, with the holy oil, for a type of the spiritual baptism. After that, either thou, O

bishop, or a presbyter that is under thee, calling and naming over them the solemn invocation of the Father and Son and Holy Spirit, shall baptize them in the water; and let a deacon receive the man and a deaconess the woman, that so the conferring of this inviolable seal may take place with a becoming decency. And after that, let the bishop anoint with chrism those that have been baptized.

CHAPTER 17

This baptism therefore is given into the death of Jesus [Rom. 6.8]: the water is instead of the burial, and the oil instead of the Holy Ghost; the seal instead of the cross; the chrism is the confirmation of the confession; 2. the mention of the Father as of the Author and Sender: the joint mention of the Holy Ghost as of the witness; 3. the descent into the water the dying together with [Christ]; the ascent out of the water the rising again with [him]. 4. The Father is the God over all; Christ is the only-begotten God, the beloved Son, the Lord of Glory; the Holy Ghost is the Comforter, who is sent by Christ, and taught by him, and proclaims him.

CHAPTER 18

But let him that is baptized be free from all iniquity; one that has left off to work sin, the friend of God, the enemy of the devil, *the heir of God the Father, the joint-heir with his Son* [Rom. 8.17]; one that has renounced Satan and his demons and deceits; chaste, pure, holy, beloved of God, the son of God, praying as a son to his father, and saying, as from the common congregation of the faithful, thus: Our Father [*etc.*].

BOOK 7

CHAPTER 22

Now concerning baptism, O bishop, or presbyter, we have already given direction, and we now say, that thou shalt so baptize as the Lord commanded us, saying: *Go ye, and teach all nations, baptizing them into the Name of the Father, and of the Son, and of the Holy Ghost (teaching them to observe all things whatsoever I have commanded you)* [Matt. 28.19]: of the Father who sent, of Christ who came, of the Comforter who testified. 2. But thou shalt first anoint the person with holy oil, and afterward baptize him with water, and finally shalt seal him with the

chrism; that the anointing with oil may be a participation of the Holy
Spirit, and the water a symbol of the death, and the chrism a seal of the
covenants. 3. But if there be neither oil nor chrism, the water is sufficient both for the anointing, and for the seal, and for the confession
of him that is dead, or indeed is dying together with [Christ]. 4. But
before baptism, let him that is to be baptized fast.

*   *   *

CHAPTER 39

2. Let him, therefore, who is to be taught the knowledge of piety
be instructed before his baptism in the knowledge of the unbegotten
God, the understanding of his only begotten Son, the certainty of the
Holy Ghost. Let him learn the order of the several parts of the
creation . . .

4. Let him that offers himself to baptism learn these and the like
things during his instruction; and let him who lays his hands upon him
adore God, the Lord of the whole world, and thank him for his creation, for his sending Christ his only-begotten Son, that he might save
man by blotting out his transgressions . . .

5. And after this thanksgiving, let him instruct him in the doctrines
concerning our Lord's incarnation, and in those concerning his passion,
and resurrection from the dead, and assumption.

CHAPTER 40

1. And when it remains that the catechumen is to be baptized, let
him learn what concerns the renunciation of the devil, and the joining
himself with Christ; for it is fit that he should first abstain from things
contrary, and then be admitted to the mysteries.

CHAPTER 41

1. Let, therefore, the candidate for baptism declare thus in his
renunciation:

2. "I renounce Satan, and his works, and his pomps, and his service,
and his angels, and his inventions, and all things that are under him."

3. And after his renunciation let him in his Act of Adherence say:
"And I adhere to Christ,

4. "And believe and am baptized into one unbegotten Being, the
only true God Almighty, the Father of Christ, the creator and maker
of all things, *of whom are all things* [1 Cor. 8.6];

5. "And into the Lord Jesus Christ, his only-begotten Son, *the
firstborn of the whole creation* [1 Cor. 1.15], who before the ages was

begotten by the good pleasure of the Father, not created, *by whom all things* [1 Cor. 8.6] were made, both those in heaven and those on earth, visible and invisible;

6. "Who in the last days descended from heaven, and took flesh, and was born of the holy Virgin Mary, and did converse holily according to the laws of his God and Father, and was crucified under Pontius Pilate, and died for us, and rose again from the dead after his passion the third day, and ascended into the heavens, and sitteth at the right hand of the Father, and is to come again at the end of the world with glory *to judge the quick and the dead* [2 Tim. 4.1], *of whose kingdom there shall be no end* [Luke 1.33].

7. "And I am baptized into the Holy Ghost, that is, the Comforter, who wrought in all the saints from the beginning of the world, but was afterwards sent to the Apostles by the Father, according to the promise of our Saviour and Lord Jesus Christ; and after the Apostles to all those that believe in the holy catholic Church;

8. "Into the resurrection of the flesh, and into the remission of sins, and into the kingdom of heaven, and into the life of the world to come."

CHAPTER 42

1. And after this vow, he comes in order to the anointing with oil.

2. Now this is blessed by the priest for the remission of sins, and the first preparation for baptism.

3. For he calls upon the unbegotten God, the Father of Christ, the King of all sensible and intelligible natures, that he would sanctify the oil *in the name of the Lord Jesus* [Acts 8.16], and impart to it spiritual grace and efficacious strength, the remission of sins, and the first preparation for the confession of baptism, that so the candidate, when he is anointed, may be freed from all ungodliness, and may become worthy of initiation, according to the command of the Only-begotten.

CHAPTER 43

1. After this he comes to the water.

2. He blesses and glorifies the Lord God Almighty, the Father of the only-begotten God; and the priest returns thanks that he has sent his Son to become man on our account, that he might save us; that he has permitted that he should in all things become obedient to the laws of that incarnation, to preach the kingdom of heaven, the remission of sins, and the resurrection of the dead.

3. Moreover, he adores the only-begotten God himself, after his

Father, and for him, giving him thanks that he undertook to die for all men by the cross, the type of which he has appointed to be the baptism of regeneration.

4. He glorifies him also, for that God who is Lord of the whole world, in the name of Christ, and by his Holy Spirit, has not cast off mankind, but has suited his providence to the difference of seasons: at first giving to Adam himself paradise for an habitation of pleasure, and afterwards giving a command on account of providence, and casting out the offender justly, but through his goodness not utterly casting him off, but instructing his posterity in succeeding ages after various manners: on whose account, in the conclusion of the world, he has sent his son to become man for man's sake, and to undergo all human passions without sin.

5. Him, therefore, let the priest even now call upon in baptism, and let him say: Look down from heaven and sanctify this water and give it grace and power, that so he that is baptized, according to the command of thy Christ, may be crucified with him, and may die with him, and may be buried with him, and may rise with him to the adoption which is in him, that he may be dead to sin and live to righteousness.

CHAPTER 44

1. And after this, when he has baptized him in the Name of the Father and of the Son and of the Holy Ghost, let him anoint him with chrism, and say:

2. O Lord God, who art without generation, and without a superior, the Lord of the whole world, who hast scattered the sweet odour of the knowledge of the gospel among all nations, do thou grant at this time that this chrism may be efficacious upon him that is baptized, that so the sweet odour of thy Christ may continue upon him firm and fixed; and that now he has died with him, he may arise and live with him.

3. Let him say these and the like things, for this is the efficacy of the laying on of hands on every one; for unless there be such a recital made by a pious priest over every one of these, the candidate for baptism does only descend into water as do the Jews, and he only puts off the filth of the body, not the filth of the soul.

CHAPTER 45

1. After this let him stand up, and pray that prayer which the Lord taught us. But, of necessity, he who is risen again ought to stand up

and pray, because he that is raised stands upright. Let him, therefore, who has been dead with Christ, and is raised up with him, stand up.

2. But let him pray towards the East . . .

3. But let him pray thus after the foregoing prayer, and say: O God Almighty, the Father of thy Christ, thy only-begotten Son, give me an undefiled body, a pure heart, a watchful mind, an unerring knowledge, the influence of the Holy Ghost for the obtaining and assurance of the truth, through thy Christ, by whom be glory to thee in the Holy Spirit for ever. Amen.

4. We have thought it proper to make these constitutions concerning the catechumens.

ST JOHN CHRYSOSTOM

In the autumn of 1955 M. Antoine Wenger visited the monastery of Stavronikita on Mt Athos and came away with the text of eight catechetical addresses by St John Chrysostom which had been hitherto unknown outside the peninsula. In 1957 he published them under the title *Huits catéchèses baptismales* in the series *Sources chrétiennes* (Vol. 50) with an introduction, French translation and notes. In the same volume M. Wenger drew attention to another series of four catechetical addresses by Chrysostom. They were also very little known, having been published only once, in 1909 at St Petersburg, by A. Papadopoulos-Kerameus in *Varia Graeca Sacra*.

Both of these series of addresses have been translated into English and edited with full notes by P. W. Harkins (*St John Chrysostom, Baptismal Instructions*, Ancient Christian Writers, Vol. 31, 1963). A useful study of the baptismal rite revealed in these addresses has been made by Fr T. M. Finn, c.s.p. in *The Liturgy of Baptism in the Baptismal Instructions of St John Chrysostom*, The Catholic University of America Studies in Christian Antiquity, No. 15, 1967.

The translation below is that of P. W. Harkins. All the addresses were delivered at Antioch. The date of the first (PK 3) is Lent 388; of the second (Stavronikita 2), Lent *c.* 390. It is clear from internal evidence that these two addresses were delivered before baptism, during Lent and not after Easter.

SERIES OF PAPADOPOULOS-KERAMEUS NO. 3

11. . . . We faithful have believed in things which our bodily eyes cannot see . . . Therefore, God has made for us two kinds of eyes: those of the flesh and those of faith.

12. When you come to the sacred initiation, the eyes of the flesh see water; the eyes of the faith behold the Spirit. Those eyes see the body being baptized; these see the old man being buried. The eyes of

C

the flesh see the flesh being washed; the eyes of the spirit see the soul being cleansed. The eyes of the body see the body emerging from the water; the eyes of faith see the new man come forth brightly shining from that sacred purification. Our bodily eyes see the priest as, from above, he lays his right hand on the head and touches [him who is being baptized]; our spiritual eyes see the great High Priest as he stretches forth his invisible hand to touch his head. For, at that moment, the one who baptizes is not a man but the only-begotten Son of God.

13. And what happened in the case of our Master's body also happens in the case of your own. Although John appeared to be holding his body by the head, it was the divine Word which led his body down into the streams of Jordan and baptized him. The Master's body was baptized by the Word, and by the voice of his Father from heaven which said: *This is my beloved Son*, and by the manifestation of the Holy Spirit which descended upon him. This also happens in the case of your body. The baptism is given in the name of the Father and of the Son and of the Holy Spirit. Therefore, John the Baptist told us, for our instruction, that man does not baptize us, but God: *There comes after me one who is mightier than I, and I am not worthy to loose the strap of his sandal. He will baptize you with the Holy Spirit and with fire.*

14. For this reason, when the priest is baptizing, he does not say, "I baptize so-and-so", but, "So-and-so is baptized in the name of the Father and of the Son and of the Holy Spirit." In this way he shows that it is not he who baptizes but those whose names have been invoked, the Father, the Son, and the Holy Spirit.

15. Therefore, my sermon today is called "faith", and I entrust nothing else to you until you shall say "I believe". This word is a foundation stone unshaken which holds up an unshaken edifice. Therefore, Paul also says: *For he who comes to God must believe that God exists.*

16. Therefore, you who are coming to God, first believe in God and then speak out that word loud and clear. For if you cannot do this, you will be able neither to speak nor understand any other . . .

18. But as regards the instruction on faith, I shall leave that task for your teacher. I will be able to speak to you of it at another time, when many of the uninitiated will be present. But what you alone must hear now and what cannot be told to you when the uninitiated are mingled together with you, these things I must tell you today.

19. What are these things? Tomorrow, on Friday at the ninth hour, you must have certain questions asked of you and you must present

your contracts to the Master . . .

21. . . . when you have all been led into [the church], then you must all together bend your knee and not stand erect; you must stretch your hands to heaven and thank God for this gift.

22. Sacred custom bids you to remain on your knees, so as to acknowledge his absolute rule even by your posture, for to bend the knee is a mark of those who acknowledge their servitude. Hear what St Paul says: *To him every knee shall bend of those in heaven, on earth, and under the earth.* And after you have bent your knees, those who are initiating you bid you to speak those words: "I renounce thee, Satan."

24. "I renounce thee, Satan." What has happened? What is this strange and unexpected turn of events? Although you were all quivering with fear, did you rebel against your master? Did you look with scorn upon his cruelty? Who has brought you to such madness? Whence came this boldness of yours? "I have a weapon", you say, "a strong weapon." What weapon, what ally? Tell me! "I enter into thy service, O Christ", you reply. "Hence, I am bold and rebel. For I have a strong place of refuge. This has made me superior to the demon, although heretofore I was trembling and afraid. Therefore, I not only renounce him but also all his pomps."

27. After these words, after the renunciation of the devil and the covenant with Christ, inasmuch as you have henceforth become his very own and have nothing in common with that evil one, he straightway bids you to be marked and places on your forehead the sign of the cross. That savage beast is shameless and, when he hears those words, he grows more wild—as we might expect—and desires to assault you on sight. Hence, God anoints your countenance and stamps thereon the sign of the cross. In this way does God hold in check all the frenzy of the Evil One; for the devil will not dare to look upon such a sight. Just as if he had beheld the rays of the sun and had leaped away, so will his eyes be blinded by the sight of your face and he will depart; for through the chrism the cross is stamped upon you. The chrism is a mixture of olive oil and unguent; the unguent is for the bride, the oil is for the athlete. And that you may again know that it is not a man but God himself who anoints you by the hand of the priest, listen to St Paul when he says: *It is God who is warrant for us and for you in Christ, who has anointed us.* After he anoints all your limbs with this ointment, you will be secure and able to hold the serpent in check; you will suffer no harm.

28. After the anointing, then, it remains to go into the bath of

sacred waters. After stripping you of your robe, the priest himself leads you down into the flowing waters. But why naked? He reminds you of your former nakedness, when you were in Paradise and you were not ashamed. For Holy Writ says: *Adam and Eve were naked and were not ashamed*, until they took up the garment of sin, a garment heavy with abundant shame.

29. Do not, then, feel shame here, for the bath is much better than the garden of Paradise. There can be no serpent here, but Christ is here initiating you into the regeneration that comes from the water and the Spirit.

STAVRONIKITA SERIES, NO. 2.

9. All of you, then, who have deserved to be enrolled in this heavenly book, bring forward a generous faith and a strong reason. What takes place here requires faith and the eyes of the soul, so that you pay heed not only to what is seen, but you make the unseen visible from the seen . . .

10. What is this I am saying and why did I say to pay no heed to visible things, but to have the eyes of the spirit? I say it in order that when you see the bath of water and the hand of the priest touching your head, you may not think that this is merely water, nor that only the hand of the bishop lies upon your head. For it is not a man who does what is done, but it is the grace of the Spirit which sanctifies the nature of the water and touches your head together with the hand of the priest. Was I not right in saying that we need the eyes of faith?

12. Now you stand at the threshold; soon you will enjoy the benefit of so many gifts. Let me instruct you, then, as far as I can, in the reasons for each of the present rites, that you may know them well and depart from here with a more certain understanding of them. You must understand why, after this daily instruction, we send you along to hear the words of the exorcists. For this rite does not take place without aim or purpose; you are going to receive the King of heaven to dwell within you. This is why, after we have admonished you, those appointed to this task take you and, as if they were preparing a house for a royal visit, they cleanse your minds by those awesome words, putting to flight every device of the wicked one and making your hearts worthy of the royal presence. For even if the demon be fierce and cruel, he must withdraw from your hearts with all speed after this awesome formula and the invocation of the common Master of all

things. Along with this, the rite itself impresses great piety on the soul and leads it to marvellous compunction.

14. See what profit those words and those awesome and wonderful invocations bring with them. But the show of bare feet and the outstretched hands point out something else to us. Those who endure captivity of the body show by their posture their dejection at the disaster which has overcome them. So, too, when the devil's captives are about to be set free from his domination and to come under the yoke of goodness, they first remind themselves of their prior condition by their external attitude . . .

15. Do you wish me to address a word to those who are sponsoring you, that they too may know what recompense they deserve if they have shown great care for you, and what condemnation follows if they are careless? . . . (16) . . . it is customary to call the sponsors "spiritual fathers" . . .

17. Now let me speak to you of the mysteries themselves, and of the contract which will be made between yourselves and the Master. In worldly affairs, whenever someone wishes to entrust his business to anyone, a written contract must be completed between the trustee and his client. The same thing holds true now, when the Master is going to entrust to you not mortal things which are subject to destruction and death, but spiritual things which belong to eternity. Wherefore, this contract is also called faith, since it possesses nothing visible but all things which can be seen by the eyes of the spirit. There must be an agreement between the contracting parties. However, it is not on paper nor written in ink; it is in God and written by the Spirit. The words which you utter here are registered in heaven, and the agreement which you make by your tongue abides indelibly with the Master.

18. See here again the external attitude of captivity. The priests bring you in. First they bid you pray on bent knees, with your hands outstretched to heaven, and to remind yourselves by your posture from what evil you are delivered and to what good you will dedicate yourselves. Then the priest comes to you one by one, asks for your contract and confession, and prepares you to utter those awesome and frightening words: "I renounce thee, Satan".

20. . . . Then the priest has you say: "I renounce thee, Satan, thy pomps, thy service, and thy works." The words are few but their power is great. The angels who are standing by and the invisible powers rejoice at your conversion, receive the words from your tongues, and carry them up to the common Master of all things.

There they are inscribed in the books of heaven.

21. Did you see what the terms of the agreement are? After the renunciation of the wicked one and of all things which are important to him, the priest again has you say: "And I enter into thy service, O Christ." Did you see his boundless goodness? Receiving only these words from you, he entrusts to you such a store of treasures! He has forgotten all your former ingratitute, he reminds you of none of your past deeds, but he is content with these few words.

22. After that contract of renunciation and attachment, after you have confessed his sovereignty and by the words you spoke have attached yourself to Christ, in the next place, as if you were a com- batant chosen for the spiritual arena, the priest anoints you on the forehead with the oil of the spirit and signs you [with the sign of the cross], saying: "So-and-so is anointed in the name of the Father and of the Son and of the Holy Spirit."

23. The priest knows that henceforth the enemy is furious, grinds his teeth, and goes about like a roaring lion when he sees those who were formerly subject to his sovereignty in sudden rebellion against him, not only renouncing him, but going over to the side of Christ. Therefore, the priest anoints you on the forehead and puts on you the sign [of the cross], in order that the enemy may turn away his eyes. For he does not dare to look you in the face when he sees the lightning flash which leaps forth from it and blinds his eyes. Henceforth from that day there is strife and counterstrife with him, and on this account the priest leads you into the spiritual arena as athletes of Christ by virtue of this anointing.

24. Next after this, in the full darkness of the night, he strips off your robe and, as if he were going to lead you into heaven itself by the ritual, he causes your whole body to be anointed with that olive oil of the spirit, so that all your limbs may be fortified and unconquered by the darts which the adversary aims at you.

25. After this anointing, the priest makes you go down into the sacred waters, burying the old man and at the same time raising up the new, who is renewed in the image of his Creator. It is at this moment that, through the words and the hand of the priest, the Holy Spirit descends upon you. Instead of the man who descended into the water, a different man comes forth, one who has wiped away all the filth of his sins, who has put off the old garment of sin and has put on the royal robe.

26. That you may also learn from this that the substance of the

Father, Son, and Holy Spirit is one, baptism is conferred in the following manner. When the priest says: "So-and-so is baptized in the name of the Father, and of the Son, and of the Holy Spirit", he puts your head down into the water three times and three times he lifts it up again, preparing you by this mystic rite to receive the descent of the Spirit. For it is not only the priest who touches the head, but also the right hand of Christ, and this is shown by the very words of the one baptizing. He does not say: "I baptize so-and-so", but: "So-and-so is baptized", showing that he is only the minister of grace and merely offers his hand because he has been ordained to this end by the Spirit. The one fulfilling all things is the Father and the Son and the Holy Spirit, the undivided Trinity. It is faith in this Trinity which gives the grace of remission from sin; it is this confession which gives us the gift of filial adoption.

27. What follows suffices to show us from what those who have been judged worthy of this mystic rite have been set free, and what they have gained. As soon as they come forth from those sacred waters, all who are present embrace them, greet them, kiss them, rejoice with them, and congratulate them, because those who were heretofore slaves and captives have suddenly become free men and sons and have been invited to the royal table. For straightway after they come up from the waters, they are led to the awesome table heavy laden with countless favours, where they taste of the Master's body and blood, and become a dwelling place for the Holy Spirit. Since they have put on Christ himself, wherever they go they are like angels on earth, rivalling the brilliance of the rays of the sun.

THE PILGRIMAGE OF ETHERIA

These extracts are taken from pages 79 and 90-4 of the translation in *The Pilgrimage of Etheria*, ed. M. L. McClure and C. L. Feltoe, S.P.C.K., 1919.

Etheria wrote an account of her experiences on pilgrimage in the Holy Land, *c.* 400, which includes these passages relating to the preparation of candidates for baptism in Jerusalem.

[THE INSCRIBING OF THE COMPETENTS]

Moreover, I must write how they are taught who are baptized at Easter. Now he who gives in his name, gives it in on the day before Quadragesima, and the priest writes down the names of all; that is before the eight weeks which I have said are kept here at Quadragesima.

And when the priest has written down the names of all, after the next day of Quadragesima, that is, on the day when the eight weeks begin, the chair is set for the bishop in the midst of the great church, that is, at the martyrium, and the priests sit in chairs on either side of him, while all the clergy stand. Then one by one, the competents are brought up, coming, if they are males, with their fathers, and if females, with their mothers. Then the bishop asks the neighbours of every one who has entered concerning each individual, saying: "Does this person lead a good life, is he obedient to his parents, is he not given to wine, nor deceitful?" making also inquiry about the several vices which are more serious in a man. And if he has proved him in the presence of witnesses to be blameless in all these matters concerning which he has made inquiry, he writes down his name with his own hand. But if he is accused in any matter, he orders him to go out, saying: "Let him amend, and when he has amended, then let him come to the font." And as he makes inquiry concerning the men, so also does he concerning the women. But if any be a stranger, he comes not so easily to baptism, unless he has testimonials from those who know him.

[PREPARATION FOR BAPTISM: CATECHIZINGS]

This also must I write, reverend sisters, lest you should think that these things are done without good reason. The custom here is that they who come to baptism through those forty days, which are kept as fast days, are first exorcized by the clergy early in the day, as soon as the morning dismissal has been made in the Anastasis. Immediately afterwards the chair is placed for the bishop at the martyrium in the great church, and all who are to be baptized sit around, near the bishop, both men and women, their fathers and mothers standing there also. Besides these, all the people who wish to hear come in and sit down— the faithful however only, for no catechumen enters there when the bishop teaches the others the Law. Beginning from Genesis he goes through all the Scriptures during those forty days, explaining them first literally, and then unfolding them spiritually. They are also taught about the resurrection, and likewise all things concerning the Faith during those days. And this is called the catechizing.

[DELIVERY OF THE CREED]

Then when five weeks are completed from the time when their teaching began, they receive the Creed. And as he explained the meaning of all the Scriptures so does he explain the meaning of the

Creed; each article first literally, and then spiritually. By this means all the faithful in these parts follow the Scriptures when they are read in Church, inasmuch as they are all taught during those forty days, from the first to the third hour, for the catechizing lasts for three hours. And God knows, reverend sisters, that the voices of the faithful who come in to hear the catechizing are louder [in approval] of the things spoken and explained by the bishop than they are when he sits and preaches in church. Then, after the dismissal of the catechizing is made, the bishop is at once escorted with hymns to the Anastasis. So the dismissal takes place at the third hour. Thus are they taught for three hours a day for seven weeks, but in the eighth week of Quadragesima, which is called the Great Week, there is no time for them to be taught, because the things that are described above must be carried out.

[RECITATION OF THE CREED]

And when the seven weeks are past, and the Paschal week is left, which they call here the Great Week, then the bishop comes in the morning into the great church at the martyrium, and the chair is placed for him in the apse behind the altar, where they come one by one, a man with his father and a woman with her mother, and recite the Creed to the bishop. And when they have recited the Creed to the bishop, he addresses them all and says: "During these seven weeks you have been taught all the law of the Scriptures, you have also heard concerning the faith, and concerning the resurrection of the flesh, and the whole meaning of the Creed, so far as you were able, being yet catechumens. But the teachings of the deeper mystery, that is, of baptism itself, you cannot hear, being as yet catechumens. But lest you should think that anything is done without good reason, these, when you have been baptized in the Name of God, you shall hear in the Anastasis, during the eight Paschal days, after the dismissal from the church has been made. You, being as yet catechumens, cannot be told the more secret mysteries of God."

[MYSTIC CATECHIZINGS]

But when the days of Easter have come, during those eight days, that is, from Easter to the Octave, when the dismissal from the church has been made, they go with hymns to the Anastasis. Prayer is said anon, the faithful are blessed, and the bishop stands, leaning against the inner rails which are in the cave of the Anastasis, and explains all things that are done in baptism. In that hour, no catechumen approaches the Anastasis, but only the neophytes and the faithful, who wish to hear concerning the mysteries, enter there, and the doors are shut lest any catechumen should draw near. And while the bishop discusses and sets forth each point, the voices of those who applaud are so loud that they can be heard outside the church. And truly the mysteries are so unfolded that there is no one unmoved at the things that he hears to be so explained.

[In an earlier passage in the book, Etheria writes:] The Paschal vigils are kept as with us, with this one addition, that the children, when they have been baptized and clothed, and when they issue from the font, are led with the bishop first to the Anastasis; the bishop enters the rails of the Anastasis, and one hymn is said, then the bishop says a prayer for them, and then he goes with them to the greater church, where, according to custom, all the people are keeping watch. Everything is done there which is customary with us also, and after the oblation has been made, the dismissal takes place.

THEODORE OF MOPSUESTIA

A. Mingana has edited and translated the Syriac text of the first and second parts of Theodore's Instructions to Candidates for Baptism (*Woodbrooke Studies*, Vols. 5 and 6, Cambridge, 1933), and the following extracts have been taken from his translation. The first part, dealing with the Nicene Creed, is translated in Vol. 5; the second part, with which we are here concerned, in Vol. 6. Part 2 consists of six sermons, of which the first relates to the Lord's Prayer, the three following to the rites of baptism, and the two last to the Eucharist. It is clear that they are intended as sermons to be delivered to candidates. Before they were translated from Greek into Syriac, they were used in the Greek Church of the Patriarchate of Antioch as a textbook for the catechumens. Theodore died in A.D. 428.

INSTRUCTIONS TO CANDIDATES FOR BAPTISM

PART 2, SERMON 2

He who wishes to draw nigh unto the gift of the holy baptism comes to the Church of God . . .

He is received by a duly appointed person—as there is a habit to register those who draw nigh unto baptism—who will question him about his mode of life in order to find out whether it possesses all the requisites of the citizenship of that great city. After he has abjured all the evil found in this world and cast it completely out of his mind, he has to show that he is worthy of the citizenship of the city and of his enrolment in it . . .

This rite is performed for those who are baptized by the person called godfather, who however does not make himself responsible for them in connection with future sins, as each one of us answers for his own sins before God. He only bears witness to what the catechumen has done and to the fact that he has prepared himself in the past to be worthy of the city and of its citizenship. He is justly called a sponsor, because by his words [the catechumen] is deemed worthy to receive baptism . . .

It is for this reason that as regards you also who draw nigh unto the gift of baptism, a duly appointed person inscribes your name in the Church book, together with that of your godfather, who answers for you and becomes your guide in the city and the leader of your citizenship therein . . .

Because you are unable by yourselves to plead against Satan and to fight against him, the services of the persons called exorcists have been found indispensable, as they act as your surety for divine help. They ask in a loud and prolonged voice that our enemy should be punished and by a verdict from the judge be ordered to retire and stand far . . . In this same way when the words called the words of exorcism are pronounced you stand perfectly quiet, as if you had no voice and as if you were still in fear and dread of the Tyrant . . . You stand therefore with outstretched arms in the manner of one who prays, and look downwards and remain in that state in order to move the judge to mercy. And you take off your outer garment and stand barefooted in order to show in yourself the state of cruel servitude in which you served the devil for a long time . . . You stand also on garments of sackcloth so that from the fact that your feet are pricked and stung by the roughness of the cloth you may remember your old sins . . . As to the words of exorcism, they have the power to induce you, after having made up your mind to acquire such a great gain, not to remain idle and without work. You are therefore ordered in those intermediary days to meditate on the words of the profession of faith in order that you may learn it, and they are put in your mouth in order that through a continuous meditation you may strive to be in a position to recite them by heart . . .

When the time for the reception of the sacrament draws nigh and the judgement and fight with the demon—for the sake of which the words of exorcism have been used—are at an end; and when by God's decision the tyrant has submitted and yielded to the shouts of the exorcist and been condemned, so that he is in nothing near to you and you are completely free from any disturbance from him; and when you have possessed the happiness of this enrolment without any hindrance—you are brought by duly appointed persons to the priest, as it is before him that you have to make your engagements and promises to God. These deal with the faith and the Creed, which by a solemn asseveration you declare you will keep stedfastly, and that you will not, like Adam the father of our race, reject the cause of all good things, but that you will remain to the end in the doctrine of the Father, the Son, and the Holy Spirit . . . When a person wishes to enter the house of a man of power in this world, with the intention of doing some work in it, he does not go direct to the master of the house and make his engagement and contract with him, as it is unbecoming to the master of the house to condescend to such a conversation, but goes to the majordomo and agrees with him about his work . . . in this same way you act who draw nigh unto the house of God . . . This majordomo is the priest who has been found worthy to preside over the Church; and after we have recited our profession of faith before him, we make with God, through him, our contract and our engagements concerning the faith, and we solemnly declare that we will be his servants, that we will work for him and remain with him till the end. After we have, by our profession of faith, made our contracts and engagements with God our Lord, through the intermediary of the priest, we become worthy to enter his house and enjoy its sight, its knowledge, and its habitation, and to be also enrolled in the city and its citizenship. We then become the owners of a great confidence.

Sermon 3

From what we have previously said, you have sufficiently understood the ceremonies which are duly performed, prior to the sacrament, and according to an early tradition, upon those who are baptized. When you go to be enrolled in the hope of acquiring the abode and citizenship of heaven, you have, in the ceremony of exorcism, a kind of law-suit with the Demon, and by a divine verdict you receive your freedom from his servitude. And thus you recite the words of the profession of faith and of prayer, and through them you make an engagement and a promise to God, before the priests, that you will remain in the love of the divine nature . . . and that you will live in this world to the best of your ability in a way that is consonant with the life and citizenship of heaven. It is right now that you should receive the teaching of the ceremonies that take place in the sacrament itself, because if you learn the reason for each one of them, you will acquire a knowledge that is by no means small. After you have been taken away from the servitude of the Tyrant by means of the words of exorcism, and have made solemn engagements to God along with the recitation of the Creed, you draw nigh unto the sacrament itself; you must learn how this is done.

You stand barefooted on sackcloth while your outer garment is taken off from you, and your hands are stretched towards God in the posture of one who prays. In all this you are in the likeness of the posture that fits the words of exorcism, as in it you have shown your old captivity and the servitude which through a dire punishment you have rendered to the Tyrant . . .

First you genuflect while the rest of your body is erect, and in the posture of one who prays you stretch your arms towards God . . .

The rest of your body is erect and looks towards heaven. In this posture you offer prayer to God and implore him to grant you deliverance from the ancient fall and participation in the heavenly benefits. While you are in this posture, the persons who are appointed for the service draw nigh unto you and say unto you something more than that which the angel who appeared to the blessed Cornelius said to him: Your prayers have been heard and your supplications answered [Acts 10.4] . . .

What are then the engagements and promises which you make at that time, and through which you receive deliverance from the ancient tribulations, and participation in the future benefits ?—

"I abjure Satan and all his angels, and all his service, and all his deception, and all his worldly glamour; and I engage myself, and believe, and am baptized in the Name of the Father, and of the Son, and of the Holy Spirit."

The deacons who at that time draw nigh unto you prepare you to recite these words . . .

When you have, therefore, made your promises and engagements, the priest draws near to you, wearing, not his ordinary garments, or the covering with which he was covered before, but clad in a robe of clean and radiant linen, the joyful appearance of which denotes the joy of the world to which you will move in the future, and the shining colour of which designates your own radiance in the life to come, while its cleanness indicates the ease and happiness of the next world . . .

And he signs you on your forehead with the holy Chrism and says: "So-and-so is signed in the Name of the Father and of the Son and of the Holy Spirit."

He offers you these first fruits of the sacrament, and he does it in no other way than in the Name of the Father and of the Son and of the Holy Spirit. Where you expect to find the cause of all the benefits, there the priest begins the sacrament. In fact, it is from there that the priest draws you nigh unto the calling towards which you must look, and in consequence of which you ought to live above all things according to the will [of God]. The sign with which you are signed means that you have been stamped as a lamb of Christ and as a soldier of the heavenly King . . .

Immediately after your godfather, who is standing behind you, spreads an *orarium* [i.e., stole] of linen on the crown of your head, raises you, and makes you stand erect . . . The linen which he spreads on the crown of your head denotes the freedom to which you have been called . . . Freemen are in the habit of spreading linen on their heads, and it serves them as an adornment both in the house and in the market place.

After you have been singled out and stamped as a soldier of Christ the Lord, you receive the remaining part of the sacrament and are invested with the complete armour of the Spirit, and with the sacrament you receive participation in the heavenly benefits. We ought to explain little by little how these things are effected, but let what has been said suffice for to-day, and let us end our discourse as usual by offering praise to God the Father, and to his Only-begotten Son, and to the Holy Spirit, now, always, and for ever and ever. Amen.

Sermon 4

Yesterday we spoke sufficiently of the signing and of the meaning of the ceremonies that take place in it, and it behoves us to speak to-day of the things which follow it . . .

You draw, therefore, nigh unto the holy baptism, and before everything you take off your garments . . .

After you have taken off your garments, you are rightly anointed all over your body with the holy Chrism: a mark and a sign that you will be receiving the covering of immortality, which through baptism you are about to put on . . .

While you are receiving this anointing, the one who has been found worthy of the honour of priesthood begins and says: "So-and-so is anointed in the Name of the Father and of the Son and of the Holy Spirit." And then the persons appointed for this service anoint all your body. After these things have happened to you, at the time which we have indicated, you descend into the water, which has been consecrated by the benediction of the priest, as you are not baptized only with ordinary water, but with water of the second birth, which cannot become so except through the coming of the Holy Spirit on it. For this it is necessary that the priest should have beforehand made use of clear words, according to the rite of the priestly service, and asked God that the grace of the Holy Spirit might come on the water and impart to it the power both of conceiving that awe-inspiring child and becoming a womb to the sacramental birth . . .

. . . the priest makes use beforehand of his priestly service and of clear words and benedictions, written for the purpose, and prays that the grace of the Holy Spirit come upon the water . . .

The priest stands up and approaches his hand, which he places on your head and says: "So-and-so is baptized in the Name of the Father and of the Son and of the Holy Spirit," while wearing the aforesaid apparel which he wore when you were on your knees and he signed you on the forehead and when he consecrated the water . . .

The priest places his hand on your head and says, "Of the Father", and with these words he causes you to immerse yourself in water, while you obediently follow the sign of the hand of the priest and immediately, at his words and at the sign of his hand, immerse yourself in water. By the downward inclination of your head you show as by a hint your agreement and your belief that it is from the Father that you will receive the benefits of baptism, according to the words of the priest . . . You therefore immerse and bow your head while the priest says, "And the Son", and causes you with his hand to immerse again in the same way . . . Then the priest says, "And of the Holy Spirit", and likewise presses you down into the water . . . After this you go out of the water.

When you go out of the water you wear a garment that is wholly radiant . . .

After you have received the grace of baptism and worn a white garment that shines, the priest draws nigh unto you and signs you on your forehead and says: "So-and-so is signed in the Name of the

Father and of the Son and of the Holy Spirit." When Jesus came out of
the water he received the grace of the Holy Spirit who descended like
a dove and lighted on him, and this is the reason why he is said to have
been anointed: "The Spirit of the Lord is upon me, because of which
the Lord hath anointed me" [Luke 4.18], and: "Jesus of Nazareth whom
God hath anointed with the Holy Spirit and with power [Acts 10.38]—
texts which show that the Holy Spirit is never separated from him, like
the anointment with oil which has a durable effect on the men who
are anointed, and is not separated from them. It is right therefore that
you should also receive the signing on your forehead.

After you have received in this way a sacramental birth through
baptism, you draw nigh unto an immortal food . . .

NARSAI

Dom R. H. Connolly has translated the Syriac text of certain sermons of
Narsai which treat of liturgical matters in *Texts and Studies*, Vol. 8, Cambridge,
1909, and the following extracts have been taken from his translation.

Narsai had been a professor in the school of Edessa from 437. In 457 the
followers of Ibas were expelled, and Narsai founded the Nestorian School at
Nisibis. He died in 502.

Connolly showed clearly that the two sermons which were numbered 21 and
22 in Mingana's printed edition of the Syriac text should in fact be the other
way round, as they are here presented.

HOMILY 22: ON BAPTISM

. . . As a pen the [divine] Nod holds him spiritually, and inscribes
[and] writes body and soul in the book of life. As with a rod it drives
from them by the word of his mouth the darkness of error which had
blinded them from understanding.

He lifts up his voice and says: "Renounce ye the Evil One and his
power and his angels and his service and his error."

They first renounce the dominion of the Evil One who brought
them to slavery: and then they confess the power of the Creator who
has set them free. Two things he says who draws nigh to the mysteries
of the Church: a renunciation of the Evil One, and a [confession of]
faith in the Maker: "I renounce the Evil One and his angels," he cries
with the voice, "and I have no dealings with him, not even in word."

The priest stands as a mediator [i.e., interpreter], and asks him: "Of
whom dost thou wish to become a servant from henceforth?" He
learns from him whom he wishes to call Master: and then he inscribes

him in the number of the first-borns of the height.

From Satan and his angels he [the priest] turns away his [the cate-chumen's] face; and then he traces for him the image of the Divinity upon his forehead.

And then he comes to the confession of the faith. The truth of his soul he reveals by the sensible voice: "Lo," he says, "I have turned away from the Evil One to the Creator." He puts the devils to shame by the utterance of his mouth [saying]: "Hearken, ye rebellious ones, I have no part with you." The assemblies of the height he makes to rejoice by the words of his faith: "Come, ye spiritual ones, rejoice with me, for I am saved alive from destruction: I am your fellowservant and a fellow-labourer in your works; and with that Lord to whom ye minister I am desirous of serving." He names himself a soldier of the Kingdom of the height—a fugitive who has returned to take refuge with the King of kings.

He first entreats the stewards of the Holy Church to present him at the door of the King, that he may speak his words. . .

The priests he asks to be as an advocate in the suit against the suit [opposed to him]; and they plead the cause for him while he is silent. As in a lawsuit the priest stands at the hour of the Mysteries and ac-cuses the devil on behalf of sinners. The sinner also stands like a poor man that has been defrauded; and he begs and entreats that mercy may help him in the judgement. Naked he stands and stripped before the Judge, that by his wretched plight he may win pity to cover him. Without covering he pleads his cause against his adversary, that the King may see him and swiftly exact judgement for him.

He bends his knees and bows his head in confusion, and is ashamed to look aloft towards the Judge. He spreads sackcloth [Connolly here adds "upon him", probably wrongly: see art. Quasten, *Harvard Theological Review*, Vol. 35]: and then he draws near to ask for mercy, making mention of his subjection to the Evil One. Two things he depicts by his kneeling down at the hour of the Mysteries: one, his fall, and one, that he is making payment as a debtor. That fall which was in Paradise he now recalls; and he pleads a judgement with Satan who led astray his father [i.e., Adam]. He is in dread of him, therefore his face is looking upon the ground till he hears the voice of forgiveness, and then he takes heart.

He waits for the priest to bring in his words before the Judge; and he [the priest] restores to him the chart of liberty with the oil and the water.

A sponsor also he brings with him into the court, that he may come in and bear witness to his preparation and his sincerity. With sincerity he protests that he will abide in love of the truth; and his companion becomes surety [saying]: "Yea, true is the protestation of his soul." He becomes as a guide to his words and actions; and he shews him the conduct of spiritual life. He calls [or reads] his name, and presents him before the guards [i.e., the priests], that they may name him heir, and son, and citizen.

In the books the priest enters the name of the lost one, and he brings it in and places it in the archives of the King's books. He makes him to stand as a sheep in the door of the sheepfold; and he signs his body and lets him mix with the flock. The sign of the oil he holds in his hand, before the beholders; and with manifest things he proclaims the power of things hidden. And as by a symbol he shows to the eyes of the bodily senses the secret power that is hidden in the visible sign...

To them [i.e. the priests] he gave the signet of the Name of the incomprehensible Divinity, that they might be stamping men with the holy Name. The stamp of his Name they lay upon his flock continually; and with the Trinity men are signing men.

The iron of the oil the priest holds upon the tip of his fingers; and he signs the body and the senses of the soul with its sharp [edge]. The son of mortals whets the oil with the words of his mouth; and he makes it sharp as iron to cut off iniquity. The three Names he recites in order, one after the other; and in triple wise [i.e., with the three Names] he completes and performs the mystery of our redemption...

The three Names he casts upon the oil, and consecrates it, that it may be sanctifying the uncleanness of men by its holiness. With the Name hidden in it he signs the visible body; and the sharp power of the Name enters even unto the soul. Ah, marvel, which a man performs by that [power] which is not of his own; signing the feeble bodies so that the inward [parts] feel the pain. The office of a physician, too, he exercises towards the members; touching the exterior and causing pain [or sensation] to reach unto the hidden parts. To body and soul he applies the remedies of his art; and the open and hidden [disease] he heals by the divine power. Divinely he mixes the drug that is given into his hands; and all diseases he heals by its power without fail. As a [drug-] shop he has opened the door of the holy temple; and he tends the sickness and binds up the diseases of his fellowservants. With the external sign he touches the hidden diseases that are within; and then he lays on the drug of the Spirit with the symbol of the water. With the open voice he preaches its hidden powers; and with his tongue he distributes hidden wealth. The words he makes to sound in the ears of the flock while he is signing it; and it hearkens with love to the three Names when they are proclaimed. With the Name of the Father and of the Son and of the Holy Spirit he seals his words; and he confirms him that is being baptized with their Names. The three Names he traces upon his face as a shield; that the tyrant may see the image of the Divinity on the head of a man. The cause of the signing on the forehead is [that it may be] for the confusion of the devils; that when they discern [it] on the head of a man they may be overcome by him [or it]. On account of these [i.e., the devils] are performed the mysteries of the oil and water, that they may be an armour against their warfare and attacks. An armour is the oil with which the earth-born are anointed, that they may not be captured by the [evil] spirits in the hidden warfare. It is the great brand of the King of kings with which they are stamped, that they may serve [as soldiers] in the spiritual contest. On their forehead they receive the spiritual stamp, that it may be bright before angels and men. Like brave soldiers they stand at the King's door, and the priest at their head like a general at the head of his army. He sets their ranks as if for battle at the hour of the mysteries, that they may be casting sharp arrows at the foe. The arrows of words he fixes [as on a bow-string, and] sets in the midst of their mouths, that they may be aiming against the Evil One who made them slaves. A mark he sets before their eyes for them to aim at; and as [arrows] on a bow-string he draws back the words on their tongues. They enter into an examination at the beginning of the warfare to which they have been summoned, being tested by the confession of their minds. In truth the priest stands at the head of their ranks, and shows them the mark of truth that they may aim aright. They renounce the standard of the Evil One, and his power and his angels; and then he [the priest] traces the standard of the King on their forehead. They confess and they renounce—the two in one, without doubting—[making] a renunciation of the Evil One, and a confession of the heart in the name of the Divinity. By the hand of the priesthood they make a covenant with the Divinity, that they will not again return to Satan by their doings. They give to the priest a promise by the words of their minds; and he brings in, reads [it] before the good-pleasure of God. The chart which is the door of the royal house he holds in his hands; and from the palace he has [received] authority to inscribe [the names of] men.

He calls the King's servants by their names and causes them to stand [forth]; and he makes them to pass one by one, and marks their faces with the brand of the oil. By the voice of his utterances he proclaims the power that is hidden in his words, [and declares] whose they are, and whose name it is with which they are branded. "Such a one", he says "is the servant of the King of [all] kings that are on high or below; and with his Name he is branded that he may serve [as a soldier] according to his will." The name of the Divinity he mixes in his hands with the oil; and he signs and says "Father" and "Son" and "Holy Spirit". "Such a one", he says, "is signed with the three Names that are equal, and there is no distinction of elder or younger between One and Another."

The priest does not say, "I sign" but, "is signed"; for the stamp that he sets is not his, but his Lord's. He is [but] the mediator who has been chosen by a favour to minister; and because it is not his it drives out iniquity and gives the Spirit. By the visible oil he shows the power that is in the Names, which is able to confirm the feebleness of men with hidden [powers]. The three Names he recites, together with the rubbing of the oil upon the whole man: that hostile demons and vexing passions may not harm him. It is not by the oil that he keeps men from harms: it is the power of the Divinity that bestows power upon [its] feebleness. The oil is a symbol which proclaims the divine power; and by outward things he [God] gives assurance of his works [done] in secret. By his power body and soul acquire power; and they no more dread the injuries of death. As athletes they descend [and] stand in the arena, and they close in battle with the cowardly suggestions that are in them. This power the oil of anointing imparts: not the oil, but the Spirit that gives it power. The Spirit gives power to the unction of the feeble oil, and it waxes firm by the operation that is administered in it. By its firmness it makes firm the body and the faculties of the soul, and they go forth confidently to wage war against the Evil One. The sign of his Name the devils see upon a man; and they recoil from him in whose name they see the Name of honour. The Name of the Divinity looks out from the sign on the forehead: and the eyes of the crafty ones are ashamed to look on it.

Homily 21: On the Mysteries of the Church and on Baptism

. . . With the Name of the Divinity, the three Names, he consecrates the water, that it may suffice to accomplish the cleansing of the defiled.

The defilement of men he cleanses with water: yet not by water, but by the power of the Name of the Divinity which there lights down. The power of the Divinity dwells in the visible waters, and by the force of his power they dissolve the might of the Evil One and of Death. The Evil One and Death are undone by baptism; and the resurrection of the body and the redemption of the soul are preached therein. In it, as in a tomb, body and soul are buried, and they die and live [again] with a type of the resurrection that is to be at the end. It [Baptism] fills for men the office of the grave mystically; and the voice of the priesthood [is] as the voice of the trump in the latter end.

In the grave of the water the priest buries the whole man; and he resuscitates him by the power of life that is hidden in his words. In the door of the tomb of baptism he stands equipped, and he performs there a mystery of death and of the resurrection. With the voice openly he preaches the power of what he is doing—how it is that a man dies in the water, and turns and lives again. He reveals and shows to him that is being baptized in whose name it is that he is to die and swiftly come to life.

Of the Name of the Divinity he makes mention, and he says three times: "Father and Son and Holy Spirit, one equality." The Names he repeats with the voice openly, and thus he says: "Such a one is baptized in the Name of the Father and the Son and the Spirit." And he does not say, "I baptize", but "is baptized"; for it is not he that baptizes but the power that is set in the Names. The Names give forgiveness of iniquity, not a man; and they sow new life in mortality. In their Name he that is baptized is baptized [and buried] as in a tomb; and they call and raise him up from his death.

Three times he bows his head at their Names, that he may learn the relation—that while They are One They are Three. With a mystery of our Redeemer he goes into the bosom of the font [*lit.*, of baptism] after the manner of those three days in the midst of the tomb. Three days was our Redeemer with the dead: so also he that is baptized—the three times are three days. He verily dies by a symbol of that death which the Quickener of all died; and he surely lives with a type of the life without end. Sin and death he puts off and casts away in baptism, after the manner of those garments which our Lord departing left in the tomb.

As a babe from the midst of the womb he looks forth from the water; and instead of garments the priest receives him and embraces him. He resembles a babe when he is lifted up from the midst of the water; and as a babe everyone embraces and kisses him. Instead of swaddling-clothes they cast garments upon his limbs, and adorn him as a bride-groom on the day of the marriage-supper. He also fulfils a sort of marriage-supper in baptism; and by his adornment he depicts the glory that is prepared for him. By the beauty of his garments he proclaims the beauty that is to be: here is a type, but there the verity which is not simulated. To the Kingdom of the height which is not dissolved he is summoned and called; and the type depicts beforehand and proclaims its truth. With a type of that glory which is incorruptible he puts on the garments, that he may imitate mystically the things to be. Mystically he dies and is raised and is adorned; mystically he imitates the life immortal. His birth [in Baptism] is a symbol of that birth which is to be at the end, and the conduct of his life of that conversation which is [to be] in the Kingdom on high.

In the way of spiritual life, he begins to travel; and, like the spiritual beings, he lives by spiritual food.

[The Homily ends with an account of the Eucharist.]

DIONYSIUS THE AREOPAGITE

Text: Migne, P. G., Vol. 3. The following extracts are based on the transla-tion of J. Parker, *The Writings of Dionysius the Areopagite*, London, 1897. *On the Ecclesiastical Hierarchy* is the title of one of the works of an unknown author who wrote in Syria about A.D. 500.

ON THE ECCLESIASTICAL HIERARCHY

CHAPTER 2

2. He, who has felt a religious longing to participate in these truly supermundane gifts, comes to some one of the initiated, and persuades him to act as his conductor to the Hierarch [i.e., presumably, the Bishop]. He also promises wholly to follow the teaching that shall be given him, and prays the initiate to undertake the superintendence of his introduction and of all his after life. Now the initiate, though he has a holy longing for his [friend's] salvation, when he measures human infirmity against the loftiness of the undertaking, is suddenly seized with fear and a sense of incapacity: nevertheless at last he agrees with a good grace to do what is requested, and takes and leads him to the chief Hierarch.

3. The Hierarch, when with joy he has received, as the sheep upon his shoulders, the two men, and has first worshipped, glorifies with a mental thanksgiving and bodily prostration the One Beneficent Source, from which those who are being called are called, and those who are being saved are saved.

4. Then collecting a religious assembly of all orders of the Church into the sacred place, so that he might have their help, and that they might celebrate together the man's salvation, and also for thanksgiving for the divine goodness, he first chants a certain hymn, found in the Oracles, accompanied by the whole body of the Church; and after this, when he has kissed the holy table, he advances to the man before him and demands of him what he wants.

5. When the man, out of love to God, has confessed, according to the instruction of his sponsor, his ungodliness, his ignorance of the really beautiful, his insufficiency for the life in God, and prays through his holy mediation to attain to God and divine things, the Hierarch then testifies to him that his approach ought to be entire, as to God who is all-perfect and without blemish; and when he has expounded to him fully the godly course of life, and has demanded of him if he would thus live—after his promise he places his right hand upon his head, and when he has sealed him commands the priests to register the man and his sponsors.

6. When these have enrolled the names, the Hierarch makes a holy prayer, and when the whole Church has completed this with him, he then looses the [candidate's] sandals and removes his clothing, with the help of the ministers [leitourgoi]. Then, when he has placed the candidate facing the west, and making a show of disdain towards the same quarter with his hands, he commands him thrice to breathe scorn upon Satan, and further, to profess the words of renunciation. When he has witnessed his threefold renunciation, he turns him back to the east, after he has professed this thrice; and when he has looked up to heaven and extended his hands thither, he commands him to make his Act of Adherence to Christ and all the divinely transmitted Oracles of God. When the man has done this, he attests him again for his threefold profession, and again, when he has thrice professed, after prayer he gives thanks and lays his hand upon him.

7. When the ministers have entirely unclothed him, the priests bring the holy oil of the anointing. Then he begins the anointing with a threefold sealing, and for the rest assigns the man to the priests for the anointing of his whole body, while he himself advances to the mother

of filial adoption, and when he has purified the water within it by the holy invocations and perfected it by three cruciform effusions of the most pure Chrism and by the same number of injections of the most holy Chrism, and has invoked the sacred melody of the inspiration of the God-rapt prophets, he orders the man to be brought forward; and when one of the priests from the register has announced him and his surety, the priests conduct him near to the water and lead him by the hand to the hand of the Hierarch. Then the Hierarch stands down [in the water] and when the priests have again called aloud to him in the water the name of him that is being perfected, the Hierarch dips him three times, invoking the threefold Subsistence of the Divine Blessedness, at the three immersions and emersions of him that is being perfected. The priests then take him and entrust him to the sponsor and guide of his introduction: and when they, with his help, have cast appropriate clothing over him that is being perfected, they lead him again to the Hierarch, who when he has sealed the man with the most divinely operating Chrism pronounces him to be henceforward partaker of the most divinely perfecting Eucharist.

JAMES OF EDESSA

The developed and lengthy Orders of Baptism and Confirmation of the Syrian Church have been collected and translated into Latin by H. Denzinger, *Ritus Orientalium*, Vol. 1, Wurzburg, 1867 (reprinted, 1961). The following account by James of Edessa is an exact description of the rite which bears his name. For the account, see *Ritus Orientalium*, Vol. 1, p. 279: for the rite itself, see p. 280.

The administration is divided into two parts. In the first part there is a prayer over the catechumens, then the priest says a prayer for himself, and then a prayer for the catechumens which is accompanied by incense. After this their names are written in a book and they are signed on the forehead in the Name of the Father and of the Son and of the Holy Ghost. As they stand, each in his place, the priest turns them to the West, and then turns himself and says the prayer which precedes the exorcism: then the exorcism against the devil, in the awful Name of the Lord: after that he bids them renounce the devil and all that belongs to him. Next they turn themselves to the East and follow Christ, confessing that they believe in him, in his Father, and in his Holy Spirit. Then a prayer is said thanking God that they have been counted worthy to be made Christians. The ancient custom was that they remained thus for a long time and during this period were called Christians; then finally they were baptized. Those who wish to receive baptism enter the baptistry and say: "We believe in one God", etc. Then the priest pronounces the Peace: he says a prayer and then signs them with holy oil, and they stand naked while another prayer is said in which he breathes thrice upon the water in the form of a cross and says: "May the head of the dragon be beaten down." After that he pours the chrism thrice in the form of a cross while he says a prayer. Then he baptizes them in the Name of the Father and of the Son and of the Holy Ghost. Next he signs them with chrism, saying: "And may they receive this sign in thy Name." Then he says a prayer of thanksgiving. Finally they go to the church and receive the holy mysteries.

3. The Armenian Rite

An English translation of the Armenian rite has been published by F. C. Conybeare and A. J. Maclean in *Rituale Armenorum*, Oxford, 1905. This translation is based on a ninth-century manuscript, and certain variant readings from another manuscript of about A.D. 1300 are provided in the notes (p.67 below). A Latin translation has been published by H. Denzinger in *Ritus Orientalium*, Vol. I, pp. 384-91, from which certain variant readings are entered into the text below under the sign D.

It will be noted that the rubrics of the following Canon (or Order) of baptism assume the baptism of adults or grown children. Before this Order the Armenian books provide two Canons to be used for infants. The first is the "Canon of an eight days old child"; the infant is brought to the door of the church by his grandmother, he is named, signed with the cross, and one prayer said. The second is a Canon for use when the child is forty days old; he is brought by his mother and his nurse, at the church door a prayer is said for the purification of the mother, they enter church where hands are laid on the child, and he is caused to prostrate himself before the altar.

THE ARMENIAN RITE

THE CANON OF BAPTISM

when they make a Christian. Before which it is not right to admit him into church. But he shall have hands laid on him beforehand, three weeks or more before the baptism, in time sufficient for him to learn from the Wardapet [Instructor] *both the faith and the baptism of the Church. First of all the Godhead of the Holy Trinity, and about the creation and coming to be of all creatures: and next about the election of just men. After that the birth of Christ, and in its order all the economy, and the great mystery of the cross, and the burial and the resurrection and ascension unto the Father, and the second coming, and the resurrection of all flesh, and the rewarding of each according to his works. In teaching this the* Wardapet *shall instruct him to be untiring in prayer.*

This is the order for those of ripe age. First the catechumen shall have hands laid upon him, whether of full age or a child. Psalm 131: Lord, my heart is not haughty.

Prayers over the catechumen before baptism. This is the beginning of baptism.

O Lord our God, God who doest good, who couldst not despise mankind that had erred and strayed from thee, driven forth and fallen from the garden of delight; but didst have pity and condescend from thy height unto our lowly nature, and taking upon thee our whole estate, except our sins, didst by thy sufferings and death on the cross purchase our salvation and return, and graciously bestow on us baptism. Accept even now, in thy goodness, O Lord, the earnest desire of this thy creature, who has resolved to draw nigh unto thy sole Godhead bearing in himself a Christian name. Give him strength and help both to become worthy and to attain unto the purity of the holy font, of thy unblemished life, and unto the inheritance of adoption in the kingdom of heaven; through Jesus Christ our Lord, to whom are due glory, rule, and honour, now and ever.

Thereafter on the day of baptism at the door of the church, the priest shall celebrate the following office in concert with the clergy over children and those of full age. Psalms are said, three in number: 25. Unto thee, O Lord, have I lifted up my soul. 26. Judge me, O Lord. 51. Have mercy upon me, O Lord, according to thy great mercy.

The deacon proclaims:
And also for this catechumen let us pray to God who loveth men, to have mercy upon him according to his great mercifulness, and to make him worthy of the washing of second birth and of the raiment of incorruption; and to number him among those who have believed in his Name, and to make him alive by his mercy. By thy grace, almighty one and creator, Lord our God, make alive and have mercy.

They shall say three times: Lord, have mercy.

The priest saith the following prayer over him:
Receive, O Lord, who lovest mankind, the catechumen here presented to thee. Cleanse his mind and conscience from all wiles of the adversary; and make him worthy by means of the font to wash away the oldness of his sins, and to be renewed by the light of the grace of thy Christ. To the end that together with us he may glorify Father, Son, and Holy Ghost, now and forever.

The deacon proclaims: And again for the forgiveness of sins, by the descending of mercy from God upon this catechumen, let us pray.

They say thrice: Lord, have mercy.

The priest shall say this prayer:
O Lord God, great and glorified by all creatures. Thy servant, taking refuge in thine awful name, hath bowed his head to thy holy *Name,*

whereunto every knee is bent of beings heavenly and earthly and of those under the earth; and let every tongue confess that Jesus Christ is Lord, unto the glory of God the Father [Phil. 2.10f]. Let him be made a partaker in that awful Name of thine, which has routed and dispelled the deceit of devils and the folly of idolatry, and has brought to nought all the snares of Satan. Look, O Lord, in thy mercy on this man; remove and set afar from him, by the all-conquering invocation over him of thy Name, the thoughts, words, and deeds of lurking unclean spirits, and all the wicked devices whereby evil demons are wont to deceive and undo mankind. To the end that, being affrighted at thy conquering Name, they may be troubled and tortured with unseen torments, driven afar from him by adjurations, and may not again return into him. Replenish him with heavenly grace, and make him to rejoice in a goodly calling, naming him a Christian. And may he become worthy, at the right season for baptism, of a second birth; so that receiving thy Holy Spirit, he may become very body and limb of thy holy Church. And may we by innocent following of Christ lead a pure and religious life in this world, and attain unto the good things to come, together with all who love thy Name; glorifying the unchangeable lordship of Father, Son, and Holy Spirit, now and ever and unto eternity of eternities.

Next he orders the catechumen to turn to the west, and he adjures him three times to say as follows:

We renounce thee, Satan, and all thy deceitfulness and thy wiles, and thy service and thy paths and thine angels.

And as he turns the catechumen the priest asks: Dost thou renounce, renounce, renounce?

And at each several question he shall say: I renounce.

Then he shall turn him towards the east, confessing the one Godhead of the holy Trinity, thrice as follows: Dost thou believe in the all-holy Trinity, in Father and Son and Holy Spirit?

The priest shall ask thus: Dost thou believe in the Father? Dost thou believe in the Son? Dost thou believe in the Holy Spirit?

And at each several question the catechumen shall say: I believe, I believe, I believe.

And once more he asks him thrice: Dost thou believe, believe, believe?

And at each several question the catechumen shall say: I believe.

And they recite the Nicene Creed in full. Then they shall say Psalm 118:

Confess ye unto the Lord, for he is good . . . *as far as the verse*, Open me the gates. *And they open the church and enter in, coming before the font* [D. *the altar*]; *and having ready the holy oil, the deacon proclaims:* And also for the coming down into this oil of the grace of thy all-holy Spirit, let us pray to the Lord.

Three times: Lord, have mercy on us.

The priest says the following prayer:

Blessed art thou, O Lord our God, who hast chosen thee a people, unto priesthood and kingship, *for a holy race and for a chosen people* [1 Pet. 2.9]. As of old thou didst anoint priests and kings and prophets with such all-holy oil, so now also, we pray thee, beneficent Lord, send the grace of thy Holy Spirit into this oil: to the end that it shall be for him that is anointed therewith unto holiness of spiritual wisdom, that he may manfully fight and triumph over the adversary, unto strength of virtuous actions, and unto his perfect instruction and exercise in the worship of God. To the end that enlightened in his understanding he may pass through the life of this world, unto the salvation of his soul, to the honour and glory of the all-holy Trinity, to become worthy of and to attain to the lot and heritage of those who love the name of Jesus Christ our Lord, with whom to thee, Father, and to the Holy Spirit, are due glory, rule, and honour.

Then he shall pour the water into the font crosswise.

[An office then follows consisting of Ps. 29; Ezek. 36.25-8; Gal. 3.24-9; Ps. 23; John 3.1-8; and a litany.]

And he shall cause him that is born anew [D. *the catechumen*] *to stand close up to the font, and shall say the following prayer:*

Thou, Lord, by thy mighty power, hast made sea and dry land, and all creatures that are in them. Thou hast divided and established the waters below the heavens for a dwellingplace of the hosts who incessantly do praise thee. Thou didst send thy holy apostles, laying on them the command to *preach and baptize in the Name of the Father, Son, and Holy Ghost all the nations* [Matt. 28.19]. But also thou hast declared, and thy word lieth not, that *except men be born of water and of spirit, we cannot enter the kingdom* [John 3.5]. In awe whereat this thy servant, desiring eternal life, is come of his own will unto baptism of this spiritual water. We pray thee, Lord, send thy Holy Spirit into this water, and cleanse it as thou didst cleanse the Jordan by thy descent into it, all-holy one, our Lord Jesus Christ, prefiguring this font of baptism and of the regeneration of all men. And graciously vouchsafe to him in this water, in which he is now baptized, means to the remission of sins, to reception of the Holy Spirit [D. and one of Conybeare's MSS. omit this phrase], to adoption as a son of the heavenly Father in heaven, and to inheriting of thy kingdom of heaven. To the end that, cleansed from sin, he may continue in this world agreeably to thy will, and in the world to come may receive thine infinite benefits together with all thy saints, and thankfully glorify Father and Son and Holy Spirit, now and ever.

Next he shall pour some of the holy oil into the font crosswise, saying, Alleluiah. *And he bids them strip off the catechumenal dress and be ready for the holy washing.*

And the priest says the following prayer over the novice:
Lord, who hast called thy servant unto the enlightenment of baptism, we pray thee, Lord, make him worthy of thy mighty grace. Strip him naked of the oldness of sin, and renew him unto new life; and fill him with the strength of thy Holy Spirit, for the adoption of the life of thy Christ. To whom are due glory, rule, and honour, now and ever.

And he maketh the novice to go down into the font. And the priest shall ask his name, and pouring some of the holy water over his head thrice, he shall say as follows:
N. or M. is [some MSS: shall be] baptized in the name of the Father, Son, and Holy Spirit, redeemed by the blood of Christ from the slavery of sin, receiving the freedom of adoption as son of the heavenly Father, having become [D. that he may become] a co-heir with Christ, and a temple of the Holy Spirit. Now and ever and for eternity.

This he shall three times repeat, and three times plunge the novice in the water, thereby signifying the three days burial of Christ and his fellowship with him. And he shall wash his whole body and say:
Ye that have been baptized into Christ, have put on Christ [Gal. 3.27].

Alleluia. *Ps. 34. Antiphon:* Many are the afflictions of the righteous [Ps. 34.19].
Ye that have been enlightened in the Father, the Holy Spirit shall rejoice in you. Alleluia.

Verse by verse they sing the same psalm, and give the "glory" with the same antiphon. And he draws up the baptized from the font, and gives him to the seal-father, and reads the gospel of Matthew, 3.13-6.

Our Father, which art in heaven . . .

And then he says the following prayer:

Thou who hast enlightened this thy creature, Christ God, darting the light of Godhood into this thy servant, hast freed him and cleansed and justified him and bestowed adoption. Graciously grant him equal participation of life; vouchsafe to him perpetual incorruptibility, mingling him with thy just ones and in the number of thy beloved ones, through our Lord Jesus Christ, with whom to thee, Father, and Holy Spirit are due glory, rule, and honour.

Peace be to all.

Let us adore.

O God, that art mighty and eternal, and who knowest all secrets, who art holy and dwellest amid the holy, Saviour of all mankind. Who dost vouchsafe thy knowledge to thy believers; and has given them authority to become the sons of God [John 1.12], through regeneration of water and spirit. Whereby thou hast renewed also this N. or M. in the purity of thy font. Render him holy by thy truth, replenish him with the grace of thy Holy Spirit, that he may become a temple of dwelling of thy holy Name; and may be able to walk in all the paths of righteousness, and to stand in confidence and cheerfulness before the dread judgement seat of thy Only-Begotten, our Lord Jesus Christ, to whom are due glory, rule, and honour.

Thereafter he anoints him with holy oil:

First the forehead, saying: A fragrant oil poured out in the name of Christ, the seal of heavenly gifts.

Next the eyes, saying: This seal which is in the name of Christ, may it enlighten thine eyes, that thou mayest not ever sleep in death.

The ears: May the anointing of holiness be for thee unto hearing of the divine commandments.

The nostrils: May this seal of Christ be to thee for a sweet smell from life to life.

The mouth, saying: May this seal be to thee a watch set before thy mouth and a door to keep thy lips.

The palms of the hands, saying: May this seal of Christ be for thee a means of doing good, of virtuous actions and living.

The heart: May this seal of divine holiness establish in thee a holy heart, and renew an upright spirit within thine interior.

The backbone: May this seal which is in the name of Christ be for thee a shield and buckler, whereby thou mayest be able to quench all the fiery darts of the evil one.

And the feet: May this divine seal guide thy steps aright unto life immortal.

And thereafter he shall say: Peace be with thee, thou saved of God.

And the person baptized saith: And with thy spirit.

Next he puts on his raiment, and saith the following prayer:

Blessed art thou, O God, who takest good care of us, and hast clothed thy servant with a garment of salvation and the raiment of gladness. And hast set the helmet of salvation and a crown of grace upon his head, armour without flaw against the adversary. Wherefore also let us thankfully glorify Father and Son and Holy Spirit.

Thereafter he leadeth him up to the bema [sanctuary] *and causeth him to bow low before the holy altar, and thrice he kisses the three sides. And he saith this prayer:*

Lord God almighty, Father of our Lord Jesus Christ, unto thee they that have believed bow their heads. Stretch forth thy unseen right hand, and bless him. Prosper the works of their hands. Fortify those who are in the estate of virginity, and strengthen all by patience and long-suffering, for all the worship of God. Preserve in peace their children, nurture and bring them to the full measure of age. Protect them all under their several roofs, in all gladness unto Christ Jesus our Lord, with whom to thee, Father, be glory, rule, and honour, now and ever.

And he communicates him (or them) in the holy mysteries, and they escort him (or them) as far as the door of the church, singing the psalm: Blessed is he whose sins are forgiven [Ps. 32].

The deacon proclaims: For the help which is from above, and for salvation and for the establishing of this our newly-sealed one, let us pray to the Lord.

Three times, Lord have mercy on us.

And he says the following prayer: Glory to thee, King eternal, *etc.*

And they are saluted by the congregation and accompanied to their houses. But for eight days the person baptized shall remain in the church, and shall cover his head with a white hood. He shall attend to the prayers of the church, being assiduous at all times in partaking of the body and blood of Christ. And after eight days the priest lifts off the crown, saying the following prayer over him: They that have been baptized, *etc.*

NOTES

The following variant readings are found in the Vatican manuscript which Conybeare calls B, and which is dated *c.* 1300.

1. The rite begins in B as follows:

Order of catechumenate which is fulfilled before the door of the church, previously to baptism, whenever they shall be pleased to make him a Christian. Before which it is not right . . . untiring in prayer.

This is the order for those of ripe age. First they shall lay hands on all catechumens, children, and those of ripe age. They are led to the door of the church and say Psalm 131: O Lord, my heart is not haughty. *Then praise and glory. And thereafter this canon is celebrated: Ps. 42: As the hart panteth . . . Lections: Isaiah; Paul Corinth.; Gospel of Matthew. If it be a Sunday another gospel is read.* O cry unto the Lord. *And then the gospel in order. The deacon proclaims:* And again for peace let us pray in concord. *Thrice:* Lord, have mercy. *And the priest says this prayer over the catechumens:*

O Lord our God, who dost good . . . now and ever.

Canon: On the day of baptism at the door, etc.

★ ★ ★

2. The interrogations in B are as follows:

Next the priest orders the catechumen to turn to the west and to stretch his hand straight out in the same direction, as if thrusting backwards the gloomy darkness. And he bids him spit three times on Satan, that is to deny him; and he adjures him thrice, saying: Dost thou renounce Satan and all his deceitfulness and his wiles and his paths and his angels?

The priest questions him thrice, and each time the catechumen shall say: I renounce, *and withal spits on Satan.*

Then he turns the catechumen to the east, and bids him raise his eyes to heaven and stretch out his hands, confessing the one Godhead of the holy Trinity, saying thrice as follows:

Dost thou believe in the all-holy Trinity, in Father, Son, and Holy Spirit?

Dost thou believe in the birth of Christ? Dost thou believe in the baptism of Christ? Dost thou believe in the crucifixion of Christ? Dost thou believe in the three days burial of Christ? Dost thou believe in the resurrection of Christ? Dost thou believe in the ascension of Christ? In his sitting at the right hand of God? In the coming again of Christ to judge the quick and the dead?

And the priest asks the catechumen thrice: Dost thou believe?

And then they say the creed throughout.

And they say Psalm 118.

[Of Conybeare's ten MSS. this is the only one which introduces the ceremony of spitting on the devil.]

★ ★ ★

D

3. After the anointing.

Next he puts on his raiment and crowns him and says the following prayer: Blessed art thou, O God . . . Father and Son and Holy Spirit.

Thereafter he leads him up to the sanctuary, and causes him to bow before the holy altar, and thrice he kisses the three sides: that is the holy altar and the holy font and the holy door of the temple. And he shall say thrice: N. or M., a servant of God, having come from the catechumenate unto baptism and from baptism to adoration of the holy altar, hath stripped off lawlessness and hath arrayed himself in light and immortality.

And he comes up to the font and door, and says: This man being baptized hath stripped off lawlessness, hath arrayed him in light and immortality. Let him adore the divine holy font and the doors of the holy temple.

And the priest says this prayer: Lord God Almighty, etc.

4. *The Byzantine Rite*

Text: Conybeare and Maclean, *Rituale Armenorum*, Oxford, 1905. The most ancient document of the rite of Constantinople is that supplied by the Barberini Euchologion, a Greek manuscript written *c.* 790.

The rite of Constantinople was derived from that current in Syria and in many respects is similar to that described by St John Chrysostom. Indeed, the literary connection between the baptismal instructions of St John Chrysostom and the first of the passages quoted below is so close as to compel the conclusion that the latter was written by Chrysostom. Unfortunately it contains only a part of the preparatory rites, and not the order of baptism itself. The second translation is of a complete baptismal rite. Conybeare has supplied the variant readings of other comparable MSS. Most of them, however, reflect only later elaborations of the same rite; such as may be of value are inserted in brackets in the text which follows.

1. THE BARBERINI EUCHOLOGION
fol. 260ff

The renunciation [of the devil] *and act of adherence* [to Christ] *take place under the presidency of the archbishop, on the day of the holy Preparation* [Good Friday] *of the Pascha, all the catechumens being gathered in the holy church.*

The archbishop begins about the sixth hour and ascends into the ambo: and after the archdeacon has said, Let us attend, *he says to them,* Peace be to you all.

And the archbishop says to the catechumens: Behave with reverence: sign yourselves: remove your clothes and shoes.

When they are ready, he begins the instruction thus:

This is the end of our instruction: the occasion of your redemption. To-day you are to publish before Christ the contract of faith: for our pen and ink we use our understanding, our tongue and our behaviour. Watch therefore how you write your confession: make no mistake, lest you be deceived. When men are about to die, they make a will and assign someone else as the heir of their possessions: to-morrow night, you are to die unto sin: now you make and ordain a will, namely your renunciation, and you assign the devil as the heir of your sins, and you dispose of your sins as a patrimony (to him). So if any of you has anything belonging to the devil in his heart, throw it to him. He that dies has no longer power over his possessions: let none of you therefore preserve in your hearts anything that is the devil's. That is why you stand and hold up your hands when I command, as though being searched lest anyone has hidden upon him anything belonging to the devil. Let no one harbour enmity or anger, let no one behave with deceit, let no one listen with hypocrisy. Throw to the devil all *filthiness and superfluity of naughtiness* [Jas. 1.21]. Conduct yourselves as prisoners, for as such Christ purchases you. Each of you shall look at the devil and hate him, and thus ye shall blow upon him. Each of you must enter into his conscience, search his heart, and see what he has done. If after you have blown upon the devil there is still anything evil in you, spit it out. Let no Jewish hypocrisy dwell in any one; have no doubts about the sacrament. *The Word of God* searches your hearts, *being sharper than any two-edged sword* [Heb. 4.12]. The devil stands now to the west, gnashing his teeth, tearing his hair, wringing his hands, biting his lips, crazed, bewailing his loneliness, disbelieving your escape to freedom. For this cause Christ sets you opposite the devil, that having renounced him and having blown upon him you may take up the warfare against him. The devil stands to the west because that is whence darkness comes: renounce him, blow upon him, and then turn to the east and join yourselves unto Christ. Be not contemptuous. Behave with reverence: all that is happening is most awful and horrifying. All the powers of the heavens are there, all angels and archangels. Unseen, the Cherubim and Seraphim record your voices: at this moment they look down from heaven to receive your vows and carry them to the Master. Take care therefore how you renounce the enemy and accept the Creator.

And after this he says to them: Turn to the west, raise your hands. What I say, do you say also. I renounce Satan and all his works and all his service and all his angels and all his pomp.

He says this three times and they all repeat it.

Then he asks them three times: Have you renounced **Satan**?

They reply: We have renounced him.

He says: Blow upon him.

Then again he says to them: Turn to the east and lower your hands. Behave with reverence. What I say do you say also. And I adhere to Christ. And I believe in one God the Father Almighty maker of heaven and earth. And in our Lord Jesus Christ, the only-begotten Son of God, *and so on to the end. He says this three times and all answer.*

And he asks them: Have you adhered to Christ?

They reply: We have adhered.

He asks this three times. And after this he says: Worship him.

And as all worship, he says this prayer: Blessed be God, *who will have all men to be saved and come unto the knowledge of the truth* [1 Tim. 2.4] now and always and unto all ages.

And he speaks to them again:

Behold, you have renounced the devil and adhered to Christ. The contract is fully written. The Master preserves it in heaven. Study the articles of your agreement: remember, it is brought forth at the day of judgement. Make no mistake about the capital, upon which interest will be required of you. Take care that you are not ashamed at that awe-ful and dreadful tribunal before which all the powers of heaven tremble, and all mankind stands to be judged, with the myriads of angels, the armies of archangels, and the companies of the heavenly powers, when there shall be a river of fire, *the unsleeping worm* [cp. Mark 9.44], and *outer darkness* [Matt. 25.30]. You must then acknowledge the bond which you have written. If you are merciful and kind, straightway you shall have the merciful for your companions. But if you are inhuman and mean, unmerciful and abusive, slandering those who have not harmed you, then the devil shall stand at thy side for thy companion and say: In his words this man renounced me for his master, but in his actions he has served me. And then, though angels mourn and all the righteous weep over thee, yet the end of the process is heavy. It is said: Whosoever in this present life shall fall into danger shall find a protector, he shall call upon his friends, he shall be helped by relations, or he shall be released by payment. But there there shall be no such thing: no father to help, no compassionate mother, no brothers to come about you, no friends to busy themselves for you; but every man shall stand naked, alone, with no one at his side, with his own works only to help him or condemn him. For a brother cannot redeem thee, shall a man be redeemed? Watch then, and secure yourselves: you have renounced the devil, hate him to the end: you have united yourselves to Christ, praise him to your last breath, sojourn with this orthodox confession to God the Master. Be not *shipwrecked concerning the faith* [1 Tim. 1.19]. Have mercy upon the poor man, do not despise the wicked, do not take other men's goods, do not slander the innocent, give not your ears to empty talk: and while you secure your own life on every occasion, contend also in defence of us who are priests. I have not hesitated to tell you the things which will help you. For the rest, it is for you to know how to watch them. For I have done what was in me, telling you these things for your benefit, lest a sword may come and take the soul out of the people of God. For the enemy watches your words and spirit and mind and movement and action. But do you so secure yourselves that, *he of the contrary part having no evil thing to say against you* [Tit. 2.8] in the day of the dreadful judgement, we may stand unashamed at the tribunal of Christ, and hear that blessed voice which we have longed for: *Come, blessed of my Father, inherit the kingdom prepared for you from the foundation of the world* [Matt. 25.34]: to him belongs all glory, honour, worship, to the Father, to the Son, and to the Holy Ghost, now and ever and unto all ages. Amen.

And after this Amen, he says to them: Raise your hands.

For the peace of the world, for the health of the holy churches, and the praise of all men, let us say,

Lord, have mercy.

For our most religious kings, for all the palace, for their armies, and for the people that love Christ, let us say,

Lord have mercy.

For the redemption of our souls, and that Satan may soon be trampled down beneath our feet, and that our city may be kept free of bloodshed, let us say,

Lord, have mercy.

And the archbishop signs the people according to custom and says this prayer: Thou God art loving and merciful, *etc.*

And after the Amen he says, Resume your clothing, take off your shoes [Greek, *hupoluo*: probably for *hupoduo*, put on your shoes].

And he enters the sanctuary: and he offers a prayer for those who are preparing for the holy enlightening, while the deacon offers his prayer according to custom: the priest says this prayer, but does not say the customary ecphonesis *at the end of the prayer.*

O Lord, our Master and our God, summon thy servants to thy holy enlightening and make them worthy of this great gift: put off from them their years and give them new birth into eternal life, and fill them with the power of the Holy Spirit, unto the praise of thy Christ: that they may be no longer children of the body but children of thy kingdom. [This prayer appears also on p. 78.]

And the deacon completes the prayer of those who are being enlightened: then, at the time of bowing of heads, he says: As many as are for the enlightenment come forward for the laying on of hands and be blessed.

And the priest lays hands on all, both men and women: he goes in again near to the holy table and completes his prayer aloud: For thou art our light, and to thee we send up our praise.

Then the priest says: Peace be to all. *And as the deacon says:* Bow your heads, *again the priest says:*

O God our saviour, *that willeth all men to be saved and come unto the knowledge of the truth* [1 Tim. 2.4]: light the lamp of knowledge in our hearts, and in the hearts of those who approach thy holy enlightening: and count them worthy of this immortal gift and unite them to thy holy catholic Church: for it is thy property to have mercy and to save, O our God, and to thee we send up our praise, to the Father and to the Son and to the Holy Ghost, now and ever and unto all ages.

2. THE BARBERINI EUCHOLOGION
fol. 170ff

A prayer for the sealing of an infant when he receives his name on the eighth day after birth.

O Lord our God, we pray and beseech thee, let the light of thy countenance be marked upon this thy servant, and let the cross of thy Only-Begotten Son be marked, in his heart and in his thoughts, unto the renunciation of the vanities of the world and all the evil schemes of the adversary, and unto the following of thy commandments. And grant, O Lord, that he may never deny thy holy Name, that he be united in due season with thy holy Church, and perfected by the dread mysteries of thy Christ: to the end that he may walk according to thy commandments, and guard the seal unbroken, and attain to the blessedness of thine elect. (*Aloud*) By the grace and mercy and love of thy Only-Begotten Son, with whom thou art blessed, *etc.*

And when the prayer is ended, he seals him upon the forehead and breast and mouth.

A prayer when the infant comes into the Church on the fortieth day after his birth.

O Lord our God, who upon the fortieth day didst come according to the law with Mary thy mother to the temple, and was laid in the arms of Symeon the just, prosper this servant of thine by thy power, that coming to the washing of immortality he may become a child of light and day: that he may attain to a portion of the heritage of thine elect and partake of thy precious Body and Blood, being guarded by the grace of the holy, consubstantial and undivided Trinity. (*Aloud*) Unto thy glory and the glory of thine Unoriginate Father and the all-holy, good, and lifegiving Spirit, now and ever, *etc.*

A Prayer for making a Catechumen

He removes his clothes and shoes, and sets him facing to the east, and breathes upon him thrice, and seals his forehead and mouth and breast, and says:

In thy Name, O Lord the God of truth, and in the Name of thy Only-Begotten Son and of thy Holy Spirit, I set my hand upon this thy servant whom thou hast been pleased to give refuge in thy holy Name and to guard him *under the shadow of thy wings* [Ps. 17.8]: remove his feet from the path of ancient error, and fill him with faith in thee, with hope and love: that he may know that thou alone art true God, with thy Only-Begotten Son our Lord Jesus Christ and thy Holy Spirit. And grant that he may go forward in all thy commandments and guard thy good things: that *according as a man shall perform them, so shall he live in them* [cp. Rom. 10.5]: and write his name in thy *book of life* [Phil. 4.3; Rev. 13.8]: and unite him to the *flock of thine inheritance* [cp. Ps. 78.71]: may thy holy Name be praised in him, with the Name of thy beloved Son our Lord Jesus Christ, and of thy life-giving Spirit: and let thy merciful eyes ever rest in pity upon him, and thine ear to hear his supplications. Give him delight in all the works of his hands and in all the ways of his life, that he may confess thee, worshipping and praising thy great and most exalted Name, and always magnifying thee all the days of his life. (*Aloud*) For all the powers of the heavens sing thy praises, and thine is the glory of the Father and the Son and the Holy Spirit, now and ever unto all ages. Amen.

The First Exorcism

The Lord rebuke thee, O devil, the Lord who came into the world and tabernacled among men to destroy thy tyranny and deliver mankind: who upon the tree did *triumph* [cp. Col. 2.15] over the powers that were against him; when *the sun was darkened* [Luke 23.45] and *the earth did quake*, when *the graves were opened and the bodies of saints arose* [Matt. 27.51]: who by death destroyed death, and left him powerless who had the power of death, that is, the devil. I adjure thee by God, who set forth the tree of life, who appointed the Cherubim and the living sword that turned to guard it: be rebuked and depart, O unclean spirit. I adjure thee by him who walked upon the surface of the sea as upon dry land, and *rebuked* the raging of *the winds* [Mark. 4.39]: whose glance doth dry up the depths and his threat *melt the mountains* [cp. Ps. 97.5]. For he himself now commands you through us. Be afraid, go hence and depart from these creatures, come not back to hide in them, approach them not, seek not to command or tear them, neither in night nor day, nor in the hour of mid-day: but depart to thine own dark abode, until the great day of judgement which is prepared for thee. Fear God that sitteth upon the throne of the Cherubim, and looks down upon the abyss, whom the angels dread, with archangels, thrones, lordships, majesties, powers, the many-eyed cherubim and the six-winged seraphim: whom the heaven doth dread, and the earth, the sea, and all that is in them. Go hence and depart from the sealed, new-chosen servants of Christ our God. I adjure thee by him who *walketh upon the wings of the wind, who maketh his angels spirits and his ministers a flaming fire* [Ps. 104.4]: go hence and depart from these creatures with all thy power and thine angels. That the name of the Father, the Son, and the Holy Spirit be glorified now and ever, unto all ages. Amen.

The Second Exorcism

God the holy, who is to be feared and glorified, who reigneth over all his works, whose power none can restrain, who is unsearchable, God who has appointed unto thee, O devil, the torment of everlasting punishment, God himself through us his *unprofitable servants* [Luke 17.10] commands thee and all thy fellows to depart from these who are but lately sealed in the name of our Lord Jesus Christ, our true God. I adjure thee, therefore, all-evil, unclean, abominable, loathsome, and alien spirit, by the power of Jesus Christ who has all power in heaven and earth, who said to the deaf and dumb spirit: *Come out from* the man *and enter no more into him* [Mark. 9.25]; depart, acknowledge that thy power is spent, that thou hast no power, not even over the swine. Remember him that did command thee, at thy request, to enter into the herd of swine. Fear God, at whose command the earth was separated from the waters, that made the heavens, that set *the mountains in scales and the hills in a balance* [Isa. 40.12], that put *the sand for a bound of the sea* [Jer. 5.22], and a safe path through the raging water: fear God, that *toucheth the mountains and they smoke* [Ps. 144.5], that *decketh himself with light as it were with a garment, that stretcheth out the heavens like a curtain, that layeth the beams of his chambers in the waters, that layeth the foundation of the earth to establish it* [Ps. 104.2f]; he shall not fail throughout all ages, that calleth upon the water of the sea and poureth it out upon the face of all the earth. Go out and depart from these who are making ready for the holy enlightening. I adjure thee by the saving suffering of our Lord Jesus Christ and by his precious Body and Blood, and by his dreadful coming: for he shall *come in the clouds* [Matt. 24.30], he shall come and shall not delay, and shall judge all the earth, and shall punish thee and all thy fellows in the Gehenna of fire, casting thee into *outer darkness* [Matt. 8.12], where is *the unsleeping worm and the fire is not quenched* [cp. Mark 9.46]. By the power of Christ our God, with the Father and the Holy Spirit, now and throughout all ages. Amen.

The Third Exorcism

O Lord of Sabaoth, the God of Israel, that healeth *all manner of sickness and all manner of disease* [Matt. 4.22], look upon thy servants: seek, search out and drive away from them all the operations of the devil. Rebuke the base and unclean spirits, pursue them and cleanse the works of thy hands: work sharply and speedily crush down Satan beneath their feet, and give them victory over him and the unclean spirits, that by thy mercy they may be found worthy of the immortal and heavenly mysteries, and send up praise to thee, *etc.*

A prayer, after the making of a catechumen, as the hour of his baptism approaches.

O Lord, who art our master, who made man after thine image and likeness, and didst give him the power of eternal life, who then didst not disregard his fall through sin, but didst bring about the salvation of the world by the incarnation of thy Christ: do thou, as thou dost redeem this thy creature from the bondage of the enemy, receive him into thy heavenly kingdom: open the eyes of his understanding that he may behold the light of thy gospel: unite his life with a shining angel, to deliver him from all the counsel of the enemy, from the encounter of the evil one, from the mid-day spirit, from evil phantoms.

And he breathes on him thrice, and seals his brow and mouth and breast, and says:

Drive away from him every evil and unclean spirit, hidden and lurking in his heart: the spirit of error, the spirit of evil, the spirit of idolatry and all covetousness, the spirit of deceit and all uncleanness, which is worked after the teaching of the devil: and make him a reasonable sheep of the flock of thy Christ, a precious member of thy Church, a *sanctified vessel* [2 Tim. 2.21], a son of light, and an inheritor of thy kingdom: that walking after thy commandments and guarding the seal unbroken, preserving the garment unspotted, he may attain the blessedness of thine elect in thy kingdom. By the grace and mercies and loving kindness of thy Only-Begotten Son, with whom thou art blessed with thine all-holy and good and lifegiving Spirit, now and for ever and throughout all ages. Amen.

And after the Amen, the candidate is stripped and his shoes removed, and the priest turns him to the west. The candidate's hands being raised, the priest says thrice:

I renounce Satan, and all his works and all his service and all his angels and all his pomp.

And the candidate or his sponsor answers each time.

And again the priest asks, saying: Have ye renounced Satan?

And he replies: We have renounced.

And the priest says: Then blow upon him.

And the priest turns him to the east, his hands being lowered, and says:

And I adhere to Christ, and I believe in one God, the Father Almighty, *and the rest.*

And when the priest has spoken thrice, again he asks them:

And have ye adhered to Christ?

And they answer: We have adhered.

And the priest says: Worship him.

[At this point, some MSS. add: *He replies,* I worship Father, Son, and Holy Ghost, the consubstantial Triad that reigneth unto eternity.]

And the priest says this prayer:

O Lord our Master and God, summon these thy servants to thy holy enlightening, and make them worthy of this great gift of thy holy baptism: wash away their years and give them a new birth into eternal life, and fill them with the power of thy Holy Spirit, that they may be one with thy Christ: that they may be no longer children of the body, but children of thy kingdom. By the good pleasure and the grace of thy Only-Begotten Son, with whom thou art blessed, with thine all-holy and good and life-giving Spirit, now and for ever and throughout all ages. Amen. [This prayer appears also on p. 73.]

[At this point, an eleventh-century MS. includes the following rubric: *The prayers of the holy baptismal rite which the patriarch says when the foregoing prayers have been said: especially on the evening of the holy Sabbath. After the evening light has been brought in, the patriarch comes down from his throne through the sacristry into the unrobing room of the great baptistry. He changes [his robes] and puts on a white vestment and white shoes, and coming out again to the font he censes round it: and he puts the censer aside: and he makes his prayer while the deacon says the litany, and signs thrice with candles.*]

The Diakonika of the Holy Sabbath at the Baptism

In peace let us beseech the Lord.

For [Greek: *hyper*, throughout this Litany] the peace from above and the salvation of our souls, let us beseech the Lord.

For this holy house, [let us beseech the Lord].

For the sanctification of these waters by the indwelling and power of the Holy Spirit, let us pray.

That the Lord may send upon them the grace of redemption, the blessing of Jordan, let us beseech the Lord.

That they may be blessed as were Jordan's waves, let us beseech the Lord.

For the descent upon these waters of the kindly cleansing of the supersubstantial Triad, let us beseech the Lord.

That all the powers of the soul-destroying enemy may be sunk deep in them, let us beseech the Lord.

That they may avail for the cleansing of the souls and bodies of all who draw and partake of them, let us beseech the Lord.

That those who are baptized therein may appear as the lights of heaven, *not having spot nor wrinkle* [Eph. 5.27], let us beseech the Lord.

That we may be delivered, [let us beseech the Lord].

A prayer which the priest makes before he baptizes: while the deacon prays, the priest says this prayer silently:

The compassionate and merciful God, that searches the hearts and reins and knoweth the secrets of men: for there is no work that is hid from thee, but all things are bare and open to thine eyes: God that knoweth my ways; abhor me not, neither turn thy face from me, but pass over mine offences, even in this hour, thou that dost overlook the sins of men unto repentance, and take away the filth of my body and the stain of my soul, make all my being holy and perfect by thine unseen power and by thy spiritual right hand: lest while I declare freedom to others, and offer it to the faith which proceeds from thine ineffable goodness, *myself* as a slave of sin may be *a castaway* [1 Cor. 9.27]. Master that alone art good and loving to mankind, let me not turn away abased, ashamed, but send upon me power from on high, give me strength to administer this great and heavenly mystery, let *Christ be formed* [cp. Gal. 4.19] in those who seek to be reborn through my piteous ministry, build them up upon the foundation of the Apostles and Prophets [Eph. 2.20], and cast them not down: plant them as a planting of truth in thy holy, catholic, and apostolic Church, and pull them not up: that as they advance in reverence they may also glorify the holy name of thee, the Father, the Son and the Holy Ghost, now and ever and unto all ages. Amen.

It must be understood that the priest does not say the ending aloud; but he says even the Amen silently. And when the deacon has finished his prayer, the priest raises his voice and says:

Great art thou: O Lord, and wonderful are thy works, and no words are sufficient to sing thy wonders: for by thy will thou dost bring into being all things from nothing, by thy power thou dost uphold the creation, and dost order the world according to thy providence. Thou hast compounded the creation from four elements, and in four seasons hast crowned the course of the year. All powers and intelligences dread thee: the sun hymns thee, the moon praises thee, the stars hold converse with thee, the light obeys thee, the depths shudder before thee, the springs of water serve thee. Thou *spreadest out the heavens like a curtain* [Ps. 104.2]: thou dost establish the earth above the waters: thou dost *set the sand for a bound of the sea* [Jer. 5.22]. Thou dost pour out the air for man's breath. The angels worship thee: the choirs of archangels praise thee: the many-eyed cherubim and the six-winged seraphim encircle thee, they wing around thee with fear and veil thy unapproachable glory. For thou that art God, being without bounds, whose beginning is past the power of human telling, didst yet come upon earth, taking *the form of a servant and wast made in the likeness of men*

[Phil. 2.7]: for in thy compassion, Lord, thou wouldest not bear to look upon the race of men in servitude to the devil, but thou didst come and save us. We confess thy love, we tell forth thy mercy, we do not hide the goodness of thy works. Thou didst set free the children of our race. Thou didst sanctify a virgin's womb by thy birth: the whole creation hymns thine appearing. For thou, our God, didst look upon the earth and dwelt among men. For thou didst sanctify the waves of Jordan, thou didst send down thy Holy Spirit from heaven and crushed down the heads of the serpents·that lurked there. Therefore do thou, our loving king, be present now in the visitation of thy Holy Spirit and sanctify this water. Give it the grace of redemption, the blessing of Jordan. Make it a fount of purity, a gift of sanctification, a way of deliverance from sins, a protection against disease, a destruction to demons, unapproachable to the power of the enemy, filled with angelic power. Let all who seek the overthrow of this thy child flee therefrom, that we may praise thy name, O Lord, which is wondrous and glorious and fearful to the enemy.

And he breathes into the water thrice and signs it with his finger thrice, and says:

May all the enemy powers be crushed down by the sign of the type of the cross of thy Christ. May all aerial and unseen shapes depart from us, may no dark demon lie hidden in this water: and we pray thee, Lord, let no evil spirit go down with him at his baptism to bring darkness of counsel and confusion of mind. But do thou, maker of all things, declare this water to be a water of rest, water of redemption, water of sanctification, a cleansing of the pollution of the body and soul, a loosening of chains, forgiveness of sins, enlightenment of souls, washing of rebirth, grace of adoption, raiment of immortality, renewal of spirit, fount of life. For thou, Lord, hast said, *Wash you and make you clean* [Isa. 1.16]. Take away the wickedness from our souls. Thou hast given us the new birth from above by water and Spirit. Be present, Lord, in this water and grant that those who are baptized therein may be refashioned, so that they may *put off the old man, which is corrupt according to the deceitful lusts* [Eph. 4.22], and put on the new man, which is restored after the image of him that created him: that being *planted together in the likeness of the death* [Rom. 6.5] of thy Only-Begotten Son, through baptism, they may share also in his resurrection: and guarding the gift of thy Holy Spirit, and increasing the store of grace, they may receive *the prize of the high calling* [Phil. 3.14] and be numbered among *the first-born who are written in heaven* [Heb. 12.23] in Christ Jesus our Lord, for with him and the all-holy and good and life-giving Spirit the glory and the power are thine, now and for ever and unto all ages. Amen.

And after the Amen the priest says: Peace be to you all.

The deacon: Let us bow our heads to the Lord.

The priest bows his head towards the vessel of olive oil which is held up by the deacon, and breathes upon it thrice and seals it thrice, and says:

O Master, Lord God of our fathers, who didst send to those who were in Noah's ark a dove bearing a twig of olive in its mouth, to be a symbol of reconciliation and of salvation from the flood, and thereby didst prefigure the mystery of grace: who hast furnished the fruit of the olive unto the fulfilment of thy holy mysteries, and thereby hast filled with the Holy Spirit those who are under the law, and hast perfected those who live in grace: do thou bless even this oil with the power and operation and indwelling of thy Holy Spirit, so that it may be a chrism of incorruption, a shield of righteousness, a renewal of soul and body, turning away every work of the devil, unto deliverance from all evil for those that are anointed in faith and partake of it: unto thy glory, and the glory of thine Only-Begotten Son, and of thy holy and good and life-giving Spirit, now, etc.

And after the Amen, the deacon says: Let us attend.

And the priest takes the bowl of holy oil and makes three crosses with it in the water: and he sings Alleluia *thrice with the congregation, and after this puts the bowl aside.*

Blessed be God that *enlightens* and sanctifies *every man that cometh into the world* [John 1.9], now and always and unto all ages. Amen.

And he that is to be baptized is brought unto the priest: and the priest takes holy oil on his finger, and makes the sign of the cross upon the forehead and breast and back of him that is to be baptized, and says: Such a one is anointed with the oil of gladness, in the Name of the Father and of the Son and of the Holy Ghost, *etc.*

[Some MSS. read: Such a one the servant of God, is anointed, etc.]

And then his whole body is anointed by the deacon, and after that the priest baptizes him, saying: Such a one is baptized in the name, *etc.*

[Some MSS. read: Such a one, the servant of God, is baptized, etc.]

And after he is baptized, the singer begins: Blessed are they whose iniquities have been forgiven [Ps. 32.1].

And after this, while the deacon recites a prayer, the priest says this prayer:

Blessed art thou, O Lord God, the Almighty, the fount of good things, *the sun of righteousness* [Mal. 4.2], that hast raised up a light of salvation to those in darkness, through the epiphany of thy Only-Begotten Son our God, and to us unworthy hast given the blessed cleansing of his holy water and divine sanctification in the life-giving chrism: who even at this moment hast been pleased to give new birth to these thy servants newly enlightened, by water and Spirit, and has bestowed upon them forgiveness of their sins, both willingly and unwillingly committed: thou therefore, Master most benevolent, give to them also the seal of the gift of thy holy and all-powerful and worshipful Spirit, and the communion of the Holy Body and Precious Blood of thy Christ. Guard them in thy sanctification: strengthen them in the right faith: deliver them from the evil one and from all his ways, and by thy saving fear keep their souls in holiness and righteousness: that being well-pleasing to thee in every work and word, they may become sons and inheritors of thy heavenly kingdom. (*Aloud*) For thou art our God, whose property is to have mercy and to save, and to thee we send up our praise, to the Father and the Son, *etc.*

And after this prayer he says: As many as are baptized in Christ have put on Christ [Gal. 3.27].

And the priest anoints those that have been baptized with the holy oil, making the sign of the cross on the forehead and eyes and nostrils and mouth and both ears, saying: The seal of the gift of the Holy Spirit.

And he retires, saying: Blessed are they whose iniquities are forgiven and whose sins are covered [Ps. 32.1].

And the priest approaches the entrance [*i.e., the door through the screen between chancel and sanctuary*] *with the neophytes, and the divine liturgy begins.*

5. Egypt

THE SACRAMENTARY OF SARAPION

Greek text: ed. F. E. Brightman, *Journal of Theological Studies*, 1899–1900. The translation of the following extracts is based upon the translation of Bishop John Wordsworth in *Bishop Sarapion's Prayer Book*, S.P.C.K., 1899.

This document is the work of Bishop Sarapion of Thmuis, and its date is about 350. It consists only of prayers, with headings to indicate the occasion of their use, but no rubrics.

7. SANCTIFICATION OF WATERS

King and Lord of all things and Artificer of the world, who gavest salvation freely to all created nature by the descent of thy Only-Begotten Jesus Christ, thou who didst redeem the creation that thou didst create by the coming of thy ineffable Word: look down now from heaven and behold these waters and fill them with Holy Spirit. Let thine ineffable Word come to be in them and transform their energy and cause them to be productive [by] being filled with thy grace, in order that the mystery which is now being celebrated may not be found in vain in those that are being born again, but may fill all those that go down and are baptized with the divine grace. O loving benefactor, spare thy own handiwork, save the creature that has been made by thy right hand. Form all that are being born again [after] thy divine and ineffable form, in order that having been reformed and born again they may be able to be saved and counted worthy of thy kingdom. And as thy only-begotten Word coming down upon the waters of the Jordan rendered them holy, so now also may he descend on these and make them holy and spiritual, to the end that those who are being baptized may be no longer flesh and blood, but spiritual and able to worship thee the uncreated Father through Jesus Christ in Holy Spirit, through whom to thee [be] the glory and the might both now and to all the ages of the ages. Amen.

8. A PRAYER ON BEHALF OF THOSE BEING BAPTIZED

We beseech thee, O God of truth, on behalf of this thy servant and pray that thou wilt count him worthy of the divine mystery and of thy ineffable rebirth. For to thee, O Lover of men, is he now offered; to thee we dedicate him: grant him to share in this divine rebirth, to the end that he may no longer be guided by anyone who is bad or evil, but may serve thee continually and observe thy ordinances as thy only-begotten Word doth guide him: for through him to thee [be] the glory and the might in the Holy Spirit both now and to all the ages of the ages. Amen.

9. A Prayer after the Renunciation

O Lord almighty, seal the Act of Adherence of this thy servant which has now been made to thee, and keep his character and his manner of life unchanged, that he may no longer minister to those that are worse, but may worship the God of truth and serve thee the maker of all things, to the end that he may be rendered perfect and thine own through thy Only-Begotten Jesus Christ, through whom to thee [be] the glory and the might in holy Spirit both now and to all the ages of the ages. Amen.

10. A Prayer after the Reception

O Lover of mankind, saviour of all those who have turned to thee for succour, be gracious to this thy servant. Guide him to the second birth with thy right hand: may thy only-begotten Word guide him to the washing: let his rebirth be honoured by thine assent, let it not be empty of thy grace: let thy holy Word accompany him, let thy Holy Spirit be with him scaring away and driving off every temptation, because through thy Only-Begotten Jesus Christ [be] the glory and the might both now and to all the ages of the ages. Amen.

11. After he has been Baptized and has come up—a Prayer

O God, the God of truth, the Artificer of all, the Lord of all the creation, bless this thy servant with thy blessing: render him clean in the regeneration, make him to have fellowship with thy angelic powers, that he may be named no longer flesh but spiritual, by partaking of thy divine and profitable gift. May he be preserved up to the end to thee the maker of the world through thy Only-Begotten Jesus Christ, through whom [is] to thee the glory and the might in the Holy Spirit both now and to all the ages of the ages. Amen.

15. Prayers of Sarapion, Bishop of Thmuis; a Prayer in regard to the Anointing Oil of those who are being Baptized

Master, *lover of men and lover of souls* [Wisd. 11.26], compassionate and pitiful, O God of truth, we invoke thee following out and obeying the promises of thine Only-Begotten who has said, *Whosesoever sins ye forgive, they are forgiven them* [John 20.23]: and we anoint with this anointing oil those who in purpose approach this divine regeneration, beseeching thee that our Lord Jesus Christ may work in them healing and strength-making power, and by this anointing oil may reveal himself and heal away from their soul, body, and spirit, every mark of sin and lawlessness or satanic fault, and by his own proper grace may afford them remission, that *dying to sin they shall live to righteousness* [1 Pet. 2.24], and being re-created through this anointing, and being cleansed through the washing, and *being renewed in the spirit* [Eph. 4.23], they shall be able henceforth to have victory over all the opposing energies and deceits of this world that assail them, and thus to be bound up and united with the flock of our Lord and Saviour Jesus Christ, because through him to thee is the glory and the might in the Holy Spirit to all ages of ages. Amen.

16. Prayer in regard to the Chrism with which those who have been Baptized are being Anointed

God of hosts, the helper of every soul that turns to thee and that cometh under the mighty hand of thy Only-Begotten, we invoke thee to work in this chrism a divine and heavenly energy through the divine and unseen powers of our Lord and Saviour Jesus Christ, in order that they who have been baptized, and who are being anointed with it with the sign of the impress of the saving cross of the Only-Begotten, by which cross Satan and every opposing power was routed and triumphed over, they also, as being regenerated and renewed through the *washing of regeneration* [Titus 3.5], may become partakers of the gift of the Holy Spirit, and being made secure by this seal, may continue *steadfast and immovable* [1 Cor. 15.58], unhurt and inviolate, free from harsh treatment and intrigue, in the franchise of the faith and full knowledge of the truth, awaiting to the end the heavenly hopes of life and eternal promises of our Lord and Saviour Jesus Christ, through whom to thee is the glory and the might both now and to all the ages of ages. Amen.

TIMOTHY, BISHOP OF ALEXANDRIA

Two books of questions and answers upon pastoral and liturgical questions have been attributed to Timothy of Alexandria, *c.* 381, and passages from both books are here translated from J. B. Pitra, *Iuris Ecclesiastici Gretorum Historia et Monumenta*, Rome, 1864.

It is probable that the second book is wrongly attributed, and was written in the fifth century.

THE CANONICAL RESPONSES OF TIMOTHY OF ALEXANDRIA

BOOK 1

Question 6. If a catechumen, a woman, gave in her name for baptism, and on the day of baptism it befell her after the manner of women, ought she to be baptized on that day, or should it be deferred, and how long deferred?

Reply. It should be deferred, until she is cleansed.

Question 38. If an infant has been baptized, and any doubt shall arise for any reason respecting his baptism, and uncertainty remains about it, ought he to be baptized [again] or not?

Reply. If any question of this kind suggests that he ought to be baptized, then whoever baptizes him shall say: "If thou has not been baptized, I baptize thee in the Name of the Father and of the Son and of the Holy Ghost."

BOOK 2

Question 4. In the event of approaching death, should a newborn child be received as a catechumen and baptized before the seventh day?

Reply. He should.

Question 8. If a presbyter is by himself and has to administer baptism, how shall he follow the customary order? Ought he to perform the renunciation of the catechumen after consecrating the water of the laver of regeneration, and then proceed to the unction of oil? Or ought he first to perform the renunciation and then to sanctify the Jordan, that is, the water of the font? Or even, shall he baptize immediately after the blessing of the water and not go out to the renunciation?

Reply. Let him first perform the renunciation, and then enter to bless the water, and so baptize.

Question 9. At a baptism, ought a priest to perform the renunciation himself, when other priests are present, or should they?

Reply. If a deacon is present, he ought to perform the renunciation: if there are two presbyters, one should concern himself with the renunciation and the other baptize: each so bearing himself as in honour to prefer the other.

Question 10. Ought a deacon to prepare catechumens for the renunciation, or not?

Reply. Certainly: for normally this is the proper work of a deacon.

Question 11. Is it permissible for a reader or a sub-deacon to hand over a catechumen for baptism and to call out his names, or not?

Reply. It is permissible for a sub-deacon to call out the names in the absence of a deacon: moreover, if a deacon cannot be found, even a reader shall do it because of the necessity.

THE CANONS OF HIPPOLYTUS

Text: H. Achelis, *Die Canones Hippolyti*, Leipzig, 1891. The date of this document is *c.* 500. The original text was written in Greek, but no copy survives. The Latin text provided by Achelis is a translation from an Arabic version: but a Coptic version intervenes between the Arabic and the original Greek.

It will be seen that the baptismal rite of the *Canons of Hippolytus* is based upon the *Apostolic Tradition* written by Hippolytus, which however has been considerably altered to suit the needs of a different place and date.

60. Those who come often to church, in order that they may be received among the Christians, should be examined with all care, to know why they forsake their own religion, and lest by any chance they come in to jeer.

61. And if anyone has come in true faith, let him be received with joy and questioned about his job and instructed by a deacon, and learn to make renunciation in church of Satan and all his pomp.

62. Let this however be observed for the whole time of his instruction, before he is numbered with the rest of the people.

68. After forty days, they are admitted to hear the instruction. If they are worthy, they are admitted to baptism. But let their teacher refer to the Church about these things.

[69–90. A list of trades and professions which disqualified the aspiring candidate from being received as a catechumen.]

91. A catechumen who is worthy of the light need not be delayed by questions of time: the Church's teacher is the person who settles this question.

92. When the teacher has completed his daily lesson, let them pray separately from the Christians.

[93–8. Regulations concerning pregnant women and the treatment of female catechumens.]

99. Let the teacher place his hand upon the catechumens before he dismisses them.

101. A catechumen who is taken and led to bear his witness and is killed before he could be baptized, let him be buried with the other martyrs: for he is baptized in his own blood.

102. A catechumen is ready for initiation in baptism if he is commended by those who present him by a good testimony, saying that during the time of his instruction he visited the sick, supported the weak, kept himself from all perverse talk, sang [God's] praises, whether he hated vain glory, despised pride, and chose humility for himself.

103. Then let him make confession to the bishop—for on the bishop alone is such duty imposed—so that the bishop may approve him and hold him worthy to receive the mysteries: for he is now made pure in truth.

104. Then let there be read over him the gospel of the season, and let him be several times questioned, thus: Hast thou a divided heart, does anything, any cause of shame, weigh upon thee?

105. For it is not permitted that anyone makes a mockery of the kingdom of the heavens: for when it comes, it drives [such things] from the hearts of all men.

106. On the fifth day of the week let those who are to be baptized be washed with water, and eat. On the sixth day, let them fast.

108. On the sabbath day, let the bishop call together those who are to be baptized, and tell them to face east and bow the knees, and let him spread out his hands over them and pray, that he may expel the evil spirit from all their limbs.

109. And let them take care that in their works and deeds they be not turned back hence to them.

110. And after he has finished adjuring them, let him breathe into their faces, and sign their breasts, their brows, their ears, and mouths.

111. And let them pass the whole night in vigil, occupied with sacred words and prayers.

112. But about cock-crow, let them stand together near the moving water of the sea . . . pure, prepared, sacred.

113. Let those who reply for small infants put off their clothes from them: but let those who are already able occupy themselves alone with this kind of preparation.

114. But let all women have other women as their companions to take off their clothes.

115. Let women put aside their ornaments and gold and the rest and loose the bands of their hair, lest there go down with them into the water of regeneration anything foreign, belonging to foreign spirits.

116. Let the bishop pray over the oil of exorcism and hand it to the presbyter.

117. Then let him pray over the oil of unction, which is the oil of thanksgiving, and hand it to another presbyter.

118. He who holds the oil of exorcism in his hand, let him stand on the left of the bishop and he who holds the oil of unction on his right.

119. He who is being baptized, let him turn his face to the west, and say: *I renounce thee, O Satan, with all thy pomp.*

120. When he has said this, the presbyter anoints him with the oil of exorcism over which he had prayed so that every evil spirit might depart from him.

121. Then he hands him to the presbyter who stands beside the water, and the presbyter performing a deacon's office takes his right hand and turns his face to the east in the water [*in aqua*].

122. Before he descends into the water, with his face turned to the east he stands beside the water and says thus after receiving the oil of exorcism: *I believe and I bow me to thee and all thy pomp, O Father, Son, and Holy Spirit.*

123. Then let him go down into the water, and let the presbyter place his hand upon his head and question him in these words:

124. *Dost thou believe in God the Father Almighty?*

125. The candidate replies: *I believe*: then he is once immersed in the water, while the presbyter withdraws the hand placed upon his head. Another time he questions him in these words:

126. *Dost thou believe in Jesus Christ the Son of God, whom Mary the virgin bore of the Holy Spirit;*

127. *who came to save the human race;*

128. *who was crucified for us under Pontius Pilate, who died and rose again from the dead on the third day and ascended to the heavens and sitteth at the right hand of God the Father, and shall come to judge the quick and the dead?*

129. He replies: *I believe*, and again he is immersed in the water. He is questioned the third time:

130. *Dost thou believe in the Holy Spirit;*

131. *the comforter, proceeding from the Father and the Son?*

132. He replies: *I believe*, and the third time he is immersed in the water.

133. Each time [*singulis vicibus*], he says, *I baptize thee in the Name of the Father and of the Son and of the Holy Spirit* [*who is equal*].

134. When he comes up from the water the presbyter takes the chrism of thanksgiving and signs his forehead and mouth and breast with the sign of the cross and anoints his whole body and his head and face, saying: *I anoint thee in the Name of the Father and of the Son and of the Holy Spirit.* [Coptic text: *in the Name of Jesus Christ.*]

135. Then he wipes him with a towel . . . and when he is dressed leads him into the church.

136. There the bishop places a hand upon all who have been baptized and says this prayer:

137. *We bless thee, Almighty Lord God, that thou hast restored these as worthy to be born again, and dost pour out upon them thy Holy Spirit, so that they are now united to the body of the Church, never to be separated by alien works.*

138. *Give more abundantly to those to whom thou hast already given forgiveness of sins the earnest of thy kingdom, through our Lord Jesus Christ, through whom to thee with himself and the Holy Spirit be glory unto all ages. Amen.*

139. Then he signs their brows with the sign of charity, and kisses them, saying, *The Lord be with you.*

140. And the baptized reply, *And with thy spirit.* He does thus to each one who has been baptized.

141. Now they pray with all the people, who are to kiss them and rejoice with them with jubilation. (*This is the kiss of peace in the Eucharist which follows. After the administration of the Eucharistic Bread and Cup, a cup or cups of milk and honey are administered to the neophytes.*)

THE COPTIC RITE

The following translation is that of R. M. Woolley, in *Coptic Offices*, S.P.C.K., 1930. It was made from the printed books in current use.

THE ORDER OF HOLY BAPTISM

A Prayer of Absolution over the Mother of the Child

The priest says:

Master, Lord God Almighty, *etc.*

A Prayer which shall be said over the Catechumens

The priest shall say:

Master, Lord God Almighty, Father of our Lord and our God and our Saviour Jesus Christ, we pray and beseech thy goodness, O Lover of men, have mercy on thy servants the catechumens who have received instruction.

The deacon shall say:

Pray for the catechumens of our people, that Christ our God may make them worthy of holy Baptism, and forgive us our sins.

The people shall say: Lord, have mercy.

The priest shall say:

Stablish them in the faith of thee; all traces of idolatry cast out of their heart. Thy law, thy fear, thy commandments, thy truths, thy holy ordinances stablish in their heart. Grant unto them that they may know the certainty of the words with which they have been instructed: and at the time appointed may they be worthy of the laver of the new birth, unto the remission of their sins; preparing them to be a temple of thy Holy Spirit. Through the grace and the mercies.

The deacon says: Pray ye.

The priest says:

Master, Lord Jesus Christ, who didst *bow the heavens and come down* [Ps. 144.5] to earth, whose word did smite the rocks more mightily than swords, before whose face *the waters were troubled* [Ps. 77.16] and *fled backwards* [Ps. 114.5]. Heal these children who come to be made catechumens. Show them the way in which it is meet for them to walk; instruct them in the grace of thy Holy Spirit that they may abide in the imperishable gift of thy Holy Spirit; and bestow upon them remission of their sins, and grant them that by thy grace they may be healed from destroying sin, that they may be made worthy of the Holy Baptism of the new birth, in order that they may receive also the washing of the spotless baptism of thy Holy Spirit; that they may see with holy vision unto sure understanding, and may give glory to thee, O God; for thine is the glory with thy good Father and the Holy Spirit, for ever. Amen.

A Prayer over the Oil of the Catechumens

Let the priest take the vessel of oil.

The deacon shall say: Pray ye.

The priest shall say:

Master, Lord God Almighty, Father of our Lord and our God and our Saviour Jesus Christ, we pray and beseech thy goodness, O lover of men, the one only true God with thy Only-Begotten Son Jesus Christ and the Holy Spirit; to look upon thy creature, this oil, and make it to become for the casting out of devils and magic and sorcery and all idolatry: and change it and manifest it as an oil for the anointing of catechumens, unto the making of the soul believing. Through Christ Jesus our Lord. Through whom.

Another Prayer over the Oil

The deacon shall say: Pray ye.

The priest shall say:
Master, Lord God Almighty, *etc.*

Here shall the priest examine the condition of the children, whether there be earrings in their ears, or ornaments on their feet, or rings on their fingers, or armlets, and shall order their removal. And he shall take the vessel of oil, and begin in order, the male children first, and then the female.

Anoint his forehead, saying:
Thou art anointed, son of N., in the Name of the Father and of the Son and of the Holy Ghost, One God, with oil of catechumens in the holy only catholic and apostolic Church of God. *Amen.*

Anoint his breast and his hands and his back, saying:
May this oil render of none effect all assaults of the adversary. *Amen.*

Here and elsewhere when the priest touches the oil or the hagielaion or the chrism let him wipe his hand or his thumb well so as not to injure the book of prayers. With this we will be content by way of warning once for all.

The deacon shall say: Let us beseech the Lord.

The priest shall say: Blessed art thou, our Master, Lord Almighty. Blessed is thy Only-Begotten Son, Jesus Christ our Lord. Through whom thou hast drawn all the nations out of darkness unto the true and wonderful light; and from error and vanity of idols unto the knowledge of the truth.

The deacon says: Pray ye.

The priest says: These thy servants hast thou called by thy holy and blessed Name. Write their name in thy book; number them with thy people and them that fear before thee. Deign to grant that they may grow in the faith, and remission of sins; preparing them to be a temple of thy Holy Spirit, through thy Only-Begotten Son, Jesus Christ our Lord. Through whom.

The deacon shall say: Let us beseech the Lord.

Let the priest enquire the name of those that are to be baptized, and pray over them saying:
And again let us beseech, *etc.*

The deacon shall say:
Pray for them that have given in their names, that the Lord may make them worthy of holy baptism unto remission of their sins.

The priest says:
Master, Lord God Almighty, *etc.*

[This and two prayers that follow are the remnant of the ancient catechetical course.]

After this let the priest lay hands upon them, saying thus:
In the Name of the Only-Begotten Son, Jesus Christ, I purify and prepare beforehand this body. In the Name of the Only-Begotten Son, Jesus Christ, let it be delivered from all demons and uncleanness. Let all darknesses flee from this body and let all unbelieving thoughts flee from this soul. In the Name of the Only-Begotten Son, Jesus Christ our Lord, mayest thou be purified, mayest thou be delivered from all demons for ever. *Amen.*

And then let him that is to be baptized be stripped: and let him look towards the west, with his right hand outstretched, and let him say thus as follows. But if he be a child, let his father or his mother or his sponsor say on his behalf thus:

I renounce thee, Satan, and all thy unclean works, and all thy wicked angels and all thy evil demons, and all thy power and all thy abominable service, and all thy evil cunning and error, and all thy host, and all thy authority, and all the rest of thy impieties.

And he shall say thrice: I deny thee.

Let the priest breathe into the face of him that is to be baptized, and say thrice:

Come out, thou unclean spirit.

After this they shall be turned to the east, with both their hands uplifted, saying thus:

I profess thee, O Christ my God, and all thy saving laws, and all thy quickening service, and all thy lifegiving works.

Again he shall bid them to confess the faith, saying:

I believe in one God, God the Father Almighty, and his Only-Begotten Son, Jesus Christ our Lord, and the holy lifegiving Spirit, and the resurrection of the flesh, and the one only catholic apostolic Church. Amen.

And thou shalt ask him thrice, saying:

Dost thou believe?

And he shall say: I believe.

After this the deacon shall say:

Let us beseech the Lord.

The priest shall say:

Master, Lord God Almighty, *etc.*

The deacon says: Bow down your heads unto the Lord.

And let them kneel and let the priest pray over them saying:

Master, our Saviour, beneficent lover of men, to thee alone is this mystery performed. To thee *all knees bow, those in heaven and those on earth, and those which are underneath the earth; and all tongues confess thee, saying, Jesus Christ is Lord, to the glory of God the Father* [Phil. 2.10f]; and thy servants who have fled to thee bow their knees to thee. Wherefore we pray and beseech thee, O lover of men, search the chambers of their souls and enlighten the eyes of their understanding with the light of knowledge. All magic, all sorcery, all workings of Satan chase from them; all traces of idolatry and unbelief cast out of their heart. Prepare their souls for the reception of thy Holy Spirit. And let them be worthy of the new birth of the laver, and of remission of sins. Preparing them to be a temple of thy Holy Spirit, according to the will of thy good Father and the Holy Spirit. Now.

After this take the agallielaion of the oil of exorcism. Anoint him that is to be baptized on his breast and his arms and over his heart behind and between his two hands in the sign of the cross, saying:

Thou art anointed, child of N. with the oil of gladness, availing against all the workings of the adversary, unto thy grafting into the sweet olive tree of the holy catholic Church of God. Amen.

The deacon says: Amen.

A prayer of the laying on of hands on the catechumens after they are anointed with the agallielaion:

Master, Lord God Almighty, *etc.*

THE HALLOWING OF THE WATER OF BAPTISM

After this the priest shall enter into the baptistry and take the unmixed oil, and pour it into the baptismal tank in the form of a cross, saying:

In the Name of the Father, *etc.*

[From this point the rite proceeds as an artificial copy of the Eucharistic rite, with four lections, psalmody, intercessions, Sursum corda, Eucharistic prayer blessing the water, infusion of chrism (= commixture in Eucharist), Baptism (= Holy Communion), prayer deconsecrating the water (= ablutions). A similar phenomenon may be observed in the Armenian rite.]

* * *

And the deacon leads him that is to be baptized from the west and brings him to the east over against the Jordan [the font], to the left hand of the priest. And the priest asks him his name, and immerses him thrice; and at each immersion he raises him up and breathes in his face.

At the first immersion he shall say:
I baptize thee, son of N. in the Name of the Father.

The second time:
And of the Son.

The third time:
And of the Holy Ghost. Amen.

And if the person that shall be baptized be a female, he shall say:
I baptize thee, daughter of N.

After he has baptized all the children, he shall pour water over his hands in the Jordan, and shall wash the surroundings of the Jordan and the cross.

Then let the priest say this prayer over the Jordan for the release [i.e., from Consecration] *of the water:*

Master, Lord God Almighty . . . we pray and beseech thee . . . to change this water to its former nature . . . now and ever. *Amen.*

Then after this he shall let the water go, taking care that none of it be put to any use at all. He shall be very careful of this.

THE SEALING WITH THE HOLY CHRISM AND THAT WHICH FOLLOWS AFTER

Then take the Holy Chrism and pray over it, saying:

O Lord who alone art mighty, who workest all marvels, and nothing is impossible with thee, O Lord, but by thy will thy power worketh in all things; bestow the Holy Spirit in the pouring out of the Holy Chrism. Let it be a living seal and a confirmation to thy servants. Through thine Only-Begotten Son, Jesus Christ our Lord. Through whom.

And after this the priest shall begin to anoint the children with the holy unction in the sign of the cross, each one with thirty and six crosses.

[He anoints the candidates at about thirty different parts of the body, as he says:]

In the Name of the Father and of the Son and of the Holy Ghost.
An unction of the grace of the Holy Ghost.
An unction of the pledge of the kingdom of heaven.
An unction of participation in eternal and immortal life.
A holy unction of Christ our God, and a seal that shall not be loosed.
The perfection of the grace of the Holy Spirit, and the breastplate of the faith and the truth.
Thou art anointed, son of N. with holy oil, in the Name of the Father and of the Son and of the Holy Ghost. *Amen.*

And when the signing of each of the children is finished, he shall lay his hand on him and say:

Mayest thou be blessed with the blessing of the heavenly ones, and the blessing of the angels. May the Lord Jesus Christ bless thee: and in his name (*here he shall breathe in the face of him that has been baptized and say*), receive the Holy Spirit and be a purified vessel; through Jesus Christ our Lord, whose is the glory, with his good Father and the Holy Spirit, now and ever.

After this he shall clothe him that has been baptized in a white garment, and he shall say:

A garment of eternal and immortal life. *Amen.*

After he has finished the signing and the breathing on all the children, he shall say over them this prayer:

The deacon says: Let us beseech the Lord.

The priest says:

Master, Lord God Almighty, who alone art eternal, the Father of our Lord and our God and our Saviour Jesus Christ; who didst command that thy servants should be born through the laver of the new birth, and hast bestowed upon them forgiveness of their sins and the garment of incorruption and the grace of sonship. Do thou again now, O our Master, send down upon them the grace of thy Holy Spirit the Paraclete; make them partakers of life eternal and immortality, in order that, according as thine Only-Begotten Son, our Lord and our God and our Saviour Jesus Christ did promise, being born again by water and spirit, they may be able to enter into the kingdom of heaven. Through the Name and the power and the grace of thine Only-Begotten Son Jesus Christ our Lord. Through whom.

After that he has clothed them with the rest of their clothing, he shall say this prayer over the crowns:

Lord God Almighty, the Father of our Lord and our God and our Saviour Jesus Christ, who hast bestowed crowns upon thy holy apostles and thy prophets and thy martyrs who pleased thee, crowns unfading: do thou again now bless these crowns which we have prepared to bestow upon thy servants who have received holy baptism that they may be unto them crowns of glory and honour. *Amen.*

Crowns of blessing and glory. *Amen.*

Crowns of virtue and righteousness. *Amen.*

Crowns of wisdom and understanding. *Amen.*

Give them strength to fulfil thy commandments and thine ordinances, that they may attain unto the benefits of the kingdom of heaven. Through Christ our Lord. Through whom.

The priest girds each one of them with a girdle in the form of a cross, and sets the crown on the head of each one of them.

[After the end of a congregational devotion, the rite continues:]

And at the end of the setting on of the crowns, the people shall finish with this sentence, saying:

Crowns unfading the Lord hath set upon them that have received
the holy baptism of Jesus Christ.

Blessed art thou in truth, O my Lord Jesus, with thy good Father
and the Holy Spirit; for thou didst receive baptism, thou didst redeem
us.

After this, give them of the Holy Mysteries.

[Note: it will be observed that three oils are used in the course of
the Coptic rite: the oil of exorcism, the Hagielaion, and the Chrism.
Hagielaion is the Greek *hagion elaion*, or holy oil. It is also called
agallielaion (Greek: *elaion agalliaseos*), meaning "oil of thanksgiving".]

6. Africa

In the sixth century, Muslim invasion obliterated Christian civilization in North Africa, and the Church ceased to exist there. No African liturgical books remain to us from those times, and our knowledge of their rite has to be gleaned from the writings of the Fathers. The chief of these is St Augustine. There are also certain sermons which have been shown to be the work of St Augustine's contemporary, Quodvultdeus, Bishop of Carthage. (See the articles by Dom Morin in *Revue Bénédictine*, Vol. 13, p. 342; Vol. 31, p. 156.) These sermons suggest that a rather different order prevailed at Carthage than that which St Augustine attests for Hippo.

A very full and valuable exposition and discussion of all the passages from St Augustine and Quodvultdeus on which our knowledge of the African rite may be built up is given by Dom Benedict Busch in *Ephemerides Liturgicae* (1938), pp. 159f, 385f, in an article entitled *De Initiatione Christiana secundum S. Augustinum*.

We set out below first those passages from St Augustine's works which are relevant to our purpose; then extracts from three sermons of Quodvultdeus; and finally extracts from correspondence between Fulgentius, Bishop of Ruspe, and Ferrandus, a deacon of Carthage from 520 to 547.

ST AUGUSTINE OF HIPPO

1. THE MAKING OF A CATECHUMEN

The principal authority for this is the book *De Catechizandis Rudibus*, which St Augustine wrote in reply to a request asking how a pagan ought to be received who seeks admission as a catechumen. He prescribes first a lengthy address (perhaps about two hours), expounding from the Bible the nature of the Christian life and faith. Speaking of the Passover Lamb, he says: "And with the sign of his Passion and Cross thou art this day to be marked on thy forehead, as on the doorpost, and all Christians are marked with it." (c. 20.)

When St Augustine has completed his outline of a suitable address, he continues: "At the conclusion of this address, the person is to be asked whether he believes these things, and earnestly desires to observe them. And on his reply to that effect, then certainly he is to be solemnly signed and dealt with in accordance with the custom of the Church. On the subject of the sacrament, indeed [reading *sane*: but some MSS. read *salis*, i.e. "of salt"], which he receives, it is first to be well impressed upon his notice that the signs of divine things are, it is true, invisible, but that the invisible things themselves are also honoured in them, and that that species, which is then to be sanctified by the blessing, is therefore not to be regarded merely in the way in which it is regarded in any common use." (c. 26.)

Whether *sane* or *salis* is the correct reading, the context makes it clear that it is salt to which St Augustine refers. Another reference to salt in the life of catechumens comes from St Augustine's reference to his own childhood, when he says: "For while yet a boy I had heard of the eternal life promised in the lowliness of our Lord God condescending to our proud minds: I was signed [*signabar*] with his cross and seasoned [*condiebar*] with his salt from my mother's womb." (*Confessions*, Book I, 11.) The custom by which catechumens in Africa regularly received salt at the Eucharist is attested by the fifth canon of the third Council of Carthage (q.v.). That sufficiently explains the significance of the imperfect tense of *condiebar*, but not of *signabar*. The following extract also possibly refers to the repeated reception of salt: "Sanctification is not received in one fashion only: for I suppose that even catechumens receive an appropriate sanctification in the sign of Christ and in the prayer of the laying on of the hand: and what they receive, though it is not the Body of Christ, is nevertheless holy, and more holy than the food with which we are nourished, because it is a sacrament." (*De Peccatorum Meritis et Remissione*, 2, 26, 42.) It is also possible, however, that the reference here is to exorcized bread, which is known to have been given to catechumens.

Another passage relating to the sign of the cross made upon a catechumen arises when St Augustine rebukes Christians who are not true to their profession: "Are you a catechumen? Has one of your foreheads received the sign of Christ, while you take another forehead to the theatre? The name of God was called upon you, Christ is called upon you, God is called upon you, and the sign of the cross is marked upon your forehead." (*Miscellanea Agostiniana*, Rome, 1930, Vol. 1, 89, 2–7.)

Two of the extracts which we have already quoted make oblique reference to exorcism at the making of a catechumen. Thus, in the passage from *De Peccatorum Meritis et Remissione*, the prayer of the laying on of the hand is a reference to exorcism: and when, in the *De Catechizandis Rudibus*, St Augustine says that the candidate is to be "dealt with in accordance with the custom of the Church" (*ecclesiae more tractandus*), we probably have a reference to the same thing. Exsufflation, as well as the laying on of the hand, is often mentioned by St Augustine, and he accepts the common interpretation of the ceremony as a sign of contempt for the devil. Thus he writes: "Exsufflation is made over infants, and they are exorcized, so that the power of the devil may be expelled from them." (*De Symbolo ad Catechumenos*, I, 13); and elsewhere he quotes the law according to which "those who made exsufflation upon the images of the emperors were guilty of treason". Exsufflation appears to have been regarded by St Augustine as a normal concomitant of exorcism.

The following passage is quoted by W. C. Bishop(*J.T.S.*, Vol. 13, pp. 250ff) as evidence that anointing was a feature of the rite whereby catechumens were made; but Dom Benedict Busch is more likely to be correct when he says that the phrases which suggest this are probably to be understood symbolically: the catechumen has placed his faith already in "the Anointed One", and is thus comparable to the blind man whose eyes were anointed. The passage in question is as follows:

The Lord came: and what did he do? He brought to our notice a great mystery. *He spat on the ground* [John 9.6] and made clay of his spittle: for *the Word was made flesh* [John 1.14]. And he anointed the eyes of the blind man. He was anointed and yet he did not see. He sent him to the pool which is called Siloam. The evangelist is careful to draw our attention to the name of the pool: he says, *Which is by interpretation, Sent.* Now you know who was sent: for none of us, unless he had been sent, would have been released from sin. And so he washed his eyes in the pool called Sent and was baptized in Christ. Now if when Christ baptized him in himself in this fashion he then also gave him sight: when he anointed him he made him, perhaps, a catechumen. The profundity of so great a sacrament may be expounded and discussed in many other ways: but let this be sufficient to your charity: you have heard a great mystery. Ask a man, Are you a Christian? He answers, No, if he is a pagan or a Jew. But if he says, I am, ask him again, Catechumen or faithful? If he answers, Catechumen, then he has been anointed, though not yet washed. But whence was the anointing? Ask, and he answers: ask him in whom he believes. In Christ [i.e., in the anointed one], he says: for he is a catechumen. I speak, you see, both to faithful and to catechumens. Why then do I speak of spittle and clay? Because the Word was made flesh. Even the catechumens hear this: but the state to which they were anointed is not enough for them: they hasten to the laver, if they seek light. (Tract on St John 44.2.)

*   *   *

In St Augustine's Africa, men might remain catechumens for many years. They would bear the name of Christian, belong to the society of the Church, attend the Mass of the catechumens, and receive there the sacrament of salt. At the beginning of Lent, the invitation was annually made to give in names for baptism. Thus Augustine says: "Lo, the Paschal season has come, give in your names for baptism." (Sermon 132, 1.) Elsewhere he says: "If the Church is a virgin, how does she bring forth children? Or if she does not bring forth children, how does it come that we give in our names, that we should be born from her bowels?" (Sermon 213, 7.)

2. PREPARATION FOR BAPTISM

A general account of the period of preparation emerges from the following passage: "Or have we so deceived ourselves that we do not notice those people who come each year to the laver of regeneration, with what ardour they approach the days when they are catechized, exorcized, scrutinized, at how many vigils they assemble?" (*De Fide et Operibus*, 6, 9.)

Nine sermons provide us with more detailed evidence of the manner and order of preparation for baptism. They are as follows:

> Sermon 216, addressed "To the Competents".
> Sermon 212, before the delivery of the Creed.
> Sermons 213, 214, at the delivery of the Creed.
> Sermon 215, at the return of the Creed.
> Sermons 56–9, at the delivery of the Lord's Prayer.

Sermon 216: Procatechesis and Scrutiny

Two views have been taken about this sermon, and it is very probable that both are correct. Thus Dom B. Busch compares it to the Procatechesis of St Cyril, because it has an introductory character. A demonstration of this would require the citation of lengthy passages, but its truth may readily be proved by reference to the sermon. A. Dondeyne in an important article in the *Revue d'Histoire Ecclésiastique* (Vol. 28, 1932) entitled "La Discipline des Scrutins dans l'Église romaine", draws attention to another aspect of the sermon. His article is devoted to a successful demonstration that the "scrutinies" of the primitive rite were primarily concerned with exorcismal exercises. They were public occasions, when the candidate underwent exorcisms of exceptional severity, in circumstances of some humiliation, standing naked and barefoot upon goatskins in some parts of the Church. Their original purpose was to satisfy the Church that the course of exorcism which the candidate had already under-gone had been effective. This was known if the candidate endured the scrutiny without showing any signs of continuing demon-possession. Certain passages in Sermon 216 indicate that the sermon was preached at the end of such an occasion:

> Being thus set about by enemies, array yourselves in goatskin and humble your minds by fasting: for that is rendered to humility which is denied to pride. Certainly you were not arrayed with goatskin when you were scrutinized, when rebukes in the Name of the dread Trinity were justly pronounced over him that incites to flight and desertion: yet with mystic meaning your feet stood upon it. Thus sin is trodden underfoot, as also the goatskin.

> Since we have ascertained that you are now free from them [unclean spirits], we congratulate you and admonish you that the health which has now been made evident in your body may be preserved also in your hearts.

If Busch and Dondeyne are both correct in affirming, first that Sermon 216 marks the first formal gathering of the *competentes*, and secondly that the sermon must be interpreted on the understanding that it was delivered in the context of a scrutiny, it seems to follow that the scrutiny was the first part of the candidates' preparation; at least so far as Hippo is concerned. There is no evidence how many scrutinies took place in the course of Lent at Hippo, but it will be shown that only one seems to have been observed at Carthage.

Sermons at the Delivery of the Creed and of the Lord's Prayer.

It is clear that one week intervened between the two deliveries, for in Sermon 213, at the delivery of the creed, St Augustine says: ". . . the Lord's Prayer, which you are to receive in a week's time" [*post octo dies*].

The evidence which will enable us to determine the dates, or the relative dates, of the two deliveries and two redditions, of the Creed and of the Lord's Prayer, may best be seen in two passages from Sermon 58. There are relevant passages in the other sermons listed above: they are consistent with Sermon 58, and add nothing to it. The first passage in question is as follows:

You have made return of the Creed, in which is contained a brief summary of the faith. . . . Therefore you must lay hold in your mind of this prayer also, and make return of it in a week's time [*ad octo dies*]. But if any of you have not made a good return of the Creed, they still have time, let them grasp it firmly: for on the sabbath, the last sabbath, the day on which you are to be baptized, you must make return of it [again] in the hearing of all who shall be there. But in a week's time from to-day [*ad octo autem dies ab hodierno die*] you are to make return of this Prayer, which to-day you have received.

The second passage, near the end of the sermon, is as follows:

When you have been baptized, you will have to say the Prayer daily. For the Lord's Prayer is said daily in Church at the altar of God, and the faithful hear it. We are not therefore disturbed by any fear, wondering whether your minds have grasped it with less care: for if any of you have not been able to grasp it perfectly, yet by daily hearing you will grasp it. That is why, on the day of the sabbath, before we keep vigil and wait on the mercy of God, it is the Creed and not the Lord's Prayer of which you are to make return. For unless you have a firm grasp of the Creed, you do not hear the Creed daily in Church among the people. So when you have grasped it, say it daily, so as not to forget it; when you rise, when you lie down to sleep, make return of your Creed, return it to the Lord, remind yourselves of it, do not tire of repeating it.

This second citation from Sermon 58 reveals what St Augustine regarded as the important reason for the ceremony of delivering the Creed. In the early Church, it had no regular liturgical recitation, and was heard only three times in the year, on the occasions of its delivery, its return, and the profession or interrogations in the actual rite of baptism. This explains for St Augustine, and possibly for other writers, the stress which they lay on the importance of learning the Creed by heart and constantly repeating it.

The Washing of Feet

Two passages from letters of St Augustine are quoted to show that the custom of washing the candidates' feet took place on Maundy Thursday:

But if you ask why the custom of washing has arisen, upon consideration the most likely explanation seems to me to be this, that the bodies of the candidates for baptism, soiled after the observance of forty days of fasting, would be very offensive to the senses when they approached the font, if upon some day they were not washed: and that day was suitably chosen for the occasion, on which the Lord's Supper is annually celebrated. And since this concession is made to candidates for baptism, many others wish to wash with them and to relax the fast. (Ep. 54, 7.)

Concerning the washing of feet . . . the question has arisen at what time so important a lesson might be given a practical demonstration, and it fell during that season in which the Lord's command might have the more exact [religiosius] expression [i.e. on Maundy Thursday]. But lest it might seem to belong to the actual sacrament of baptism, many declined to accept this into their customs. But there were some who sought to commend the observance by a more sacred season [reading sacratiore: but some MSS. read secretiore] and yet to distinguish it from the sacrament of baptism, and appointed either the third day of the octave or the octave day itself for its observance. (Ep. 55, 18, 33.)

*   *   *

3. THE RITE OF BAPTISM

In extracts from Sermon 58 we have seen that a return of the Creed was made on Easter Eve and that the night was spent in vigil.

It is difficult to construct a clear picture of the rites which accompanied the baptismal washing. From the following passages we gather something about interrogations relating to renunciation, to faith, and perhaps also about turning to God. References to the baptismal formula are not as clear as they may seem and must be understood in the light of other evidence from Africa. (See E. C. Whitaker, "The History of the Baptismal Formula", in The Journal of Ecclesiastical History, Vol. xvi, p. 1; J. N. D. Kelly, Early Christian Creeds, p. 57.) The rites following the baptismal washing evidently included unction, the imposition of the hand, and an invocation of the sevenfold Spirit.

For what reason therefore should he [the godparent] say that he [the child] renounced the devil, if there was nothing of the devil in him? that he should be turned towards God, if he was not turned away from him? that he believed in the remission of sins (among the rest), when none could be attributed to him? (*De Peccatorum Meritis et Remissione*, I, 34, 63.)

And so you put on not us but Christ. I did not ask you whether you turned towards me, but towards the living God: not whether you believed in me, but in the Father and the Son and the Holy Spirit. (*Contra litt. Pet.*, 3, 8, 9.)

The symbolism by which in his renunciation a man relinquishes night and the setting sun, and turns towards the light. (*Enarratio in Ps.* 76, 4.)

. . . for we ask the sponsors who bring the children, and say, Does he believe in God? And although the child is of an age when he does not even know whether there be a God, they reply, He believes. And they reply in like manner to each of the other questions which are asked. (Ep. 98.)

For, renouncing the devil and withdrawing your mind from his pomps and angels, you must forget past things. (Sermon 215.)

Suddenly, however, with death threatening, he begins to be disturbed and demands baptism. He receives it in such haste that the danger scarcely leaves time for the few words of the necessary interrogation. (*De Bapt.* I, 13, 21.)

And so if Marcion consecrated baptism with the gospel words, "In the name of the Father and of the Son and of the Holy Spirit", the sacrament was sound: although the faith he understood by the words was not sound, since he held other opinions than catholic truth teaches, tainted with lies and fables. For if it were possible to make a careful examination not only of Marcion or Valentinus or Arius or Eunomius but of the very children of the Church (carnal children, to whom the Apostle said, *I could not speak unto you as spiritual but as carnal* [I Cor. 3.1]) upon these same words, that is to say, In the name of the Father and of the Son and of the Holy Spirit, you would probably count as many opinions as you had people. (*De Bapt. contra Donat.* 3,20.)

Those gospel words, without which baptism cannot be consecrated, have such power that, just as by the name of Christ the devil is expelled, so by these words our prayer is cleansed of anything harmful and contrary to the rule of faith which it may contain . . . Who does not know that that is not the baptism of Christ, if the gospel words upon which the creed is grounded should be lacking (*verba evangelica quibus symbolum constat*). (*De Bapt. contra Donat.* 6, 47.)

I have learned to recognize one baptism, consecrated and signed in the name of the Father and of the Son and of the Holy Spirit. Where I find this form I cannot but approve. (Ep. 23.)

He was baptized, he was sanctified, he was anointed, the hand was laid upon him. (Sermon 324.)

He is the sevenfold Spirit, who is called down upon the baptized. (*Miscellanea Agostiniana*, Vol. 1, 490.)

Remember, you did not exist, and you were created: you were carried to the Lord's threshing floor . . . when you were set aside as catechumens you were stored in his barn. You gave in your names: you began to be ground with fasting and exorcism. After that you came to water, were moistened and made one. You were cooked then, when the ardour of the Holy Spirit came near, and now have been made the Lord's bread. (*Miscellanea Agostiniana*, Vol. 2, 6-19.)

THE RITE OF CARTHAGE

Relevant extracts from the sermons of Quodvultdeus and from one letter of Ferrandus are not sufficient grounds upon which to construct an account of the whole rite. But they afford evidence which suggests a rather different order of procedure from that which obtained at Hippo. The letter of Ferrandus indicates that there was only one scrutiny at Carthage, and this may very well have been the case at Hippo. But the sermons of Quodvultdeus, which were concerned with the Delivery of the Creed, indicate that the Creed was delivered at Carthage in the context of the scrutinial rite, and that a renunciation of the devil was made at the scrutiny. Ferrandus appears to confirm this.

QUODVULTDEUS

1. SERMON ON THE CREED. (MPL 42, col. 1117.)

. . . The presence of this great assembly demands that I explain to you the significance of the past night; of this day also, in which ye have received so great a sacrament of which I shall now explain the true and eternal salvation. For if we consider the works of the past night, and attempt to explain what, by God's gift, we then did; we shall find that in the night we performed the works, not of the night but of the day. For our senses were not lulled with the delight of sleep nor our minds deceived with dreams . . . but in watching and praying, with psalms, in strife with our adversary the devil; we felt a great light flooding our hearts, and in the night we performed the works of the day. For what did we do in the night? We put the devil to flight and brought Christ in ... What was done in the night? Pride was destroyed, humility brought in. The chief of all evil was expelled, the fount of all goodness received. You see what good things are prepared for you, and from what labour and what burden of sin you are raised by him who calls you to take upon you his light yoke and his light burden. *Casting off therefore the works of darkness, put on the armour of light* [Rom. 13.12]. The meaning of this has been explained to you, as you know in the words of the Creed which you have just received. What is, Cast off the works of darkness, but, Renounce the devil, his pomps and his angels? What is, Put on the armour of light, but, Believe in God the Father Almighty?

2. SERMON UPON THE CREED. (MPL 40, col. 637.)

I am to explain to you the sacraments of the past night and of the present holy Creed ... For you are not yet re-born in holy baptism, but by the sign of the cross you have been conceived in the womb of holy mother Church. And so this mother seeks to feed with suitable food those whom she carries, that after birth she may have joy to have brought forth those whom she has spiritually fed. What is it that has been performed upon you? What is it which in this night has happened about you, that did not happen in past nights: that from hidden places you were brought forward one by one in the sight of the whole Church, and then, with bowed head (which once had been held too high), with lowly feet, upon strewn sackcloth, examination was made upon you, the proud devil was driven out of you, and the lowly, most high Christ was called down upon you ... If our help is in his name, let us renounce the devil, his pomps, and his angels. You have heard this, it has indeed been your profession, to renounce the devil, his pomps, and his angels.

3. SERMON UPON THE CREED. (MPL 40, col. 659.)

... All the sacraments which are wrought over you are wrought by the ministry of the servants of God, in exorcism, prayers, spiritual songs, insufflations, sackcloth, bowing the head, lowliness of feet.

*   *   *

FULGENTIUS, BISHOP OF RUSPE
FERRANDUS, A DEACON OF CARTHAGE

In a letter to Fulgentius, Ferrandus submitted the case of a man baptized in
unusual circumstances and asked whether he had been truly baptized or not.
The correspondence is printed in Migne, *P.L.* 65, 378, 387.

This man, then, is handed over to the Church to receive the Church's
sacraments: he becomes a catechumen in customary fashion: after a
short time, with the approach of the Paschal solemnities, he is offered
among the competents, enrolled, instructed. Then, when he knows
and understands the universal and venerable mysteries of the Catholic
religion, the scrutiny is celebrated and he is delivered by exorcism
from the devil: and before he hears the creed, he declares as custom
requires that he will constantly renounce the devil. Moreover, he
confesses the exact words of the holy creed from memory in a clear
voice in the presence of the faithful: he receives the pious rule of the
Lord's prayer. Knowing now both what he should believe and what
he should pray, he is ready to be baptized, when suddenly he is smitten
with a severe fever . . . Then, at his last gasp, deprived of speech and of
the power to move and feel, unable to answer the questions of the
priest, he is carried by bearers, and while we make his answers as
though for an infant, with his mind quite gone he is baptized. Soon
afterwards he died, and in my opinion he never knew in this present
life that he had been baptized.

And now my question is whether or not his lack of speech damaged
his hope of eternal blessedness.

In the course of a long letter, Fulgentius replied:

We do not hesitate to say that the man was saved, because he understood, he believed, he affirmed his belief by his own profession
[i.e. in the *Redditio Symboli*]: in these circumstances, while still alive
but not understanding, he received the sacrament of holy regeneration...

. . . We believe that he was saved, and our belief is just. Before his
baptism he believed and did not fail to make confession of what his
intelligence showed him: and at the time of his baptism, though sick
and fevered, he was still alive. In the life which contracted original sin
he gave, when he was able to do so, the testimony of his conscience
and intellect [i.e. in the *Redditio Symboli*]: and so when he could no
longer make his profession [i.e. in reply to the credal interrogations]
yet by virtue of the testimony which he had given he laid hold on the
remission of original sin.

7. *Spain*

ST ISIDORE OF SEVILLE

Text: Migne, P. L., Vol. 83. St Isidore, who died in 636, wrote the *De Ecclesiasticis Officiis* in reply to an enquiry regarding the origins of the Church's institutions. In the introduction to the work he says that he has made use of the most ancient writings and that he has sometimes expressed them in his own words but that in some cases he quotes *verbatim*: but he does not generally acknowledge his sources. In the excerpts which follow, the only passages from ancient writers which are identified are those from the *Ad Competentes* of Nicetas of Remesiana (*c.* 400), a work which survives to-day only in brief fragments.

CONCERNING THE CHURCH'S INSTITUTIONS, THE SECOND BOOK

21. CONCERNING CATECHUMENS, EXORCISM, AND SALT

1. Let us now describe the order of the sacraments and the progress of those who come to faith. The first degree are the catechumens, the second the *competentes*, the third those who have been baptized. The catechumens are those who come fresh from gentile surroundings with the wish to believe in Christ; and because the first admonition in the Law of God is: *Hear, O Israel, the Lord thy God is one God* [Deut. 6.4], thence it is that he to whom God speaks for the first time, through the priest as if through Moses, is called a catechumen, that is to say, a hearer: doubtless in order that having acknowledged the one Lord he may relinquish the various errors of idolatry.

2. It is my view that all who were baptized unto repentance by John prefigured the catechumens. The catechumens then are first exorcized, then they receive salt, and are anointed. Exorcism is a rebuke against the unclean spirit, delivered over those who are possessed and over catechumens, by means of which the abominable power of the devil, his agelong malice and violent assault, may be cast out of them and put to flight.

3. This is exemplified by that madman whom Jesus *rebuked and the evil spirit departed from him* [Matt. 17.18]. The power of the devil is

exorcized, insufflation is performed over them, so that they may renounce him and being *delivered from the power of darkness may be translated unto the kingdom* of their Lord [Col. 1.13], through the sacrament of baptism. And because children are not able to make renunciation themselves, this rite is performed through the hearts and mouths of those that carry them. The giving of salt in our ministration to the catechumens was instituted by our forefathers, so that by tasting it they receive a seasoning of wisdom, and may not stray in folly from the flavour of Christ; that they may not be foolish and look backward, as did Lot's wife, lest giving a bad example they may themselves remain to infect others.

22. CONCERNING THE COMPETENTES

1. After the catechumens, the second rank is that of the *competentes*. The *competentes* are those who after instruction in the faith, being started upon a life of discipline, hasten to receive the grace of Christ. And they are called *competentes* because they seek [*petentes*] the grace of Christ: for catechumens listen only, they do not seek at that stage. They are *as it were the guest and neighbour of the faithful, they hear the mysteries and grace from the outside, but are not yet called faithful.*

2. But the *competentes* are occupied with seeking and finding, they are catechized, that is to say, they are initiated into the knowledge of the sacraments. For to them is delivered the saving *creed, a compendium* as it were *of the faith*, a token of the *holy profession*: and being instructed in it they may know in what sort they must present themselves to the grace of Christ.[1]

25

4. The font is the source of all graces. It has seven steps: three downwards for the three things which we renounce, three others upwards for the three things which we confess: the seventh is also the fourth, like that of the son of man, extinguishing the *furnace of fire* [Dan. 3.15], a sure ground for the feet, a foundation for the water, in which *dwelleth all the fullness of the godhead bodily* [Col. 2.9]. The saving gifts of baptism are founded upon the Father and the Son and the Holy Ghost. Thus one is by no means sanctified by the performance of washing [*baptisma*] unless he is dipped [*tingitur*] in the sacrament of the Trinity; as the Lord says: *Go, teach all nations, baptizing them in the*

[1] The passages italicized in sections 1 and 2 above are quotations from Nicetas of Remesiana.

Name of the Father and of the Son and of the Holy Ghost [Matt. 28.19].
And so it follows that if baptism shall be conferred and any person of
the Trinity omitted, then plainly nothing happens in the solemn
performance of regeneration, unless the whole Trinity is invoked.

5. For . . . there are two covenants for those that believe. The first
is that in which he renounces the devil and his pomps and all his manner
of life. The second is that in which he confesses his belief in the Father
and the Son and the Holy Ghost.

26. CONCERNING THE CHRISM

2. But according as our Lord was anointed by God the Father,
being [*or*, to be] true king and eternal priest, with a celestial and mystic
unguent, so now not only pontiffs and kings, but the whole Church
is consecrated with the unction of chrism, because it is a member of the
eternal king and priest. Therefore, because we are a *priestly and royal
nation* [1 Pet. 2.9], after baptism we anoint [*ungimus*: perhaps for
ungimur, we are anointed] that we may be called by the name of
Christ [i.e., anointed one].

27. CONCERNING THE IMPOSITION OF HANDS, OR CONFIRMATION

1. But since after baptism the Holy Spirit is given through the
bishops with the laying on of the hand, we recall that the apostles did
this in the Acts of the Apostles. For thus it is written: [Isidore proceeds
to quote Acts 19.2-8 and 8.14-17].

ST HILDEPHONSUS OF TOLEDO

Text: Migne, P. L., Vol. 96. St Hildephonsus died in 669. His treatise *De
Cognitione Baptismi*, though primarily theological, provides us with an account
of baptism as it was administered in Toledo in his day. Hildephonsus quotes
extensively from Isidore: where parallel passages are translated in the following
extracts, variations in the translation indicate variations in the original Latin of
the two writers. The passages quoted are noted in the extracts below.

In 1860, Adolf Helfferich propounded the view that the *De Cognitione
Baptismi* was based upon a lost work of Justinian of Valencia (*c.* 546), called
Liber Responsionum. In 1913, Paul Glaue contended that Helfferich was mistaken.
Both views are discussed by Sister A. Braegelmann in *The Life and Writings
of Hildephonsus of Toledo* (Washington, U.S.A.): Sister Braegelmann accepts
the position of Glaue.

DE COGNITIONE BAPTISMI

[Hildephonsus writes of two stages between Gentile status and baptism, i.e., catechumens, or hearers, and the *competentes*.]

They are called catechumens, in other words hearers, because the first commandment of the Law which they hear read is: *Hear, O Israel* [Deut. 6.4]. [c. 20, cf. Isid., *De Eccl. Off.*, 2, 21, 1.]

THE SCRUTINY

[THE LECTIONS]

Hence on the occasion of the exorcisms, in the assembly of the Church, before the exorcisms are pronounced, the lesson of Isaiah the prophet is read, in which it is said: *Shall the prey be taken from the mighty or can the captive of the strong be delivered? For thus saith the Lord, Yea, the captivity shall be taken from the mighty, and what was taken by the strong shall be delivered* [Isa. 49.24f].

Then [the lesson] of Peter to the peoples: *But ye are a chosen generation, a royal priesthood, an holy nation, a peculiar people: that ye should tell the virtues of him who has called you out of darkness into his own marvellous light* [1 Pet. 2.9].

The lesson also of Mark the evangelist, who sets out the sacrament of this *Effetatio* which is described and discussed above (i.e., in c. 27 below). [c. 28.]

[THE EXORCISMS]

The bishop rebukes, saying: *The Lord rebuke thee, O Satan, even he who hath chosen Jerusalem rebuke thee* [Zech. 3.2].

Then a second time, with authority, he says: To thee it is said, O Satan, *Get thee behind me* [Matt. 4.10].

Then on the trumpet note of victory the third time he proclaims: *The lion of the tribe of Judah hath conquered, the root of Jesse* [Rev. 5.5].

Then this exorcism is begun by the ministers: *Thy snares are discovered, etc.* And thus the same rebuke is pronounced by the exorcists to the end, until all the catechumens have been exorcized [c. 25].

[The manual act is stated (c. 22) to be the imposition of a hand, or hands (*potestas imponendi manus*), upon the catechumens.]

[INSUFFLATION]

Exorcism is performed, that is, the power of the devil is rebuked, and insufflation is made over those in whom the domination of his power is expelled, that they may renounce him beneath whose sway they were held in servitude, and *being delivered from the power of darkness* by the sacrament of baptism they may be *translated to the kingdom* [Col. 1.13] of their Lord. In some places, so it is reported, they receive salt [*sales*], signifying as it were the seasoning of wisdom. Possibly the custom is permissible: ancient custom alone commends it: it has no other grounds. For by no document of holy scripture can it be shown that salt was given to catechumens as they attained to the sacraments of faith: and where that is absent there can be no obligation [c. 26, cf. Isid., *De Eccl. Off.*, 2, 21, 3].

[THE EFFETA]

Concerning John and the baptism of repentance, of which the token is the carpet of goatskin over which children are led to the anointing.

And so our Lord, coming to perfect our salvation, not for his own sake but for ours, received in his own person and himself sanctified the sacrament of baptism, sending John before him, whose baptism was the pattern [*figura*] of the truth, and not the truth itself, who warned sinners to repent but gave no remission of sins, as John himself said: *I baptize in water unto repentance* [Matt. 3.11]. Hence it is then that children are led by priests to the anointing over a carpet of goatskin, that they may have token of penitence, since by reason of their age they cannot do the works of penitence [c. 14].

After the rebuke of the exorcisms they come in due order to the unction of the oil [c. 21].

If they are young [*minores*], they are led by ministers to the bishop over a carpet of goatskin in token of repentance [c. 21].

After the exorcisms . . . the catechumens are anointed with oil which has been blessed by a priest. This unction is commended by the excellent example of our Lord's deed: for when as the evangelist Mark reports, they had led to Jesus a deaf and dumb man, they besought him that he might place his hands upon him [etc. Mark 7.32f]. [c. 27.]

For after the exorcisms, the ears of him that is converted from gentile error are anointed with oil, that he may receive the hearing of faith . . . likewise his mouth is touched [c. 29].

The Delivery and Return of the Creed

The Creed which the *competentes* receive on the day of their anointing is recited and returned on the fifth day of the week [i.e., Maundy Thursday] before Easter [*Pascha*] either by themselves if they are of age, or if they be infants by the mouth of those that carry them [c. 34].

Baptism

[During Lent, baptisteries were shut and sealed with the bishop's ring (c. 107). Baptism was to be administered only "at the seat of legitimate bishops, and in their presence", or "in the churches of distant parishes" (c. 108).]

The priest approaches the font . . . he touches the water in the sign of the tree of the cross . . . he exorcizes it . . . he pours in oil . . . he gives it his blessing [c. 109].

Chapter 110. Concerning the Steps of the Font

This font is the source of all glories [*gloriarum*: Isidore, *gratiarum*]. It has seven steps: three as you go down for the three at which renunciation is made, that is, at which the devil is renounced, and his angels and his works and his commands. Three others as you go up for the three at which confession is made of the Father, the Son, and the Holy Ghost, who is one God in Trinity. The seventh is also the fourth, like unto a son of man, extinguishing *the furnace of fire* [Dan. 3.15], a sure ground for the feet, a foundation for the water, in which *dwelleth the fullness of the godhead bodily* [Col. 2.9]. And so when the candidate goes down those steps, when he has renounced three times, he leaves the heights which belong to the devil, and goes down to the humility of Christ's baptism. And so at the fourth step finding solid ground he stands free from the things which he has renounced. Then he ascends by his confession of the Trinity. And that step is the seventh at the perfection of liberation which was also the fourth when he reached the peace of liberty [cf. Isid., *De Eccl. Off.*, 2, 25, 4].

Two covenants are made: the first, in which the devil is renounced, when it is said: *I renounce thee, devil, and thy angels and thy works and thy commands*: the second, in which belief is declared in God in the name of the Trinity [c. 111, cf. Isid., *De Eccl. Off.*, 2, 25, 5].

Then according to the commandment of the Lord, who said: *Go, teach all nations, baptizing them in the Name of the Father and of the Son* and of the Holy Ghost [Matt. 28.19], the priest adding: *that thou mayest have life eternal*, the person is sprinkled with water [c. 112].

That he is once immersed, he is sprinkled in the name of the one Deity. But if he were thrice immersed, the number of the three days of the Lord's burial is shown forth. And therefore within the limits of our faith differing customs are not opposed to one another. But because the heretics by this number of immersions are accustomed to rend the unity of the Godhead, it is by God's guidance that the Church of God observes the practice of one sprinkling only [c. 117].

While a hymn of joy at liberation is sung, he is taken to the touch of the holy chrism [c. 122].

After the washing, we are anointed with chrism, that from the name of Christ we may be called Christians [c. 123].

It is therefore wholesome that after the example of Christ [Mark 10.13] a hand in blessing is placed upon the faithful by the priest [c. 127].

After the washing at the font, after the renewal of life, after the unction of the Spirit, the person is taught to pray with the words of truth [c. 132].

[He is taught the Lord's Prayer: the Eucharist is administered.]

When the foregoing sacraments have been quite completed, the reborn person will hold for several days unceasingly to the Mass and Offices [*conventui et choro*] of the Church, vested in white raiment [c. 139].

[Chapter 142 is headed: *A sermon to be given to the infants on the third day after Easter (Pascha), for the removal of the white garments.*]

THE *LIBER ORDINUM*

Text: *Monumenta Ecclesiae Liturgica*, edd. Cabrol and Leclerq, Vol. 5, ed. Dom M. Ferotin, Paris, 1904.

The *Liber Ordinum* is virtually a pontifical. Our knowledge of it comes principally from a manuscript of 1052, with which Dom Ferotin has compared certain other incomplete manuscripts of the same period.

Two baptismal orders are set out in the *Liber Ordinum*: the first is translated from column 24ff of Dom Ferotin's edition, and is a form for occasional use; the second is set into the round of the Church's year, and is translated from columns 73ff, 184ff, and 208ff.

Notes on the *Liber Ordinum*

1. Item 2: the *Ordo* for Palm Sunday *ad Matutinum.*

It will be noticed that the material in sections 16-20 below corresponds with what in our extracts from St Hildephonsus we have called "The Scrutiny". This correspondence is even closer when we add to the *Liber Ordinum* the evidence of the lectionary which goes with it: for the *Liber Comicus* (*Anecdota Maredsolana*, Vol. 1, ed. Dom Morin) provides the same three lections for the occasion as are specified by Hildephonsus. In each document, the ceremony consists of the same three specified lections; the same specified exorcisms, of great solemnity; the Effeta: and St Hildephonsus mentions in the same context the "carpet of goatskin" over which children were led to the anointing of the Effeta.

There are no good grounds for regarding this ceremony as the formal occasion for the making of catechumens. Nowhere does the *Liber Ordinum* suggest that the ceremony on Palm Sunday morning was for this purpose: nowhere does St Hildephonsus state that the similar ceremony which he describes was designed to that end. The fact that St Hildephonsus makes a reference (even a disparaging one) in this context to the giving of salt is no ground for supposing that the making of catechumens is under discussion: for the giving of salt was part of the continuing régime of catechumens, both in Africa and Rome. Moreover, the absence of any mention of a signing with the cross militates against supposing that this was a ceremony for making catechumens: and so does the date which the *Liber Ordinum* assigns to it (Palm Sunday, *ad Matutinum*).

On the other hand, the solemnity of the exorcisms and the mention by St Hildephonsus of the carpet of goatskin (cf. the African rite) do positively suggest that we have here an account of the scrutiny: and we are therefore left to conclude that neither Hildephonsus nor Item 2 of the *Liber Ordinum* preserves any reference to any *Ordo ad Catechumenum Faciendum*, although its traces are to be seen in the first two prayers of Item 1 of the *Liber Ordinum.*

2. The *Traditio Symboli.*

The introduction to the Creed, beginning, "Dearly beloved, receive the rule," etc., is borrowed from the opening words of St Augustine's sermon *De Symbolo ad Catechumenos.*

3. The final rubric.

"*Baptism is then celebrated in order.*" Dom Ferotin supposed that the order referred to is the full order of baptism for occasional use which constitutes sections 1-14 below. It seems more probable that the contents of sections 11-14 is what is meant. Another possibility is that the expression *per ordinem* means "one by one", and refers to the candidates.

An Order of Baptism for Occasional Use

The infant is handed to the priest to be exorcized: and the priest to whom he is handed blows upon him three times in the face, and says this exorcism:

I exorcize thee, unclean spirit, thou enemy of the human race, by God the Father Almighty, who *made heaven and earth, the sea and all that in them is* [Ex. 20.11], and by Jesus Christ his Son, and by the Holy Spirit. All ye armies of the devil, every power of the adversary, every violent clash of the enemy, every blind disordered phantasm, be ye rooted out and put to flight from this creature [*plasma*], that by the remission of all his sins he may become a temple of the living God; through the justification of Jesus Christ our Lord and Saviour, who shall come to judge the world by fire. Amen.

He signs him upon the forehead and gives him his name in this exorcism: he asks his name and says to him as follows:

N., receive the sign of the cross: observe the commandments of God: this day by the word of God thou art reborn and strengthened by the light of the Spirit. Enter the temple of the living God, and with the errors of darkness removed joyfully acknowledge that thou hast escaped the toils of death. May the Almighty God dwell in thee, God who designed the human body and made it to be a dwelling for the divine Spirit. Reverence therefore the celestial commandments, and await the coming of our Only-Begotten Saviour, who was born of a Virgin and conceived by the Holy Ghost: by whose light thou art enlightened, by whose power thou art strengthened, by whose sign thou art signed upon thy brow, that under his protection thou mayest come to the grace of baptism. I sign thee therefore in the Name of the Father and of the Son and of the Holy Ghost, that reigneth unto all ages of ages. Amen.

Then the priest faces to the west and says to him this exorcism:

Bethink thee, Satan, what pains await thee: look upon the man whom my Lord doth deign to call to his grace, fall back and depart in confusion. Let no mistake deceive thee; Christ awaits thee in the judgement that is prepared. Thou shalt render account to the living God: thou shalt not cross out the sign of the cross upon this vessel: thou art adjured in the Name of the Father and of the Son and of the Holy Ghost, of whom this sign and Name is unconquered.

Then the priest touches him with the blessed oil, upon the mouth and ears only, saying:

Effeta, effeta, with the Holy Spirit unto the odour of sweetness, effeta. *He hath done all things well: he maketh the deaf to hear and the dumb to speak* [Mark 7.37].

5   *After this he places his hands upon him and says:*

Blessed be the Lord God of Israel, who dost visit the redemption of thy people and dost raise up a horn of salvation for us in thy house: who didst send thy servant John before the coming of thy majesty *in the spirit and power of Elias to prepare thy ways, to give knowledge of salvation by the remission of sins* and by the revelation of thy name: *to turn the faithless to the wisdom of the just: to make ready a perfect people for thee through thy tender mercy:* whose voice was heard saying: *Prepare ye a way for the Lord, make his paths straight* [Luke 3.4]. [Cento of Luke 1.17, 68–78.]

Behold, O Lord, we also humbly observing the commandment of thy majesty have prepared a way through which we lead thy people who *like as the hart* [Ps. 42.1] thirst for the fountains of waters. Do thou, O Lord, forgive their iniquity, cover their sins, and lead them as thou hast sworn into the land of promise, that flows with milk and honey. Thou art *the Lamb of God that takest away the sins of the world* [John 1.29]: thou, who hast granted that they who know thee should become *the sons of God* [John 1. 12]: thou who art anointed by the Father with *the oil of gladness above thy fellows* [Ps. 45.7]. O Lord, pour upon these people the blessing of thy grace. Lest they die in their old sins, let them be cleansed in the blessing of the fount of waters: let them be reborn in the Holy Spirit, and let them see the everlasting altar of Jerusalem: and may the *power of the highest overshadow them* [Luke 1.35]. Blessed be their generation and *blessed be the fruit of the womb* [Luke 1.42] of their mother the Church: for the Lord shall magnify his servants in good things, and *of his kingdom there shall be no end* [Luke 1.73].

6   *When the laying on of hands is finished, he delivers to him the Creed, saying:*

Will N. believe in God? *and so on to the end.* [Another MS. reads: "Does *N.* believe?" *etc.*]

7   *When these things have been done, the priest comes near to the font and blows upon it three times, or upon the vessel where the infant is to be baptized, and says this exorcism, turning his face to the west:*

Depart, unclean spirit, from all who in this sacrament are blessed with the joy of faith: bring forward no accusation of sin, thou that dost acknowledge the power of the Saviour. For our confidence is not in our merit but in his command: may the power of ministry be the dignity of the minister. Therefore, O creature of water, I call upon thee, through God who is God of all, that thou refuse not to impart thy lively motion and know that thou hast a service to perform in which we seek to please God. Purge out from thyself the whole communion of demons, the whole society of iniquity, thou that art fitted for the Lord's use, destroy all stain of evil spirits: so that having received the grace of sanctification thou mayest restore in innocence to God, who is both thine and mine alike, those whom thou dost receive in their sins. Amen. Through our Lord Jesus Christ who liveth.

Then he says this blessing:

8
A. 19

The Blessing of the Font

This blessing is to be said in the same manner as they are said in the Mass.
O celestial flood, be sanctified by the Word of God; O water that wast trodden by the feet of Christ, be sanctified; thou upon whom the mountains weigh down, yet thou art not shut up; thou art dashed against the rocks yet thou art not destroyed; thou art spread abroad upon the earth and yet dost not fall. Thou art held up by the firmament on high; thou dost wash the whole universe about, cleansing all things yet none cleanses thee. Thou when the people of the Hebrews took their flight wast held back and hardened into ice. Thou melting upon the high peaks dost bring ruin upon the dwellers of the Nile, and with thy fierce raging dost ever torment the world as it were thine enemy. Thou art one and the same: the salvation of the faithful, the avenger of the wicked. Moses smote the rock and the rock poured thee forth: the majesty of God commanded thee to come forth and thou couldest not hide among the boulders. Thou art borne upon the clouds and dost make fruitful the fields with joyful showers. Through thee a draught bringing grace and life is poured out upon bodies hot with summer heat. Thou dost move quietly upon thy tiny courses bringing life and fruitful sap, lest the dry lifeless earth deny their proper victuals to our bodies. The beginning of all things and their end exult in thee, yet God has provided that by thee we might know no end.

Yet thou, O Lord, Almighty God, whose power we do not forget while we proclaim the merits of water and declare its marvellous works, look with favour upon sinners and of thy wonted goodness loose the captive. Restore the innocence which Adam lost in paradise, which his wife let go, which the intemperance of gluttony devoured. Give a healthful draught to men who are upset by the bitterness of the

9
A. 20

apple; purge the disorders of mortal men and with a divine antidote
cure their agelong distemper. Wash away the filth and squalor of the
world: make a way through the wall of fire which protects the garden
of paradise and open a flower-strewn path unto them that return. May
they receive the likeness of God, which once was lost by malice of the
serpent: may the iniquities which follow upon their disobedience be
carried away in this pure stream. May they rise up unto rest: may they
be brought forward unto pardon: that being renewed in the mystic
waters they may know themselves to be redeemed and reborn. Amen.

*After this the priest makes the sign of the cross over the font, or the vessel
from which he is to baptize, with the blessed oil, saying:*

In the Name of the Father and of the Son and of the Holy Ghost,
God that reigneth unto all ages of ages.

After the mixture of the water and oil, he says this blessing:

10   *The Blessing*

Foul with the squalor of our offences, stirred by the consciousness of
sin, abject and humble, we pray and beseech thee Almighty God that
of thy mercy thou wilt look down with favour upon us. Breathe
kindly upon these waters mixed with the oil of sanctification, bless them
with thy power, and from thy throne pour upon them the grace of
holiness: that whoever shall go down into this tide upon which the
most exalted Name of the Trinity is called may be loosed from man's
ancient offence and pardoned by thine everlasting blessing, that being
cleansed from all their sins and strengthened with spiritual gifts they
may be written in the pages of heaven. Grant that those who take from
this laver a new life and set aside the record of the old and are accorded
the gift of the Holy Spirit by the laying on of hands may both put
away their present faults and lay hold on eternal gifts, happy in thy
continual and everlasting succour. Amen.

Who ever liveth and reigneth over all things, one God in Trinity,
through the infinite ages of ages.

11   *Then the infant is carried naked to the priest in the arms of the minister
who waits upon the priest. And the priest asks these questions:*

N., thou servant of God, dost thou renounce the devil and his
angels?

The ministers reply: I renounce.

And all his works? R̷. I renounce.

And all his commands? R̷. I renounce.

What is thy name? R̲. *N.*

N., dost thou believe in God the Father Almighty? R̲. I believe.

And in Jesus Christ his only Son our Lord? R̲. I believe.

And in the Holy Ghost? R̲. I believe.

Then I baptize thee in the Name of the Father and of the Son and of the Holy Ghost, that thou mayest have life eternal.[1]

When the infant is baptized, he who received him from the font comes to the priest holding the infant, now clothed, with his head uncovered, on his right arm. The priest anoints him with chrism, making the sign of the cross on his forehead alone, saying:

12

The sign of eternal life which God the Father Almighty has given through Jesus Christ his Son to them that believe unto salvation.

Then he lays his hand upon him and says:

13

O God, who in this sacrament wherein men are reborn dost send thy Holy Spirit upon water, in such fashion that the Creator commands his creature and by its office cleanses those who are washed thereby, whom thou wouldest perfect [*confirmaret*] with thy bountiful gift; thou who by water wouldest take away the stain of sin and by thine own self wouldest complete the grace of the sacrament, and therefore hast commanded that the unction of chrism shall follow the ministration of baptism: we therefore pray and beseech thee, O Lord, following thy commandments according as we are able, to pour thy Holy Spirit upon these thy servants. Amen.

The spirit of wisdom and understanding. Amen.

The spirit of counsel and might. Amen.

The spirit of knowledge and godliness. Amen.

Fill them, both men and women, with the *spirit of thy fear* [Isa. 11.2, 3], who dost inspire men to follow thy saving commandment and

[1] [Other contemporary MSS. provide the following formularies in place of those above.]

Does this servant of God renounce the devil and his angels?

The ministers reply: He does renounce.

And his works? R̲. He renounces.

And his commands? R̲. He renounces.

What is he called? R̲. *N.*

N., dost thou believe in God the Father Almighty? R̲. He shall believe.

And in Jesus Christ his only Son our Lord? R̲. He shall believe.

And in the Holy Ghost? R̲. He shall believe.

Then I baptize him in the name of the Father and of the Son and of the Holy Ghost, that he may have life eternal.

dost breathe upon them a heavenly gift. And so grant that being strengthened in the Name of the Trinity, they may by this chrism be accounted worthy to become Christs, and by the power of Christ to become Christians.

14   *Then the priest sets a veil over the head of the baptized infants, and communicates them.*

15   *The third day after baptism these infants are brought to the priest and he says this prayer over them:*

Blessing over the White Robes

O Lord Jesus Christ, Redeemer of the world, whom God the Father declared to be his Son, though thou wast truly man and truly born of man, strengthen these thy servants and handmaids whom thou hast signed with thy Name and cleansed with sacred water: let them live wholly in thy Spirit, who even now are nourished and redeemed by thy Body and Blood: that these sacraments which they have received at the beginning of their new life they may unceasingly receive unto their salvation and so come safe to the reward of blessedness.

After this the Lord's Prayer is not said, but the blessing only:

The Lord Jesus Christ who hath washed you with water from his side, and redeemed you by the outpouring of his blood, confirm in you the grace of redemption. Amen.

May he by whom ye are reborn of water and the Holy Spirit bring you to the heavenly kingdom. Amen.

May he who has given you a beginning of the holy faith give you also perfection of this work and abundance of love.   Amen.

Then the priest divests him of the robes and departs whither he will.

*   *   *

The Order to be Observed over One Vexed with an Unclean Spirit

16   *First they place the man or woman who suffers in this way in the west, so that he faces towards the altar. Then the clerks and deacons or presbyters arrange themselves in two choirs, as the custom is at the Effetatio on Palm Sunday.*

17   *Then a deacon standing before the choir and facing towards the aforesaid sick person makes the sign of the cross with his hand as he recites and declaims this exorcism:*

Bethink thee, Satan, what pains await thee: look upon the man whom my Lord and God doth deign to call to his grace, fall back and depart in confusion. Let no mistake deceive thee: Christ awaits thee in the judgement that is prepared. Thou shalt render account to the living God; thou shalt not cross out the sign of the cross upon this vessel: thou art adjured in the Name of the Father and of the Son and of the Holy Ghost, of whom this sign and Name is unconquered.

The choir replies and sings this anthem: 18
Stand fast against the devil, and he shall flee from us: draw near to God, and he shall draw near to us [Jas. 4.7].

Then the deacon: Bethink thee, Satan.

The choir: Stand fast.

Then the deacon, a third time: Bethink thee, Satan.

The choir: Stand fast.

Then the bishop comes in, or the senior priest in his place, from within the   19
altar, and stands before the choir where the deacon had stood and recites an exorcism in these three parts, making the sign of the cross westwards towards the aforesaid sick man:

1. *The Lord rebuke thee, O Satan, even* the Lord *who hath chosen Jerusalem rebuke thee* [Zech. 3.2].
2. To thee it is said, O Satan: *Get thee behind me* [Matt. 4.10].
3. *The Lion of the tribe of Judah hath conquered the root of Jesse* [Rev. 5.5].

And when the bishop or some other priest in his place has said this, he   20
makes the sign of the cross westwards: and he pauses a little between each part. And immediately when he has finished, a deacon with the clerks recites this exorcism: Thy snares are discovered, etc.

[Two exorcisms follow, of very great length, and the ceremony then ends with a very long prayer said by the bishop.]

*   *   *

THE DELIVERY OF THE CREED

[This took place on Palm Sunday: after the Blessing of the palms, Mass proceeded to the end of the gospel.]

Then this sermon is read, with the Apostles' Creed: 21

Dearly beloved, receive the rule of faith, which is called the Creed: and when you have received it, write it upon your heart and say it daily to yourselves. Before you sleep, before you go forth, arm yourselves with your Creed. For no one writes the Creed so that it can be read: but it is to be thought about, lest forgetfulness obliterate things which your eyes have not read. Let your memory be your book. What ye are to hear, that ye will believe: and what ye are to believe, that ye will recite and make return of it. For the Apostle says: *With the heart man believeth unto righteousness, and with the mouth confession is made unto salvation* [Rom. 10.10].

22   This is the Creed which ye are to believe, and of which ye are to make return. So sign yourselves, and repeat:

> I believe in God the Father Almighty.
> And in Jesus Christ his only Son, our God and Lord.
> Who was born of the Holy Ghost and the Virgin Mary.
> He suffered under Pontius Pilate, was crucified and buried.
> He descended into hell.
> The third day he rose living from the dead.
> He ascended into heaven, he sitteth at the right hand of God the Father Almighty.
> From thence he shall come to judge the quick and the dead.
> I believe in the Holy Ghost,
> The Holy Catholic Church,
> The Remission of all sins,
> The Resurrection of this flesh, and eternal life.
> Amen.

That your memories may lay hold the more easily upon what has been said, let us repeat the Creed in order:

> I believe in God the Father Almighty.

And let us repeat the words of the Creed a third time; so that, since the Creed contains the faith of the divine Trinity, so the number of our repetitions may correspond with the sacrament of the Trinity.

> I believe in God the Father Almighty.

23   You are to hold fast to this rule of faith which your mother the Church has now delivered to you, with all the powers of your mind: let no doubt or scruple arise in your heart. For if, which God forbid, the slightest doubt were to arise, the whole foundation of the faith is undermined, and the soul threatened with danger. And therefore, if any of you feels thus moved, let him consider that it is on account of his failure to understand: but let him believe that everything that he has heard is true.

May Almighty God so enlighten your heart that ye may believe and understand what we have said, and preserve a right faith, and shine forth with good works: that so ye may come to blessed life. By his help, who is glorified unto all ages, one God in Trinity. Amen.

[The Mass continues: a rubric provides that the Creed which would normally be said at the Mass is omitted.]

* * *

The Order to be Observed on the Sabbath of the Paschal Vigil

24

On the Sabbath day, when the ninth hour approaches, at the beginning of the vigil, a bell is rung.

[The above rubric is followed by a series of prayers and rubrics relating to the lighting of the Paschal Candle. Then begins the reading of a series of twelve lessons, each followed by an intercession. During the third lesson, the bishop goes to the font.]

25

After the beginning of the third lesson aforesaid, the bishop, the presbyters and deacons, each holding his candle, go in procession to the chapel of St John,[1] where the chrism and the Holy Communion are lying upon the altar.

26

And going down to the font, the deacons stand around the font, and when the infants have been arranged in order in the agnile, *the bishop rises and says this prayer:*

Almighty God, that rulest all things, we hasten with eager steps to the venerable font of eternal salvation, and beseech thy magnificence that thou command that this font which has been sealed may be re-opened with the keys of thy mercy, and impart to those that thirst a most sweet cup of water. May the voice of thy divinity sound upon these waters, may the Spirit of thy sanctification dwell therein and bring healing to all ills. May the abundant streams of paradise flow from it, that by thy goodness heavenly graces may be bestowed upon these new-born children.

27

Another Prayer

Dearly beloved brethren, let us join in humble prayer and beseech God, whose gifts are immortal and whose graces are for our salvation, that through Jesus Christ his only Son our Lord, who is his Word, his Wisdom, and his Power, he may bestow the grace of his new creation upon his people that hasten to saving baptism: that he may speedily turn hence the approach of evil thoughts and pour his Holy Spirit upon

[1] In the cathedral of Toledo, this was adjacent to the font.

the life-giving laver: so that when his people that thirst after faith enter the saving water they may truly be *born again*, as it is written, *of water and the Holy Ghost* [John 3.5], and, being buried in the laver unto their Redeemer, in the manner of a holy and reverend mystery, they may die with him in their baptism and rise again into his kingdom. Amen.

28

Baptism is then celebrated in order

[The vigil service then continues with the prayer following the third lesson.]

8. *Milan*

ST AMBROSE

The extracts which follow are taken from the two works known as *Concerning the Sacraments* and *Concerning the Mysteries*. The translation is that of the Reverend T. Thompson, in *St Ambrose on the Sacraments and on the Mysteries*, ed. J. H. Srawley, S.P.C.K. First edition, 1919: second edition, 1950.

Modern scholarship has concluded that both of these works are to be attributed to St Ambrose. Both cover the same ground, although the *De Mysteriis* shows more reserve in the detail it reveals than its companion document. It has been suggested that the *De Sacramentis* is simply a transcript of St Ambrose's actual addresses to neophytes in Easter Week, when the *disciplina arcani* no longer prevented him from speaking plainly to them: its six books correspond to the six days of the week after Easter Day. The *De Mysteriis* on the other hand is a considered work for general reading.

Two notes on the Text of St Ambrose

De Sacramentis, Book I, 1. "At Rome": Latin, *Romae*. Some MSS. read *recto nomine*, or *recte*, in which case the full sentence would read: "The title of faithful is properly given only to those who have been baptized."

De Mysteriis, 7. "Whom thou mayest suppose that thou shouldst renounce to his face": Latin, *cui renuntiandum in os putares*. Some MSS. read *sputares* for *putares*, and Dom Morin has accordingly proposed the emendation *cui renuntiando in os sputares*, i.e., "by way of renouncing him to spit in his face". But the recent edition of the *De Mysteriis* in the Vienna Corpus prefers the reading *putares*.

For another example of spitting on the devil, see the variant readings of the Armenian rite, No. 2, which is found in a MS. of about 1300.

CONCERNING THE SACRAMENTS

Book I

1. The sacraments which you have received are the theme of my discourse. To have given a reasoned account of these earlier would not have been right; for in a Christian man faith is first. Therefore at Rome the title of faithful is given to those who have been baptized; and also our Father Abraham was justified by faith, not by works. So you

received baptism; you believed. For it is wrong for me to think otherwise; for thou wouldest not have been called to grace, had not Christ thought thee worthy of his grace.

2. Therefore, what did we do on the Saturday? What but the "opening"? Which mysteries of "opening" were performed, when the priest touched thine ears and nostrils? It is this which our Lord Jesus Christ indicates in the gospel when a *deaf and dumb* [Mark 7.32] man was brought to him, and he touched his ears and his mouth: the ears, because he was deaf, the mouth because he was dumb: and said, *Ephpheta*. It is a Hebrew word, which rendered into Latin is *adaperire*, that is, *be opened*. The reason therefore that the priest touched thine ears was that thine ears might be opened to the discourse and the address of the priest.

3. But thou sayest to me, "Why the nostrils?" In that case, because he was dumb, he touched his mouth; that, since he could not speak heavenly mysteries, he might receive utterance from Christ. Also in that case because it was a man: in our case, because women are baptized and there is not the same purity in the servant as in the Lord (for what comparison can there be, when the latter forgives sins, the former has them remitted?), therefore, on account of the grace bestowed by his act and office, the bishop touches not the mouth but the nostrils; that thou mayest receive a *sweet savour* of eternal godliness, and that thou mayest say, *For we are a sweet savour of Christ unto God* [2 Cor. 2.15], as the holy Apostle said; and there may be in thee the full fragrance of faith and devotion.

4. We came to the font; thou didst enter. Consider whom thou sawest; consider what thou saidst, recall it carefully. A levite met thee, a presbyter met thee. Thou wast anointed as Christ's athlete; as about to wrestle in the fight of this world, thou didst profess the objects of thy wrestling. He who wrestles has something to hope for; where the contest is, there is the crown. Thou wrestlest in the world, but thou art crowned by Christ, and thou art crowned for contests in the world; for though the reward is in heaven yet the earning of the reward is placed here.

5. When he asked thee, "Dost thou renounce the devil and his works?" what didst thou reply? "I renounce." "Dost thou renounce the world and its pleasures?" what didst thou reply? "I renounce." Be mindful of thy words, and never let the contents of thy bond pass from thy memory . . .

*   *   *

9. Then thou drewest near; thou sawest the font, thou sawest also the priest above the font. Nor can I doubt that this may have occurred to thy mind, which occurred to the Syrian Naaman; for although he was cleansed, he doubted previously. Why? I will tell; listen.

10. Thou didst enter, thou sawest the water, thou sawest the priest, thou sawest a levite. Let not someone say haply, "Is this all?" Yes, it is all . . .

* * *

18. Why did Christ descend first, the Holy Spirit afterwards, since the form and practice of baptism provides that the font should be consecrated first, and then the person to be baptized should descend? For as soon as the priest enters, he makes an exorcism over the element of water; afterwards he offers an invocation and a prayer, that the font may be consecrated and the presence of the eternal Trinity may come down. But Christ descended first, the Spirit followed. For what reason? That the Lord Jesus might not seem himself to need the mystery of sanctification; but that he might sanctify and the Spirit also sanctify . . .

BOOK 2

14. Now, then, let us consider. The priest comes; he says a prayer at the font; he invokes the Name of the Father, the presence of the Son, and of the Holy Ghost; he uses heavenly words. What heavenly words? They are those of Christ, that we should *baptize in the Name of the Father and of the Son and of the Holy Ghost* [Matt. 28.19]. If, therefore, at the word of men, at the invocation of a saint, the presence of the Trinity came down, how much more does it come where the eternal word is acting! . . .

* * *

16. Now let us examine what it is that is called baptism. Thou camest to the font, thou wentest down in it; thou didst watch the high priest, thou didst see the levites and the presbyter in the font . . .

* * *

20. Thou wast asked, "Dost thou believe in God the Father Almighty?" Thou saidest, "I believe", and didst dip, that is, thou wast buried. Again thou wast asked, "Dost thou believe in our Lord Jesus Christ, and in his cross?" Thou saidst, "I believe", and didst dip:

therefore thou wast also *buried with Christ* [Rom. 6.4; Col. 2.12]: for he who is buried with Christ, rises again with Christ. A third time thou wast asked, "Dost thou believe also in the Holy Ghost?" Thou saidst, "I believe", and didst dip a third time, that the triple confession might absolve the fall of thy former life.

＊　　　＊　　　＊

24. Therefore, thou didst dip, thou camest to the priest. What did he say to thee? "God the Father Almighty," he saith, "who hath regenerated thee by water and the Holy Ghost, and hath forgiven thee thy sins, himself anoint thee unto eternal life." See whereunto thou art anointed: "unto eternal life", he saith.

Book 3

1. Yesterday we discoursed on the font, whose appearance is somewhat like that of a tomb in shape; into which, believing in the Father and the Son and the Holy Ghost, we are received and plunged, and we emerge, that is, we are raised up. Moreover, thou receivest *myron*, that is, ointment upon the head. Why upon the head? Because *the senses of a wise man are in his head* [Eccles. 2.14, LXX], says Solomon. For wisdom is lifeless without grace: but when wisdom has received grace, then its work begins to be perfect. This is called regeneration.

＊　　　＊　　　＊

4. Thou camest up out of the font. What followed? Thou hast heard the lesson. The high priest was girt up (for though presbyters also carried it out, yet the ministry is begun by the high priest); the high priest, I say, was girt up and washed thy feet . . .

5. We are not ignorant that the Roman Church has not this custom. Her type and form we follow in all things; however, she has not this custom of washing the feet. See then, perhaps she has declined it on account of the numbers. There are, however, some who say and try to urge that this ought to be done, not as a sacrament, not at baptism, not at the regeneration; but only as we should wash the feet of a guest. The latter is an act of humility, the former a work of sanctification. Accordingly, learn how it is a sacrament and a means of sanctification: *Unless I wash thy feet, thou wilt have no part with me* [John 13.8]. This I say, not to find fault with others, but to recommend my own usage. In all things I desire to follow the Roman Church. Yet we too are not

without discernment; and what other places have done well to retain, we, too, do well to maintain.

6. It is the Apostle Peter himself that we follow; to his devotion we cling. What does the Roman Church answer to this? Certainly the Apostle Peter himself supports us in this claim, he who was a priest of the Roman Church. Peter himself says, *Lord, not my feet only, but also my hands and head* [John 13.9]. Look at his faith. His demurring at first showed his humility, his offer afterwards showed his devotion and faith.

*　　　*　　　*

8. There follows the spiritual seal, which you have heard mentioned in the lesson to-day. For after the font, it remains for the "perfecting" to take place, when, at the invocation of the priest, the Holy Spirit is bestowed, *the spirit of wisdom and understanding, the spirit of counsel and strength, the spirit of knowledge and godliness, the spirit of* holy *fear* [Isa. 11.2f], as it were the seven virtues of the Spirit.

*　　　*　　　*

10. These are the seven virtues, when thou art sealed; for, as the holy Apostle saith, *The wisdom of* our God *is manifold* [Eph. 3.10] . . .

11. After this, what follows? Thou has come to the altar, whither thou hast not come before . . .

CONCERNING THE MYSTERIES

3. . . . in performing the mystery of the "opening" we said, "*Ephpheta*", which is, "Be opened" . . .

5. After this, the *Holy of holies* [Heb. 9.3] was unbarred to thee, thou didst enter the shrine of regeneration; remember what thou wast asked, recollect what thou didst answer. Thou didst renounce the devil and all his works, the world and its luxury and pleasures. Thy answer is kept, not in the tomb of the dead, but in the book of the living.

6. Thou sawest there a levite, thou sawest a priest, thou sawest the high priest . . .

7. Thou didst enter, therefore, to look upon thine adversary, whom thou mayest suppose that thou shouldest renounce to his face; thou dost turn to the east. For he who renounces the devil turns to Christ, looks at him with direct gaze.

8. What sawest thou? Water, to be sure, but not water only;

F

levites ministering there, the high priest questioning and consecrating
. . .

20. But even a catechumen believes in the cross of the Lord Jesus,
wherewith he is also signed; but unless he is *baptized in the Name of the
Father and of the Son and of the Holy Ghost* [Matt. 28.19], he cannot
receive the remission of sins nor imbibe the gift of spiritual grace.

21. So the Syrian dipped seven times under the Law. But thou
wast baptized in the Name of the Trinity, thou didst confess the
Father—remember what thou didst—thou didst confess the Son, thou
didst confess the Holy Spirit . . .

28. Thou didst descend, then; remember what thou didst answer,
that thou believest in the Father, thou believest in the Son, thou
believest in the Holy Spirit. It is not a case of, I believe in a greater
and a less and a least; but thou art bound by the same pledge of thine
own voice to believe in the Son exactly as thou believest in the Father,
to believe in the Holy Spirit exactly as thou believest in the Son;
with this one exception, that thou confessest the necessity of belief
in the cross of the Lord Jesus alone.

29. After all this, thou didst go up to the priest. Consider what
followed. Was it not that which David said, *It is like the ointment upon
the head, that ran down unto the beard, even unto Aaron's beard?* [Ps.
133.2] . . .

30. Understand why this is done, because *the wise man's eyes are in
his head* [Eccles. 2.14]. It flowed down into the beard—that is, unto the
grace of youth—even unto Aaron's beard, for this purpose, that thou
mayest become *a chosen generation*, priestly, *precious* [1 Pet. 2.9]; for we
are all anointed with spiritual grace unto the kingdom of God and the
priesthood.

31. Thou didst go up from the font. Remember the gospel lesson.
For our Lord Jesus in the gospel washed the feet of his disciples . . .

32. Peter was clean, but he needed to wash his feet; for he still had
sin by derivation from the first man, when the serpent tripped him and
led him into trespass. His foot is washed that hereditary sins may be
removed; for our own sins are remitted by baptism.

34. Thou receivedst after this white raiment . . .

41. Whence the Lord Jesus himself also, attracted by the zeal of such
love, by the beauty of comeliness and grace (since there is no longer
the foulness of sins in those who are washed), says to the Church:
Set me as a seal upon thine heart, as a signet upon thine arm [Cant. 8.6] . . .

42. Wherefore, recollect that thou has received the spiritual seal, *the*

spirit of wisdom and understanding, the spirit of counsel and strength, the spirit of knowledge and godliness, the spirit of holy *fear* [Isa. 11.2f], and preserve what thou hast received. *God* the Father *hath sealed* thee. Christ the Lord hath *confirmed* thee, *and hath given the earnest of the Spirit in* thine *heart* [2 Cor. 1.21f], as thou hast learned from the Apostolic lesson.

43. Rich with these adornments the cleansed people hastens to the altar of Christ . . .

THE AMBROSIAN MANUAL

Text: M. Magistretti, *Monumenta veteris liturgiae Ambrosianae*, Vol. 3, Milan, 1904. The following extracts are translated from pages 122–4, 142–3, 168–70, 205–10, 266ff.

This tenth-century document provides two baptismal orders. The first is spread over Lent and culminates at the Paschal season: the second is in one rite for occasional use.

It will be found that this account of baptism at Milan and that of Beroldus in the succeeding document are complementary. Each reveals a virtually identical rite, and what is not clear in one (and the Manual in particular is somewhat confused) is made clear by reference to the other.

The following table may help to clarify the Lent Calendar at Milan:

Lent 1	Sunday at the beginning of Lent.
	Feriae 2–6.
	The first Saturday of Lent.
Lent 2	Sunday of the Samaritan Woman.
	Feriae 2–6.
	The second Saturday.
Lent 3	Sunday of Abraham.
	Feriae 2–6.
	Saturday of the Blind Man.
Lent 4	Sunday of the Blind Man.
	Feriae 2–6.
	The fourth Saturday (of Lazarus).
Lent 5	Sunday of Lazarus.
	Feriae 2–6.
	Saturday for the Delivery of the Creed.
Lent 6	Palm Sunday.

The names of some of the Sundays refer to their liturgical lessons.

1

SUNDAY AT THE BEGINNING OF LENT

[Propers are provided for Mattins, Mass, and Vespers. Then:]

In the first week, after Psalm 50 [Hebrew: 51] has been sung at Mattins, the presbyter says: The Lord be with you.

And with thy spirit.

Let the deacon also say in a moderate voice: Let the *competentes* go forth, *once: but next week, twice. And the doorkeeper at the porch:* Let no catechumen, *etc.*

And likewise at Vespers.

2   *On the Sunday of the Samaritan Woman, after the gospel the deacon says:* Whoso wishes to give in any names, let him bring them forward now.

3   *On the second Saturday, after the scrutiny, the deacon says in a loud voice at the end of the altar:*
Raise yourselves, ye faithful. Pray, ye *competentes.* Bow your heads.

Then the infants are told by an acolyte to bow their heads: again the deacon says in a loud voice:
Raise yourselves before the Lord, likewise give honour to God.

And the clerks reply: Amen.

And the deacon says in a loud voice: Bow yourselves for the blessing.

When the blessing has been given, again the deacon says in a loud voice: Let the *competentes* go forth.

And the acolytes reply likewise. Then they go out. The same order is to be observed at each scrutiny and [or, even] on Sundays, after the gospel, up to Palm Sunday.

4   *In the third week, on each day at Mattins or Vespers, the deacon says in a moderate voice:*
Let the catechumens go forth.
once: but next week, twice:
Let the catechumens go forth: let the catechumens go forth.

And the acolytes reply likewise, from the chancel doors.

5   *On the Friday, at each lection, and on Sundays at each prayer, the doorkeepers vociferate three times, through each porch:*
Let no catechumen, *etc.*

After the middle of Lent, the aforesaid doorkeepers add: Let no catechumen. Let no. *up to Palm Sunday.*

*   *   *

The Second Saturday   6

[Propers are provided for Mattins and Mass. Then:]

The Exorcism of the Ashes

I exorcize you, O ye ashes, in the Name of God the Father Almighty, and of Jesus Christ his Son, and of the Holy Ghost: who has ordained that by fire you should be made into ashes: that, just as by the commandment of God through his holy servant Moses the ashes of a heifer scattered upon the people sanctified the whole congregation of Israel, so also now, because you are exorcized in the Name of the Trinity and scattered upon this earth and this sackcloth, the devil may not lurk in those who stand over you, or those who pass by you as they undergo the scrutiny: but that he may be shown forth and expelled, that they may be found pure and true. We pray and beseech thee, Almighty Father, that as the people of Nineveh at the preaching of the prophet Jonah besought thy mercy, O Lord, and had pardon of their sins; so also those who seek to come to receive thy grace, their carnal sins being taken away, may set an end to their wickedness in the regeneration of sacred baptism. Through the same. In the unity.

The deacon, standing at the end of the altar, says in a loud voice:
Raise yourselves, ye faithful. Pray, ye *competentes*. Bow your heads. Raise yourselves before the Lord, likewise give honour to God.

A Prayer over the Competentes   7

Hear, Lord, the supplication of thy servants who desire to be united to the congregation of thy faithful: that on the day of the holy solemnity of thy clemency they may be found worthy to receive the gift of baptism. Through.

Another Prayer   8

Almighty, everlasting God, look with favour from the high throne of thy majesty upon these thy servants the *competentes* who hasten to thy Church: grant them, Lord, that beneath the protection of thy hand they may attain to the grace of holy baptism. Through.

And the clerks reply: Amen.

Then the deacon says: Let the *competentes* go forth

*   *   *

9 ## ON THE SATURDAY AT THE DELIVERY OF THE CREED

[Propers for Mattins and Mass. Then:]

After Mass has been sung, the deacon says first:
Let all catechumens go forth.

II. Let all Jews go forth.

III. Let all heathen go forth.

IV. Let all heretics go forth.

V. Let him who has no business [here] go forth.

10 *The refrain:* Come, ye children, hearken unto me:
I will teach you the fear of the Lord.

Verse 1. Come, ye children, hearken unto me:
I will teach you the fear of the Lord.

Verse 2. I will always give thanks unto the Lord:
His praises shall ever be in my mouth.
Come. Come.

Verse 3. My soul shall be praised in the Lord: the humble shall
be glad.
Come.

Verse 4. Glory be to the Father and to the Son and to the Holy
Ghost, now and always, and unto the ages of ages.
Amen.
Come. Come.

[The above anthem is based on Ps. 34. 1, 2, 11.]

11 *The second Saturday of Lent, the blessing of the ashes;* I exorcize you,
O ye ashes.

There follows, Our Father, *three times* [?tribus vicibus].

There follows, I breathe upon you, ashes scattered on sackcloth, *from
the three sides* [of the *chrismon*].

12 *After the Mass has been sung, two subdeacons vested in albs come with two
hebdomadary deacons to the doors of the church, where the children* [pueri]
stand.

Then the deacon asks the subdeacons:

What do they seek?   R̹. Faith.

Q. Are their parents worthy?   R̟. They are worthy.

Q. Do they renounce the devil
     and his works?   R̟. They renounce.

Q. His world and his pomps?   R̟. They renounce.

Be mindful of your words, that they never depart from you.

The same order is to be observed on the Saturdays of the Blind Man and of Lazarus.

When they are led in, and signed, they are to be carried before the altar. The priest behind the altar gives them the salutation. A deacon at the end of the altar says: 13

Raise yourselves, *etc.* R̟. Amen.

Bow yourselves, *etc.*

Prayer: Almighty, everlasting God.

Then the deacon says:
Let the *competentes go forth.*

The two acolytes likewise.

In the morning at Mass, after the gospel has been read, the same order is observed.

On the fifth Saturday, when the Creed is delivered, after Mass has been sung, the priest behind the altar gives the salutation. The deacon at the end of the altar shall say: Let all catechumens, *and the other sentences that follow. Then the master of the singers begins:* Come, ye children. *Then the archbishop goes into the vestry, and the chief of the readers: they vest themselves in chasubles and come to take permission from the archbishop to open the doors to the children. And as they go they pray at three places: first in the choir, again at the gradus, and a third time near the porches: and they open the doors to the children, and say:* Children, enter the house of the Lord: hear your father teaching you the way of knowledge. *And on the way back likewise they pray three times, and the primicerius carries all the time the tablets and a hazel wand green with leaves. Then the Creed is begun by the archbishop or hebdomadary presbyter. When the Creed has been delivered, the archbishop says:* The Lord be with you. Raise yourselves.   14

*   *   *

HOLY SATURDAY

[The Manual provides the order for Mattins, the blessing of new fire, the blessing of the candle, the vigil service; then:]

15
G. 89
S. 21

Prayers at the Blessing of the Font

Almighty, everlasting God, be present at the mysteries of thy great
goodness, be present at thy sacraments, and for the creation of the new
people which the fount of baptism brings forth to thee, send down the
Spirit of adoption [Rom. 8.15]: that those things which our lowly
ministry performs may be perfected by the operation of thy power.
Through our Lord.

16

Another Prayer

We humbly beseech the great God of eternal majesty, that through
our Lord Jesus Christ, his Word, his Power, and his Wisdom, he will
grant remission of all sins in this healthful laver, and give his sanctification to the waters: that whoever shall go down into them may attain
the blessing of remission of sins: through the same our Lord Jesus
Christ his Son, who liveth and reigneth with him, God, in the unity
of the Holy Spirit, through all ages of ages.

17

Another Prayer

Let us pray and beseech the goodness of God the Father Almighty
that to these *competentes* his servants and handmaidens, whom in this
hour by the protection of his right hand he has brought to the font of
blessed regeneration, he will give the grace of his mercy: that he will
endue them with such spiritual perception that they may receive the
heavenly sacrament with hearty faith and a sure mind; that to us his
servants he will give pardon for all our sins and the presence of his
glory, that we may blamelessly celebrate the mysteries of holy baptism;
through our Lord Jesus Christ his Son, who liveth and reigneth with
him, God, in the unity of the Holy Spirit, through all ages of ages.

18
G. 91
S. 17, 18,
24

You breathe into the water, and say:

I adjure thee, O creature of water, through the true God, God the
living, God the holy: who in the beginning did separate thee from the
dry land, who brought thee forth from the fountain of Paradise and
commanded thee in four rivers to water the whole earth: I adjure thee
through our Lord Jesus Christ, the Son of the living God, who in
Cana of Galilee in a wonderful sign did change thee into wine: who
walked upon thee with his feet: and was baptized in thee by John: who
sweetened thy great bitterness by the tree of his Passion: and brought
thee forth from the rock to satisfy a thirsty people: and cleansed
Naaman the Syrian in thee from his leprosy: and gave thee the name

Siloam, wherein he commanded the blind man to wash his eyes that he might receive light: who shed thee forth from his side with his blood: who said to his disciples, *Go, teach all nations, baptizing them in the Name of the Father and of the Son and of the Holy Ghost* [Matt. 28.19]. Be thou therefore exorcized and effective to put to flight every diabolic infestation, every phantasm of the enemy: and root out the enemy himself from the servants of God who are this day to be baptized in thee, receiving remission of all their sins, in the Name of God the Father Almighty and in the Name of Jesus Christ the Son of the living God, who shall come in the Holy Spirit to judge this world by fire.

O celestial flood, be sanctified by the Word of God: O water that wast trodden by the feet of Christ, be sanctified: though upon whom the mountains weigh down yet thou art not shut up: thou art dashed against the rocks yet thou art not destroyed: thou art spread abroad upon the earth and yet dost not fail. Thou art held up by the firmament on high: thou dost wash the whole universe about, cleansing all things yet none cleanses thee. Thou when the people of the Hebrews took their flight wast held back and hardened into ice. Thou melting upon the high peaks dost bring ruin upon the dwellers of the Nile, and with thy fierce raging dost ever torment the world as it were thine enemy. Thou art one and the same: the salvation of the faithful, the avenger of the wicked. Moses smote the rock and the rock poured thee forth: the majesty of God commanded thee to come forth and thou couldest not hide among the boulders. Thou art borne upon the clouds and dost make fruitful the fields with joyful showers, lest the dry lifeless earth might deny their proper victuals to our bodies. The beginning of all things and their end exult in thee, yet rather it is through thee we know no end. For, O Lord, Almighty God, we do not forget thy power while we proclaim the merits of water: but in these things we declare the wonders of thy work.

Look therefore with favour upon sinners, and loose the captive. Restore the innocence which Adam lost in Paradise, which his wife let go, which cruel incontinence spoiled. Give a healthful draught to men who are upset by the bitterness of the apple: purge the disorders of mortal men and with a divine antidote cure their agelong distemper. Wash away the filth and squalor of the world: make a way through the wall of fire which protects the garden of Paradise, and open a flower-strewn path to them that return. May they receive the likeness of God, which once was lost by envy of the serpent: may the iniquities which

19
LO. 18

20
LO. 9

follow upon their disobedience be carried away in this pure stream. May they rise up unto rest: may they be brought forward unto pardon: that being renewed in the mystic waters they may know themselves to be redeemed and reborn. Through Christ thy Son our Lord, who liveth and reigneth with thee, God, in the unity of the Holy Spirit, through all ages of ages.

After this the chrism is poured into the water.

[From this point to the beginning of the litany which follows the administration of baptism, Magistretti's principal text is so corrupt that it is incapable of translation. The readings of three other comparable MSS. are therefore supplied, as follows:]

I.

21 *Then when the presbyters and deacons have entered the font, they are questioned by him who blessed the font:*

What have ye come to do? R̟. To baptize.

The Interrogations of the Creed

Dost thou believe in God the Father Almighty, maker of heaven and earth. R̟. I believe.

And in Jesus Christ, his only Son our Lord, who was born and suffered. R̟. I believe.

And dost thou believe in the Holy Ghost, the Holy Catholic Church, the remission of sins, the resurrection of the flesh, and everlasting life? R̟. I believe.

Then the presbyter says: Baptize them in the Name of the Father and of the Son and of the Holy Ghost.

Then the Litany.

2.

Then when the presbyters and deacons have gone into the font, they are questioned by him who blessed the font:

What have ye come to do?

They reply and say: To baptize.

He says to the fathers: Go, lead them down in the Name of the Father and of the Son and of the Holy Ghost.

Again he asks the fathers: What are their names? R̟. Such and such.

So the father names the names, and he says:

Do ye believe in God the Father Almighty? R̠7. We believe.

And in Jesus Christ, his only Son our Lord, who was born and suffered? R̠7. We believe.

Do ye believe in the Holy Spirit, the Holy Catholic Church, the remission of sins, the resurrection of the flesh, everlasting life? R̠7. We believe.

The presbyter says: Baptize them in the Name of the Father and of the Son and of the Holy Ghost.

Then the Litany.

3.

The Bishop's Questions

What have ye come to do?

They reply and say: To baptize.

He says to the fathers: Go, lead them down in the Name of the Father and of the Son and of the Holy Ghost.

Again he asks the fathers: What are their names? R̠7. Such and such.

The father names the names, and the bishop says:
Do ye believe in God the Father Almighty? R̠7. We believe.

And in Jesus Christ his only Son, our Lord, who was born and suffered? R̠7. We believe.

Do ye believe in the Holy Ghost, the Holy Catholic Church, the remission of sins, the resurrection of the flesh, everlasting life? R̠7. We believe.

Then the Bishop says: Baptize them in the Name of the Father and of the Son and of the Holy Ghost.

The Litany is said over the infants.

Lord, have mercy.	St Raphael.	St Nazarius.	22
Christ, deliver us.	St John.	St Celsus.	
St Mary.	St Peter.	St Protasius.	
St Michael.	St Paul.	St Gervasius.	
St Gabriel.	St Andrew.	St Ambrose.	
	St Stephen.	All Saints.	

Then the presbyter makes a cross with chrism on the infant's head, and says this prayer:

Almighty God, the Father of our Lord Jesus Christ, who has

23
G. 94
S.28
B. 249

regenerated you by water and the Holy Ghost, and who has given you remission of all your sins, himself anoints you with the chrism of salvation, in Christ Jesus our Lord unto eternal life. Amen.

24 *Here shall the bishop wash the feet of the infants after baptism.*

25 ## A Prayer upon Returning to the Font

The Lord be with you.

Let us who have performed and completed the sacraments of divine baptism give unwearied thanks to the Lord of heaven and earth, to God the Father Almighty: and let us humbly beseech him that he may grant us and all his household to be partakers of the glorious resurrection of our Lord Jesus Christ. By the favour of the same our Lord Jesus Christ his Son, who liveth and reigneth with him, God in the unity of the Holy Spirit, through all ages of ages. Amen.

* * *

[The following baptismal office is found near the end of the Manual.]

THE MAKING OF A CATECHUMEN

26
G. 22
S. 5
The Exorcism of the Salt

I exorcize thee, creature of salt, in the Name of God the Father Almighty, and in the love of our Lord Jesus Christ, and in the power of the Holy Spirit. I exorcize thee by the true God, who has created thee for the welfare of the human race and has commanded thee to be consecrated by his servants for those who come to faith. And therefore we ask thee, O Lord our God, that in the Name of the Holy Trinity this creature of salt may be a saving sacrament to drive away the enemy: do thou, O Lord, sanctify it and bless it that it may remain a perfect medicine in the bowels of all who receive it, in the Name of our Lord Jesus Christ who shall come in the Holy Spirit to judge the world by fire.

27
G. 129
The Exorcism of the Oil

I exorcize thee, creature of oil, through God Almighty, who made *heaven and earth, the sea and all that in them is* [Ex. 20.11]. All ye powers of the adversary, thou whole army of the devil, every assault and every phantasm of Satan, be ye rooted out and put to flight from this creature of oil, that to all who are anointed therewith it may be unto the

adoption of the sons of God through the Holy Spirit. In the Name of
God the Father Almighty and in the love of our Lord who shall come
to judge the world by fire.

First you question him, and say: 28

Who offers him [her]? R̵. I do [we do].

Q. What does he wish to become? R̵. A Christian.

Q. Are his parents worthy? R̵. They are worthy.

Q. Does he renounce the devil and
his works? R̵. He renounces.

Q. His world and his pomps? R̵. He renounces.

Now call upon him and say: Be mindful of thy words, that they never
depart from thee.

R̵. I will be mindful.

Then touch his ears and nostrils with spittle and say: 29
G. 71
Epheta, that is, Be opened, unto the odour of sweetness. LO. 4

Blow upon him, from head to foot, to mock the devil: 30

I blow upon thee, most unclean spirit, in the Name of our Lord
Jesus Christ. Thou, however, O devil, take flight: for the judgement
of God has drawn near.

Here take the sanctified oil and anoint him with the thumb between his 31
shoulders and upon his breast:

I anoint thee with the oil of salvation in Christ Jesus our Lord unto
eternal life.

The Lord be with you. 32
G. 32
Prayer. O Lord holy, Father Almighty, everlasting God of light and
truth, I call upon thy eternal and most just piety for this thy servant:
that thou wouldest enlighten him with the light of thy understanding.
Cleanse and sanctify him: give him true knowledge, that he may come
worthily to the grace of thy baptism, and let him hold a firm hope,
right counsel, holy doctrine, that he may be fitted to receive thy grace.
Through.

Then you breathe into his face in the likeness of a cross: 33
LO. 1
I exorcize thee, most unclean spirit, in the Name of our Lord Jesus B. 240
Christ: O every assault, all wrath, every phantasm, be ye rooted out
and put to flight from this creature of God, whom our Lord Jesus
Christ has to-day deigned to call unto his holy temple: that he may be

a temple of the living God, and the Holy Spirit may dwell in him: in the Name of God the Father Almighty and in the Name of Jesus Christ his Son, who shall come in the Holy Spirit to judge the world by fire.

Here give him his name [pone ei nomen], *and sign him and say his name:*

Receive the sign of the holy cross: observe the commandments of God: this day by the word of God thou art reborn, and reformed by celestial light. Enter the temple of the living God, and with the darkness of error removed joyfully acknowledge that thou hast escaped the toils of death. Await now the heavenly promises, the coming of Almighty God: that thou mayest be able to hope that the Word shall come, that was begotten, brought forth of a virgin, declared by believers: by whose invocation thou art enlightened, by whose sign thou art signed upon the brow, with this sign of the cross which shall not be crossed out: in the Name of God the Father Almighty and in the Name of Jesus Christ his Son, who shall come in the Holy Spirit to judge the world by fire.

The Lord be with you.

Prayer. God, unto whom none is so small that thou dost not favourably receive him, who of thy goodness dost admit every age and sex to the worship of thy majesty, we dedicate to thee this beginning of a new man, the wholeness of this infant life. Grant that this little one who knows no evil may be protected by the sign of the holy cross of thy Only-Begotten: may he be thine, may he grow up unto thee, may he fear thee and love thee, may he ever acknowledge thee to be his creator: and by thy guidance may he come to the holy laver of regeneration. Through the same.

Take the sanctified salt and place it in the infant's mouth: hear and repeat his name:

Receive the salt of wisdom: may it be propitious unto thee for life eternal.

The Lord be with you.

Prayer. O God of our fathers, O God the founder of truth, we humbly beseech thee to look favourably upon this thy servant, and grant that he who has taken this first morsel of salt may hunger only until he may be satisfied with heavenly food: until then O Lord may he ever be *fervent in spirit, rejoicing in hope,* always *serving* [Rom. 12.11] thy Name. Lead him to the laver of the second birth, that with thy faithful people he may be worthy to receive the eternal rewards of thy promises. Through.

The Exorcism of St Ambrose   *38*

O Almighty Lord, Word of God the Father, Christ Jesus, God and Lord of the whole creation, who didst give to thy holy Apostles the *power to tread upon serpents and scorpions* [Luke 10.19]: who amongst thine other marvellous sayings didst say, Put the devils to flight: by whose power Satan was conquered and *fell as lightning from heaven* [Luke 10.18]: with fear and trembling humbly I beseech thy name that as to me, most unworthy, thou hast given pardon of all my sins, so thou wouldest give boldness and power that I may go out against this cruel dragon, in trust and faith being armed by the power of thy right hand.

[An exorcism of great length follows.]

When they go into church, say: *39*

Enter, my child, into the house of the Lord: hearken to thy Father teaching thee the way of knowledge.

Prayer over the *Competens*   *40*

Almighty everlasting God, look with favour from the high throne of thy majesty upon this thy servant N., a *competens*, who has hastened to thy Church: grant him, Lord, that beneath the protection of thy hand he may attain to the grace of holy baptism. Through.

Another   *41*

Hear, Lord, the supplication of thy servant, who desires to be united to the congregation of thy faithful: that on the day of the holy solemnity of thy clemency he may be found worthy to receive the gift of baptism.

Baptism for a sick person starts at this point.

Prayer over the Water   *42*
B. 235
G. 89
S. 21

Almighty, everlasting God, be present at the mysteries of thy great goodness, be present at thy sacraments, and for the creation of the new people which the fount of baptism brings forth to thee send down the *Spirit of adoption* [Rom. 8.15]: that what is performed by the mystery of our lowliness may be perfected by the operation of thy power. Through.

You blow upon the water crosswise: *43*

I blow upon thee, most unclean spirit, in the Name of our Lord Jesus Christ.

44

Exorcism of the Water

I exorcize thee, creature of water, in the Name of God the Father Almighty and in the Name of Jesus Christ his Son and of the Holy Spirit. May every phantasm, every power of the enemy, every assault of the devil be rooted out and put to flight from this creature of water, that it may be a *well of water springing up unto everlasting life* [John 4.14]: and when this servant of God shall have been baptized, no infirmity of the body may master him, no enemy of the human race oppose him: but when he has been *born again of water and the Holy Ghost* [John 3.5], let him become a temple of the living God in the remission of sins. in the Name of God the Father Almighty and in the Name of Jesus Christ his Son, who shall come in the Holy Spirit to judge this world by fire. R⁊. Amen.

45

Then take the chrism, pour it over the water crosswise, and mix it: and before you immerse him in the water, address him by name and question him about his faith:

What dost thou seek? R⁊. To baptize. [Other MSS: to be baptized.]

Dost thou believe in God the Father Almighty, maker of heaven and earth? R⁊. I believe.

And in Jesus Christ his only Son our Lord, who was born and suffered? R⁊. I believe.

Dost thou believe in the Holy Ghost, the Holy Catholic Church, the remission of sins, the resurrection of the flesh, everlasting life? R⁊. I believe.

Let the priest say: the first dipping: I baptize thee in the Name of the Father: *the second dipping:* and of the Son: *the third dipping:* and of the Holy Ghost.

46

Then the Litany.

Lord have mercy (*thrice*).

St Mary.	St John.	St Stephen.	St Gervase.
St Michael.	St Peter.	St Nazarius.	St Ambrose.
St Gabriel.	St Paul.	St Celsus.	All Saints.
St Raphael.	St Andrew.	St Protasius.	

47
G. 94
S. 28
B. 249

Then make the sign of the cross on the head of the infant with chrism, and say:

Almighty God the Father of our Lord Jesus Christ, who has regenerated thee *by water and the Holy Ghost* [John 3.5], and has given thee remission of all thy sins, himself anoints thee with the chrism of salvation, in Christ Jesus our Lord.

Prayer after Baptism 48

Almighty, everlasting God, who hast regenerated thy servant N. *by water and the Holy Ghost* [John 3.5], and who hast given him remission of all his sins, grant him an abiding wisdom to acknowledge the truth of thy divinity. Through our Lord.

Communicate him: The Body of our Lord Jesus Christ, with his Blood, 49 preserve thy soul unto eternal life. Amen.

BEROLDUS

Text: *Beroldus sive Ecclesiae Ambrosianae Mediolanensis Kalendarium et Ordines Saec. xii*, ed. M. Magistretti, Milan, 1894.

Beroldus was an official of the Cathedral at Milan in the twelfth century. He wrote this detailed account of the ceremonies of the Cathedral church to guide those who had to use them. A highly organized and flourishing cathedral community is reflected in the many titles of office to which the members of the various orders of the ministry are assigned. In explanation of them, it is sufficient to say that *Primicerius* means "chief", and that the word "cardinal" originally denoted a member of the clergy who was permanently attached to the church which he served: a hebdomadary priest or deacon was one who was appointed to special office or duty for the period of a week. The decumanary presbyters were the chief presbyters: the "cimiliarch" was the official who had charge of the Cathedral treasures.

BEROLDUS

In the first week, after Psalm 50 [Hebrew: 51] has been sung at Mattins, the presbyter says: *The Lord be with you* . . . Then the deacon says in a moderate voice: *Let the competentes go forth*, once; in another week, twice. And the doorkeeper at the porch: *Let no catechumen* . . . And likewise at Vespers.

On the Sunday of the Samaritan Woman, after the gospel, the deacon says: *Whoso wishes to give in any names, let him bring them forward now.*

On the second Saturday, after the scrutiny, the deacon says in a loud voice at the end of the altar: *Raise yourselves, ye faithful. Pray, ye* competentes. *Bow your heads.* Then the infants are told by an acolyte to bow their heads: again the deacon says in a loud voice: *Raise yourselves to the Lord, likewise give honour to God:* and the clerks reply: *Amen.* And the deacon says in a loud voice: *Bow yourselves for the blessing.* When the blessing has been given, again the deacon says in a loud voice: *Let the* competentes *go forth:* and the acolytes reply likewise. Then they go out.

The same order is to be observed at each scrutiny and [*or*, even] on Sundays, after the gospel, up to Palm Sunday.

In the third week, on each day at Mattins and Vespers, the deacon says in a moderate voice: *Let the catechumens go forth*, once: in another week twice: *Let the catechumens go forth: Let the catechumens go forth.* And the acolytes reply likewise from the chancel doors.

On the Friday, at each lection, and on Sundays at each prayer, the doorkeepers vociferate three times through each porch, *Let no catechumen* . . .

After the middle of Lent, the aforesaid doorkeepers add: *Let no catechumen* . . . *Let no* . . . up to Palm Sunday.

*   *   *

OF THE FIRST, SECOND, AND THIRD SCRUTINIES

On the second Saturday of Lent, two lesser caretakers in the weekly course, who are called from outside, shall seek a goatskin from the archbishop, and shall take it into the midst of the church, and make upon it a *chrismon* of ashes; and two caretaker-watchmen, who are called from outside, shall take care of the church when the mystery is being performed, both on Saturday up to the time when the deacon asks the subdeacon at the door of the church about the faith of the children, and on Sundays up to the end of the Gospel. On that Saturday, when the greater Mass is ended, the presbyter who sang the Mass comes to where the ashes are scattered and blesses the ashes: *I exorcize you, O ashes.* Then two subdeacons with the hebdomadary deacons come to the door of the church where the boys stand, the subdeacons outside, the deacons within: then the deacon questions the subdeacons, saying: *What do they seek?* R7. *Faith.* He asks: *Are their parents worthy?* R7. *They are worthy.* Again he asks: *Do they renounce the devil and his pomp?* R7. *They renounce.* He asks: *The world and its pomp?* R7. *They renounce.* And the deacon says: *Be mindful of your words, that they may never leave you.* R7. *We shall be mindful.* Then they come to the door where the girls stand, and say likewise, the chief of the readers always guiding their words.

They all go into the church, male and female alike, and come where the *chrismon* is, and stand males on one side, females on the other, the males on the south, the females on the north. Then a reader arranges them round the edge of the *chrismon* in the manner of a crown. One cardinal and two decumanary presbyters come prepared on three sides where the *chrismon* is, and say all together: *Our Father*. When they have finished the prayer, they breathe out in the form of a cross, and say: *I breathe upon you, ashes scattered on sackcloth, in the Name of the Father and of the Son and of the Holy Ghost*. Then they and others who shall come in pray outside the crown, before the altar, saying: *We confess to the Lord*. When the confession and absolution are said, straightway they begin *Our Father* and *I believe in God*. Then *Almighty Lord, the Word of God*, to *I shall go in peace*. Straightway the senior presbyter takes the book of the gospels and kisses it, and goes down and makes a circuit of the children, signing continually and saying the exorcism of St Ambrose, *I adjure thee*: they are preceded by a clerk who holds out the book as they enter and takes it back as they go out. The other presbyters follow, and two of them, or three from each part, make the sign of the cross on the foreheads of the children, on three or four [at a time?], and say, *I sign thee with the sign of the cross, in the Name of the Father and of the Son and of the Holy Ghost. Amen*. Then three deacons preceded by a reader and as many subdeacons vested in albs make a circuit of the children on the outside, signing similarly and saying continually the exorcism of St Ambrose. At the first scrutiny the signing is done by the hebdomadary priest with three cardinal deacons and three subdeacons and six presbyters of the "hundred", three times: at the second, twelve ordinaries with as many presbyters, six times: at the third, the archbishop with the chief of the presbyters with all the presbyters and the cardinal deacons, with all the subdeacons, and with the presbyters of the "hundred", nine times.

When the signing is done, the *competentes* come before the altar, outside the chancel, and the hebdomadary priest behind the altar says: *The Lord be with you*, and all the clerks reply *And with thy spirit*. And a deacon at the side of the altar says in a loud voice: *Raise yourselves, ye faithful. Pray, ye* competentes. *Bow your heads. Raise yourselves before the Lord, likewise give honour to God*. And the whole choir: *Amen*. And the deacon says: *Bow yourselves for the blessing*. Then the catechumens are told by the acolytes to bow the head. Then the presbyter says the prayer: *Hear, Lord, the supplication*. When the prayer has been said, the deacon says in a loud voice: *Let the* competentes *go forth*. When all this has been done, the children go out, and the subdeacon comes out from the sacristy with lighted candles, and vespers begins.

At every scrutiny a lesser notary with a mace precedes the cardinal presbyter or the bishop with the decumanary presbyters, to clear the way round the *chrismon*: so that at the first signing, thrice, the lesser notary precedes; at the second signing, six times, the lesser notary and a second precede; and at the third signing, nine times, a lesser notary and a second and a third precede. Similarly readers precede the deacon and subdeacon, beginning from the last, in the same way.

CONCERNING THE SATURDAY OF LAZARUS

On the Saturday of Lazarus, all the children, male and female, are to be enrolled, and after the deacon's questioning, two presbyters vested in alb and stole stand at the doors where the catechumens are to enter, and two doorkeepers hold the sanctified oil, and anoint the children on the breast and say: *I anoint thee with the oil of salvation in Christ Jesus the Lord unto eternal life*. Then the infants are to be signed according to custom. The archbishop and all the cardinal presbyters and the chief of the presbyters with the decumanary presbyters of the "hundred" shall sign, and three lesser notaries shall go before them. And outside, all the deacons and subdeacons shall sign likewise, and they shall be preceded by three lesser readers.

LIKEWISE AT THE DELIVERY OF THE CREED

It is to be understood that on the day of the delivery of the Creed all the bells are to be sounded after Mass and all the doors shut: but none is to be put out except the catechumens. And the hebdomadary priest, vested in cope and stole, gives the salutation from behind the altar, and the deacons vested in stoles say: *Let all catechumens go forth, Let all Jews go forth, Let all heathen go forth, Let all heretics go forth, Let him who has no business* [here] *go forth*. And the acolytes likewise. And before they say these sentences, and then after each one, let the deacons kiss the altar: and when the sentences are said, there is sung: *Come, children*. Then the archbishop enters the office to prepare himself, and the *Primicerius* and his readers vest themselves with chasubles, and they come to take from the archbishop his permission to open the doors to the children: and as they go, they pray in three places, first in the choir, then at the *gradus*, a third time near the porches, and then they open the doors to the children and say: *Children, enter the house of the Lord. Hearken to your father, teaching you the way of knowledge.* And as they go back they likewise pray in the three places: and all the time the *Primicerius* bears the tablets and a hazel wand green with leaves. Then the archbishop begins the Creed, from a place prepared on a platform: and if he is absent, the hebdomadary presbyter, vested at the altar, recites it; he turns to the west, and says: *For those that are to be reborn*, in the solemn tone of the gospels. There follows: *Sign yourselves and hear the Creed. I believe in God the Father Almighty*, and all is thus sung. Again: *Sign yourselves and hear the Creed. I believe in God. Sign yourselves and hear the Creed. I believe in God.* And always the acolytes shall tell the women that at each time they are to sign the children on the brow. When *I believe in God the Father* has thus been finished for the third time, then shall be said *I believe in God* in the ferial tone of the gospels, and its tract in the solemn tone of the gospels. When both the text and the tract are finished, then the archbishop recites in a loud voice: *Beloved, ye have received the Creed*, in the solemn tone of the gospels.

When the Creed has been delivered, the archbishop or hebdomadary presbyter and the deacon and two hebdomadary caretakers say those things which they have said on the other Saturdays. The archbishop goes down from his throne to the altar, or, if he is absent, the hebdomadary priest says his part. Turning to the east he says: *The Lord be with you.* The reader who keeps the keys, whose week it is, ascends the *gradus* to sing the hymn of evening light: *Since thou dost illuminate*, and the choir R̂. *And with thy spirit.*

HOLY SATURDAY

[Beroldus gives an account of the striking of the new fire, the lighting of the paschal candle, the night vigil service, and then:]

When this is finished, straightway the archbishop puts on the sacred vestments ... and goes to the fonts ... The archbishop begins the blessing and exorcism [*adjuratio*] of the water. After this the cimiliarch standing beside him with the chrism and a silver spoon holds out the empty spoon to the archbishop, and while the cimiliarch holds the chrism the archbishop pours the chrism into the fonts with the aforesaid spoon in the form of a cross, saying: *May this font be holy, sanctified, truly anointed, in the Name of the Father and of the Son and of the Holy Ghost. Amen.* So three times he pours the chrism, saying: *May this font* ... When this is done, straightway the archbishop goes to another part of the fonts, that is, to the east, and two cardinals, that is, a minor presbyter and a minor deacon enter the fonts. And three caretaker-watchmen of of the eight juniors go through the church to find, if they can, three boys who are to be called first *Peter*, second *Paul*, and third *John*. And they shall hold them out to the cardinals in the fonts and while they hold the boys the archbishop asks them: *What do ye seek?* They reply: *To be baptized*. Again he asks: *Do ye believe in God the Father Almighty, Maker of heaven and earth?* They reply: *We believe*. He asks: *And in Jesus Christ his only Son our Lord, who was born and suffered?* They reply: *We believe*. He asks: *Do ye believe in the Holy Ghost, the Holy Catholic Church, the communion of Saints, the remission of sins, the resurrection of the flesh, everlasting life?* They reply: *We believe*. And straightway he continues: *Baptize them in the Name of the Father and of the Son and of the Holy Ghost*. And straightway they baptize them, saying their names: *I baptize thee*, the first dip: *in the Name of the Father*, the second dip: *and of the Son*, the third dip: *and of the Holy Ghost. Amen*. The archbishop kneels down facing the east. Then straightway the chief of the readers begins the litanies, and after the litanies the archbishop rises and anoints the aforesaid baptized children on their foreheads in the form of a cross, saying this prayer: *God the Almighty Father of our Lord Jesus Christ, who has regenerated you with water and the Holy Ghost*. The aforesaid caretakers shall take the aforesaid boys from the hands of their fathers who took them to the font: and two of the greater caretakers of the eight lesser shall be ready, one with a vessel of water, the other with a towel from the archbishop's closet. And then the archbishop washes the feet of the three boys aforesaid and dries them with the towel and kisses them: and three times he places the heels of each upon his head.

[The Mass follows.]

9. *Rome*

THE LEONINE SACRAMENTARY

Text: *Sacramentarium Leonianum*, ed. C. L. Feltoe, Cambridge, 1896.
Sacramentarium Veronese, ed. L. C. Mohlberg (*Rerum Ecclesiasticarum Documenta*, Vol. 1), Rome, 1956.

The attribution of this document to Pope Leo has no foundation in history and was made at the time of its discovery in 1735. A number of dates have been proposed for it, ranging from 366 to 594. It is a collection of Masses and other liturgical material which does not reflect the official use of the Church in Rome.

Unfortunately, the manuscript is damaged, and those parts which might have included the Paschal and baptismal rites are missing. That part which remains, however, includes a Baptismal Mass for Pentecost, consisting of Collect, Secret, Preface, *Hanc igitur*, *Communicantes*, and a Blessing of water, honey, and milk. Only those parts of the Mass which particularly relate to baptism are here translated. A form for the Blessing of the Font appears, rather oddly, on the last page of the manuscript, and that also is translated here.

At Pentecost, for those that come up from the Font

[*The Collect*]

O ineffable and merciful God, grant that the children of adoption whom thy Holy Spirit has called unto itself [*id ipsum*] may harbour nothing earthly in their joy, nothing alien in their faith; through.

[*In the Canon*]

We beseech thee graciously to accept this oblation which we offer to thee for these whom thou hast deigned to regenerate by water and the Holy Spirit, granting them remission of all their sins; and command their names to be written in *the book of the living* [Ps. 69.28]; through.

[*A Blessing of Water, Honey, and Milk*]

Bless also we beseech thee, O Lord, these thy creatures of water, honey, and milk, and give thy servants drink of this fount of water of everlasting life, which is the spirit of truth, and nourish them with this milk and honey according as thou didst promise to our fathers, Abraham, Isaac, and Jacob, to lead them into the land of promise, a land flowing with honey and milk. Therefore, O Lord, unite thy servants to the Holy Spirit, as this honey and milk is united, wherein is signified the union of heavenly and earthly substance [*substantia*] in Christ Jesus our Lord, through whom all these, *etc.*

*　　*　　*

The Blessing of the Font

We offer thee [this] prayer, O Lord, the eternal begetter of [all] things, Almighty God, whose *Spirit was borne upon the waters* [Gen. 1.3 Vulg.], whose eyes looked down from on high upon Jordan's stream when John was baptizing [*tingeret*] those who in penitence confessed their sins: and therefore we pray thy holy glory that thy hand may be laid upon this water that thou mayest cleanse and purify the lesser man who shall be baptized therefrom: and that he, putting aside all that is deathly, may be reborn and brought to life again through the new man reborn in Christ Jesus, with whom thou livest and reignest in the unity of the Holy Spirit, unto the ages of ages.

JOHN THE DEACON

Text: Dom A. Wilmart, *Analecta Reginensia* (*Studi e Testi*, Vol. 50), Rome, 1933.

The internal evidence of this letter, written to Senarius, a Roman nobleman, shows clearly that it was written in Rome. The date of the letter is about 500.

2. You ask me to tell you why before a man is baptized he must first become a catechumen; or what the meaning is of the word or of the word "catechizing"; in what rule of the Old Testament it is set out; or whether indeed the rule is a new one, deriving rather from the New Testament. Also you ask what a scrutiny is, and why infants are scrutinized three times before the Pascha: and what purpose is served by this care and preoccupation with these examinations.

3. Here is my reply. I am confident that you are sufficiently versed in such matters as to know that the whole human race, while still so to speak in its cradle, should properly have fallen in death through the waywardness of the first man: and no rescue was possible except by

the grace of the Saviour; who although he had been begotten of the
Father before the worlds yet for our salvation did not disdain to be
born in time, man of a virgin mother alone. There cannot therefore
be any doubt that before a man is reborn in Christ he is held close in
the power of the devil: and unless he is extricated from the devil's
toils, renouncing him among the first beginnings of faith with a true
confession, he cannot approach the grace of the saving laver. And
therefore he must first enter the classroom of the catechumens.
Catechesis is the Greek word for instruction. He is instructed through
the Church's ministry, by the blessing of one laying his hand [upon
his head], that he may know who he is and who he shall be: in other
words, that from being one of the damned he becomes holy, from
unrighteousness he appears as righteous, and finally, from being a
servant he becomes a son: so that a man whose first parentage brought
him perdition is restored by the gift of a second parentage, and becomes
the possessor of a father's inheritance. He receives therefore exsufflation and exorcism, in order that the devil may be put to flight and
an entrance prepared for Christ our God: so that being delivered from
the power of darkness he may be *translated to the kingdom* [Col. 1.13]
of the glory of the love of God: so that a man who till recently had
been a vessel of Satan becomes now a dwelling of the Saviour. And so
he receives exsufflation, because the old deceiver merits such ignominy.
He is exorcized, however, that is to say he is adjured to go out and
depart and acknowledge the approach of him whose upright image
he had cast down in the bliss of Paradise by his wicked counsel. The
catechumen receives blessed salt also, to signify that just as all flesh is
kept healthy by salt, so the mind which is drenched and weakened by
the waves of this world is held steady by the salt of wisdom and of the
preaching of the word of God: so that it may come to stability and
permanence, after the distemper of corruption is thoroughly settled by
the gentle action of the divine salt. This then is achieved by frequent
laying on of the hand, and by the blessing of his Creator called over
his head three times in honour of the Trinity.

4. And so by the efforts of himself and others the man who recently
had received exsufflation and had renounced the toils and the pomps
of the devil is next permitted to receive the words of the Creed
[*symbolum*] which was handed down by the Apostles: so that he who
a short time before was called simply a catechumen may now be called
a competent, or elect. For he was conceived in the womb of Mother
Church and now he begins to live, even though the time of the sacred

birth is not yet fulfilled. Then follow those occasions which according to the Church's custom are commonly called scrutinies. For we scrutinize their hearts through faith, to ascertain whether since the renunciation of the devil the sacred words have fastened themselves on his mind: whether they acknowledge the future grace of the Redeemer: whether they confess that they believe in God the Father Almighty. And when by their replies it becomes clear that it is so, according as it is written: *With the heart man believeth unto righteousness, but with the mouth confession is made unto salvation* [Rom. 10.10]: their ears are touched with the oil of sanctification, and their nostrils also are touched: the ears because through them faith enters the mind, according as the apostle says: *Faith cometh by hearing, and hearing by the word of God* [Rom. 10.17]: so that, the ears being as it were fortified by a kind of wall of sanctification, may permit entrance to nothing harmful, nothing which might entice them back.

5. When their nostrils are touched, they are thus without doubt admonished that for as long as they draw the breath of life through their nostrils they must abide in the service and the commandments of God. Whence that holy man says: *As God liveth, who hath taken away my judgement: and the Almighty who has vexed my soul; all the while my breath is in me, and the Spirit of God is in my nostrils; my lips should not speak wickedness nor my tongue utter deceit* [Job 27.2–4]. The unction of the nostrils signifies this also, that since the oil is blessed in the Name of the Saviour, they may be led unto his spiritual odour by the inner perception of a certain ineffable sweetness, so that in delight they may sing: *Thy Name is as ointment poured forth: we shall run after the savour of thine ointments* [Cant. 1.3]. And so the nostrils, being fortified by this mystery, can give no admittance to the pleasures of this world, nor anything which might weaken their minds.

6. Next the oil of consecration is used to anoint their breast, in which is the seat and dwelling place of the heart; so that they may understand that they promise with a firm mind and a pure heart eagerly to follow after the commandments of Christ, now that the devil has been driven out. They are bidden to go in naked even down to their feet, so that having put aside the carnal garments of mortality they may acknowledge that they make their journey upon a road upon which nothing harsh and nothing harmful can be found. The Church has ordained these things with watchful care over many years, although the old books may not show traces of them [*quamvis horum vestigia vetus pagina non ostendat*]. And then when the elect or cate-

chumen has advanced in faith by these spiritual conveyances, so to speak, it is necessary to be consecrated in the baptism of the one laver, in which sacrament his baptism is effected by a threefold immersion. And rightly so: for whoever comes to be baptized in the Name of the Trinity must signify that Trinity in a threefold immersion, and must. acknowledge his debt to the bounty of him who upon the third day rose from the dead. He is next arrayed in white vesture, and his head anointed with the unction of the sacred chrism: that the baptized person may understand that in his person a kingdom and a priestly mystery have met. For priests and princes used to be anointed with the oil of chrism, priests that they might offer sacrifices to God, princes that they might rule their people. For a fuller expression of the idea of priesthood, the head of the neophyte is dressed in a linen array: for priests of that time used always to deck the head with a certain mystic covering. All the neophytes are arrayed in white vesture to symbolize the resurgent Church, just as our Lord and Saviour himself in the sight of certain disciples and prophets was thus transfigured on the mount, so that it was said: *His face did shine as the sun: his raiment was made white as snow* [Matt. 17.2]. This prefigured for the future the splendour of the resurgent Church, of which it is written: *Who is this that riseth up* [Cant. 3.6; 8.5] all in white? And so they wear white raiment so that though the ragged dress of ancient error has darkened the infancy of their first birth, the costume of their second birth should display the raiment of glory, so that clad in a wedding garment he may approach the table of the heavenly bridegroom as a new man.

7. I must say plainly and at once, in case I seem to have overlooked the point, that all these things are done even to infants, who by reason of their youth understand nothing. And by this you may know that when they are presented by their parents or others, it is necessary that their salvation should come through other people's profession, since their damnation came by another's fault . . .

*   *   *

12. You ask why milk and honey are placed in a most sacred cup and offered with the sacrifice at the Paschal Sabbath. The reason is that it is written in the Old Testament and in a figure promised to the New People: *I shall lead you into a land of promise, a land flowing with milk and honey* [Lev. 20.24]. The land of promise, then, is the land of resurrection to everlasting bliss, it is nothing else than the land of our body, which in the resurrection of the dead shall attain to the glory of incorruption

and peace. This kind of sacrament, then, is offered to the newly-baptized so that they may realize that no others but they, who partake of the Body and Blood of the Lord, shall receive the land of promise: and as they start upon the journey thither, they are nourished like little children with milk and honey, so that they may sing: *How sweet are thy words unto my mouth, O Lord, sweeter than honey and the honeycomb* [Ps. 119.103; 19.11]. As new men therefore, abandoning the bitterness of sin, they drink milk and honey: so that they who in their first birth were nourished with the milk of corruption and first shed tears of bitterness, in their second birth may taste the sweetness of milk and honey in the bowels of the Church, so that being nourished upon such sacraments they may be dedicated to the mysteries of perpetual incorruption.

NOTE.

A valuable article elucidating the *Letter to Senarius* has been published by Antoine Chavasse in *Études de critique et d'histoire religieuses* (Lyon, 1948) under the title *Les deux rituels romain et gaulois* etc.

It should be observed that at one point Chavasse appears to assume a different translation from that which is offered above. Near the end of chapter 3 [p. 155], the Latin text runs: *accipit iam catechumenus benedictum sal, in quo signatur, quia sicut omnis caro sale condita servatur,* etc. In the translation above, the verb *signare* is translated as meaning "to signify", and its construction in this sense with *quia*, though not classical, is also exemplified at the beginning of the same chapter: *Studium vestrum nosse confidimus quia omne genus humanum . . . in morte fuerit collapsum,* etc. Chavasse, however, appears to detect in the verb *signare* a reference to the Sign of the Cross, and to translate as follows: "The catechumen receives blessed salt also, during which he is signed, since . . ." etc.

It should also be observed that the anointing which follows the scrutinies (sections 4, 5) was understood by John the Deacon to be designed to close the ears and the nostrils rather than to open them. It does not therefore seem likely that he was acquainted with the form, *Effeta, quod est adaperire* . . .

10. *Gallican Documents*

THE *MISSALE GOTHICUM*

Text: H. M. Bannister, *Missale Gothicum*, Vol. 1 (H.B.S. 52). See also *Missale Gothicum*, ed. L. C. Mohlberg (*Rerum Ecclesiasticarum Documenta*, Vol. 5), Rome, 1961. This is a pure Gallican sacramentary and its date is about 700.

The sacramentary provides propers for five *Missae Jejunii* which may fairly be ascribed to the first five Sundays of Lent: the next Mass, for the Sunday before Easter, has the title *Missa in Symboli Traditione* (Mass at the Delivery of the Creed). It consists of a set of Gallican propers, namely, *Prefatio, Collectio, Collectio post Nomina, Collectio ad Pacem, Immolatio, Post Secreta, Ante Orationem Dominicam, Post Orationem Dominicam*. The themes of the propers are the Raising of Lazarus and the Entry into Jerusalem. The only mention of the delivery of the Creed is that provided by the title. The presence of the candidates at the Mass is indicated in the *Collectio post Nomina*, which reads as follows:

Behold, O Lord, the unwitting prophecy of Caiaphas the high priest is fulfilled in thy people: that as one man thou shouldest die for the people, lest all equally should perish: so thou a single grain in the earth didst die, that much corn should spring up. Suppliant we pray thee, who wast slain a sacrifice for the world's salvation, that thou who offered thyself for us wilt give us pardon. And grant we beseech thee that those whose names we recite before the holy altar, who have passed from the bonds of the body and now rest in peace, may have thee for their deliverer whom in baptism they had for their Redeemer. And we pray thee O Lord our God for those here present who are prepared for the saving sacraments of baptism, that being instructed in the faith, disciplined in the body, and strengthened in grace, and so being prepared to receive the fullness of thy grace by the gift of thy Spirit, in obedience to thy will they may be reborn in the fount of the holy laver which they have longed for. 198

[The Mass *in Symboli Traditione* is followed by the propers for the Maundy Thursday Masses, and formularies for Good Friday and Easter Eve. Then comes the Easter vigil; after the Blessing of the Candle and a series of prayers to be said in the vigil service, there follows:]

252   ## [ORDER] FOR THE MAKING OF A
                              CHRISTIAN

O Lord, condescend to bless this child thy servant *N.* forasmuch as
neither his estate nor age doth prevent it: according as thy most dearly
beloved Son our Lord hath said: *Forbid not* the children *to come unto me*
[Matt. 19.14]. Let these children, Lord, before they know good or evil
be signed with the sign of thy cross, and even in this tenderness of age
may they be counted worthy to receive the baptism of thy holy
Name. Through Jesus Christ our Lord.

253   *Another Collect*

Receive the sign of Christ: accept the words of God: receive the
light of the Word of God: for this day doth Christ confess thee to be
his own. Through Jesus Christ our Lord.

254   *Another Collect*

I sign thee in the Name of the Father and of the Son and of the
Holy Spirit, that thou mayest be a Christian: [I sign] thine eyes to see
the clearness of God; thine ears to hear the voice of the Lord; thy nose
to savour the sweetness of Christ; thy mouth to confess the Father, the
Son, and the Holy Spirit; thine heart to believe in the holy and undivided Trinity. Peace be with thee, through Jesus Christ our Lord,
who with the Father and the Holy Spirit liveth . . .

255   *Collect for the Blessing of the Fonts*

Dearly beloved brethren, ye stand by the shore of a life-giving
fount, ye are to lead new voyagers to embark and ply their trade upon
a new sea. They set sail with the cross for their mast, with heavenly
desire to guide them, with no staff but the sacrament. The place indeed
is small, but full of grace: the Holy Spirit has brought them on a fair
course. Let us therefore pray our Lord God to bless this font, that to all
who go down therein it may be a laver of rebirth unto the remission
of all their sins. Through the Lord . . .

256   *This collect follows:*

O God, who for the salvation of men's souls didst sanctify the waters
of Jordan, may there descend upon these waters the angel of thy
blessing, that thy servants over whom it has been poured may receive

remission of their sins, and being *born again of water and the Holy Spirit* [John 3.5] may serve thee faithfully for ever. Through the Lord . . .

Contestatio   257

It is meet and right, O Lord holy, Father Almighty, everlasting God, the author and Father of holy chrisms, who through thy only Son our Lord and God hast given us a new sacrament, who before the beginning of the world didst bestow thy Holy Spirit upon the waters which supported him, who by thy angel of healing didst watch over the waters of Bethsaida, who by the condescension of Christ thy Son didst sanctify the bath of Jordan: look down, O Lord, upon these waters which are made ready to blot out men's sins; may the angel of thy goodness be present in these sacred fonts, to wash away the stains of the former life and to sanctify a little dwelling for thee: so that the souls of them that are reborn may flourish unto eternal life and may truly be renewed by the newness of baptism. O Lord our God, bless this creature of water, may thy power descend upon it, pour down from on high thy Holy Spirit the Comforter, the Angel of truth, sanctify O Lord the waves of this flood as thou didst sanctify the stream of Jordan, so that all who go down into this font in the Name of the Father and the Son and the Holy Spirit shall be counted worthy to receive the pardon of their sins and the infusion of the Holy Spirit, through Jesus Christ our Lord, who with the Father and the Holy Spirit is blessed throughout all the ages of the ages.

Then you make a cross with the chrism and say: 258

I exorcize thee, creature of water, I exorcize you, all ye armies of the devil, all ye shades and demons, in the Name of our Lord Jesus Christ of Nazareth, who was incarnate in the Virgin Mary, to whom the Father *hath put all things in subjection* [1 Cor. 15.27] both in heaven and earth. Do thou fear and tremble, thou and all thy wickedness, give place to the Holy Spirit, so that for all who go down to this font it may be a laver of the baptism of regeneration, unto the remission of all their sins, through Jesus Christ our Lord who shall come *in the throne of his Father's glory* [Matt. 19.28] with his holy angels to judge thee, thou enemy, and this world, by fire unto the ages of ages.

Then you breathe thrice upon the water and pour in chrism in the form of a   259
cross, and say:

The infusion of the saving chrism of our Lord Jesus Christ, that to all

who descend therein it may be a *well of water springing up unto everlasting life* [John 4.14]. Amen.

260   *While you baptize him you question him and say:*

I baptize thee, *N.*, in the Name of the Father and of the Son and of
the Holy Ghost, unto the remission of sins, that thou mayest have
eternal life. Amen.

261   *While you touch him with chrism you say:*

I anoint thee with the chrism of holiness, the garment of immortality [cf. Gel. 60], which our Lord Jesus Christ first received from the
Father, that thou mayest bear it entire and spotless before the judgement
seat of Christ and live unto all eternity.

262   *While you wash his feet, you say:*
B. 251
S. 36   I wash thy feet as our Lord Jesus Christ did to his disciples. So mayest
thou also do unto pilgrims and strangers, that thou mayest have
eternal life.

263   *While you place the robe upon him, you say:*
B. 250
S. 33   Receive the white robe, and bear it spotless before the judgement
seat of our Lord Jesus Christ. Amen.

264   *A Collect*

Dearly beloved brethren, let us pray to our Lord and God for his
neophytes who are now baptized, that when the Saviour shall come
in his majesty he may clothe with the garments of eternal salvation
those whom he has regenerated with water and the Holy Spirit.
Through the Lord.

265   *Another Collect*
B.253
S.39   For those who are baptized, who seek the chrism, who are crowned
in Christ, to whom our Lord has been pleased to grant a new birth, let
us beseech Almighty God that they may bear the baptism which they
have received spotless unto the end. Through the Lord.

[The first Mass of Easter follows next in the sacramentary; baptismal
references are found in the Preface and *Immolatio*.]

MASS AT THE VIGIL OF THE
HOLY PASCHA

266   *[Preface]*

Dearly beloved brethren, who by the grace of this holy and sacred
night are freed from the darkness of this world, and chosen unto the

promised grace of righteousness and heavenly light, let us beseech the tireless goodness of Almighty God the Father, through Christ his Son, that he may take under the protection of his majesty his holy catholic Church spread throughout all the world, which he sought by the Passion and most glorious Blood of his most loving Son, and may keep it safe and secure against all the snares of the world, and grant it perpetual tranquillity. Through the rising [Lord], *etc.*

*   *   *

Immolatio

270

It is meet and right, fitting and right, that here and in all places we should thank thee, should sing thy praises and offer sacrifices and confess thy mercies, O Lord holy, Father Almighty, everlasting God, *for thou art great and doest wondrous things, thou art God alone* [Ps. 86.10], *thou in thy wisdom madest the heavens* [Ps. 136.5], thou didst form the earth above the waters, thou madest *great lights, the sun to rule the day, the moon* and stars *to rule the night* [Gen. 1.16]; *it is thou that hast made us and not we ourselves* [Ps. 100.3]; *disregard not the work of thine own hands* [Ps. 138.8]. *The day is thine and the night is thine* [Ps. 74.17], *thou hast granted thy lovingkindness in the daytime and in the nightseason* [Ps. 42.10], thou hast declared what we celebrate in to-day's vigil, in the festival of this light. For this is the night which has knowledge of the saving sacraments, the night in which thou dost offer pardon to sinners, dost make new men from old, from worn out old men dost restore full-grown infants, whom thou dost bring from the sacred font renewed unto a new creature. On this night thy people are new born and brought forth unto eternal day, the halls of the kingdom of heaven are thrown open, by thy blessed ordinance human conversation is changed to divine. For this is the night which was made in joy, in which thou hast *made us glad through thy works* [Ps. 92.4], the night in which hell opened its gates, the night in which Adam was set free, the night in which the piece of *silver which had been lost was found* [Luke 15.8], the night in which the *lost sheep was carried upon the shoulders of the good shepherd* [Luke 15.5], the night in which the devil slept and Christ the *sun of righteousness* [Mal. 4.15] arose, when the bonds of hell were burst and its bars broken, and *many bodies of the saints broke out from their tombs and entered the holy city* [Matt. 27.52]. O truly blessed night, which alone was found worthy to witness the time and the hour in which Christ arose, of which it had been foretold in the Psalm, that the *night shall be as clear as the day* [Ps. 139.11]; the night in which the resurrection to eternal life took its beginning; for thee, Almighty God, the multitude of heavenly beings and the innumerable choir of angels unceasingly do praise, saying, Holy . . .

THE LETTERS OF ST GERMANUS OF PARIS

Text: Migne, P.L. 72. These letters are wrongly ascribed. It has been demonstrated by Dom A. Wilmart (*D.A.C.L.*, Article, *Germain, Lettres de Saint*) that these letters include certain quotations from the works of St Isidore, none of which, however, appear in the following extracts. St Isidore died in the year 636, and Dom Wilmart shows reason for attributing the letters to the South of France, about 700.

THE SECOND LETTER

In an earlier letter, by God's grace, we touched upon the order of the Holy Oblation, with brief explanations: now in this brief note we set before you various *charismata* of the Church and their purpose, so far as God has enabled us to understand them.

*　　*　　*

Sanctus Deus Archangelorum is sung in Lent, and not the song of Zacharias, because that song is a supplication for the people, according to its words. And the prophecy [i.e., the *Benedictus*] is not sung for the same reason as the baptistry is shut: because the canons so order, and because baptism does not belong to Lent.

The oil which is blessed with the chrism is spoken of in the Psalm which is quoted about Christ: *God hath anointed thee with the oil of gladness above thy fellows* [Ps. 45.8], and again: *With my holy oil have I anointed him* [Ps. 89.21]. Thus we see the men of old time were first anointed with oil and then bathed in unguent. The Greek *oleum* [*sic*] corresponds to the Latin word "pity" [*misericordia*], and by oil [*oleum*] is indicated the grace of the Holy Spirit. For God has consecrated this liquid in the Church for the making of unguents, for the preparation of lights, and for healing the wounds of sin.

On this day also the Creed is delivered to the *competentes* so that just as upon the first day God said *Let there be light* [Gen. 1.3], (by which is signified the light of faith), so then upon that day the light of faith may appear. The seventh day he blessed and hallowed with rest: and so upon this day the faith of the people is strengthened and fed with the Creed and the milk of chrism, because upon the seventh day the rest of Christ in the sepulchre is the theme of our worship: and as evening draws on the triumph of his resurrection is observed. And so when the priest comes to deliver the Creed, soft feather cushions and white towels are spread out over the screen around the choir, vessels of chrism and oil are poured into chalices for blessing, and the book of the Holy Gospel, covered in red: for the people as they approach the faith may be likened to an infant. For as an infant is delicate and new in body, so a catechumen is delicate and new in the faith. Infant limbs are rested on pillows, that they may thrive the better: the more gentle words of the Lord are proffered to the catechumen, that he may be enticed the more. For he cannot sustain the more vigorous injunctions before he is strengthened in grace through the baptism of the Holy Spirit. The infant's limbs are wiped dry with towels, that is the white linen cloths, lest his tender flesh be harmed: so the depths of the faith are opened to the catechumen in the Creed, that through his faith he may be wiped free of all sin. [There is a gap in the next sentence which makes it impossible to read.] The infant is nourished with milk: the catechumen is anointed with chrism. Milk is drawn from the mother's breasts: so chrism is consecrated in the bosom of our holy mother the Church.

The book of the Gospel is covered in red in the likeness of the body of Christ, signifying his blood. The vessels of chrism are brought in chalices because all the sacraments of baptism are founded in the Passion of Christ. The glass or crystalline vessels used for chrism signify the brightness of baptism. The chrism is made from balsam. The gum of balsam is made from a tree called the *lentiscus*, and there is a tradition that the part of the Lord's Cross to which the wicked man nailed the Lord's hands was made from the *lentiscus*. [There is a gap in the next sentence which makes it impossible to read.] For the angel of God comes down over the altar at our prayer, as though over the tomb, and blesses the sacrifice, after the example of that angel who announced the resurrection of Christ. And then with clear and unrestrained voices all those hymns which in Lent had fallen silent are raised again, the Drowning of Pharaoh, the *Sanctus de caelis*, the *Alleluia*, for joy that the Lord is risen. These things are performed through the night, because through the night the Saviour broke the bonds of hell. Then the faithful feed sweetly on the Flesh and Blood of the Lamb, by which the whole world is redeemed at great price: and at the first light of dawn the resurrection of the Lord is celebrated with clear songs of praise and blessing.

11. Hybrid Documents

Few ancient documents of pure Roman or Gallican origin survive to-day. But the dissemination of Roman documents in France and Western Europe has left behind it a crop of documents in which Roman and Gallican elements are mingled. The "Gelasian Sacramentary", the *Ordo Romanus XI*, the Bobbio and Stowe Missals, are among the most notable of these. Unfortunately, since our evidence for the Roman and Gallican rite in its pure form is so slight, it is not always easy to discern the two elements in the mixed documents, or to appreciate with certainty the proportions in which they appear.

The Gelasian Sacramentary is the name commonly given to a Vatican manuscript (*Reginensis* 316) edited by H. A. Wilson and published under that title. The manuscript was made in the region of Paris in the eighth century. It is accurate to describe this as a hybrid document since it may be clearly seen that sections 66-76 include Gallican elements. Nevertheless, the rite set out in sections 26-44 is certainly Roman. See A. Chavasse, *Le Sacramentaire Gélasien*, Tournai, 1957.

The *Reginensis* 316 is an edition of a rite which in its original Roman form was first drawn up in the early sixth century: the *Ordo Romanus XI* followed it at the end of the century. But our knowledge of the *Ordo* rests upon a collection of French manuscripts of the ninth century and later. It will be seen that the *Ordo* employs the same formularies which we find in the Gelasian Sacramentary: but again it is not clear to what extent the original Roman form of the *Ordo* has been revised in France.

In the Bobbio Missal, of which the date is about 700, it is not for the most part difficult to distinguish the elements which it has in common with the Gelasian Sacramentary and with the Gallican *Missale Gothicum*. This is a case where a Gallican book such as *Missale Gothicum* has clearly been used as a basis for Roman additions.

The Stowe Missal was written in Ireland, about 800. Here we see material from Gallican and Roman sources combined in a highly individual manner.

THE GELASIAN SACRAMENTARY

Text: The Gelasian Sacramentary, ed. H. A. Wilson, Oxford, 1894; see also *Liber Sacramentorum*, ed. L. C. Mohlberg (*Rerum Ecclesiasticarum Documenta*, Vol. 4), Rome, 1960.

BOOK I

XXVI

1

THE THIRD SUNDAY [IN LENT]

The Mass is celebrated for the scrutinies of the elect.

We beseech thee O Lord, bestow upon these elect right hearts and wise minds as they come to confess thy praise: so that man's ancient dignity, which once by sin they had lost, by thy grace may be restored in them. Through . . .

The Secret

2

O God we beseech thee, bring thy servants in pity to these mysteries, and at all times lead them in the way of devotion. Through . . .

Within the Canon, when he says

3

Remember Lord thy servants, both men and women, who are to bring the elect to the holy grace of baptism: and all this congregation here present. *And you keep silence. And the names are read of the men and women who are to receive the infants from the font. And you continue:* whose faith is known to thee.

Again within the Canon

4

We pray thee therefore, O Lord, that thou wilt favourably receive this oblation, which we offer to thee for thy servants, both men and women, whom thou hast deigned to choose and to call to eternal life and to the blessed gift of thy grace. Through Christ.

And the names of the elect are read. And when they have been recited you say, We pray thee, Lord, for these who are to be renewed in the fount of baptism, and by the gift of thy Spirit make them ready for the bounty of thy sacraments. Through . . .

The Postcommunion

5

O Lord we beseech thee, watch over the work of redemption, and graciously shield the preparation of those whom thou dost raise up by the sacraments of eternity. Through . . .

[*The Collect*] ad Populum

6

Suppliant, O Lord, thy holy family awaits thy gifts and thy compassion: bestow upon it, we beseech thee, those things which thou dost bid it to desire. Through . . .

XXVII
THE FOURTH SUNDAY [IN LENT]

7

[*The Mass is*] *for the second scrutiny.*

Almighty everlasting God, send thy Holy Spirit to bless thy Church with increase, and grant that those who by birth are earthly may by a second birth be made heavenly. Through . . .

8   [*The Secret*]

We joyfully present before thee, O Lord, the elements of the ever-lasting remedy, and pray that in a right spirit we may revere them and acceptably set them forth for those that are to be saved. Through . . .

9   *Within the Canon, as above.*

10   *The Postcommunion*

We beseech thee O Lord, do thou of thy goodness alway support thy family: place it beneath thy correction; guard it in its subjection; and of thy perpetual goodness guide it in the way of salvation. Through . . .

11   [*The Collect*] ad Populum

We beseech thee O Lord, let it be thy pleasure to set thy servants in the right way: endue them with such virtues as please thee, that having overcome all things they may attain to thy reward. Through . . .

XXVIII

12   THE FIFTH SUNDAY [IN LENT]

[*The Mass is*] *for the Scrutiny.*

Grant O Lord to the elect that being throughly taught in thy mysteries they may be renewed at the fount of baptism and numbered with the members of thy Church. Through . . .

13   *The Secret*

Hear us, Almighty God, and by the power of this sacrifice cleanse thy servants in whom thou hast sown the first seeds of the Christian faith. Through . . .

14   *Within the Canon, as above.*

15   *The Postcommunion*

O Lord we beseech thee, may thy people live at peace among them-selves; and serving thee with a pure heart and being free from all strife, may they both take a ready delight in their own salvation and with good will pray for those who await their second birth. Through . . .

[*The Collect*] ad Populum   16

O God who at all times art busy with the work of man's salvation, and who at this present time with more abundant grace dost multiply thy people: look favourably on these whom thou hast chosen, that, being helped by thy fatherly protection, they may be conceived and born again. Through . . .

XXIX

NOTICE OF THE SCRUTINY   17

Which begins in the third week of Lent on the second day.

Dearly beloved brethren, take notice that the day of scrutiny is at hand, when the elect are instructed in divine things. With watchful devotion therefore, let us meet on (such and such) day following, at about the sixth hour of the day: so that the heavenly mystery, when the devil with his retinue is destroyed and the door of the heavenly kingdom is opened, may by God's help be perfectly performed. Through our Lord Jesus Christ, who with the Father and the Holy Spirit liveth and reigneth with God throughout all ages. Amen.

When they have come to the Church, the names of the infants are written   18
down by the acolyte, and they are called into the church by name as they are
written. And males are stood on the right side, females on the left, and the
priest says a prayer over them.

XXX

PRAYERS OVER THE ELECT

For making a Catechumen   19
                                         S. 7

Almighty everlasting God, Father of our Lord Jesus Christ, look upon these thy servants whom thou hast called to the elements of faith. Drive from them all *blindness of heart* [Mark 3.5; Eph. 4.18]: loose the bonds of Satan with which they were bound: open to them, O Lord, the door of thy religion: that, bearing the sign of thy wisdom, they may turn from the squalor of fleshly lusts and delight in the sweet savour of thy commandments and joyfully serve thee in thy church: that first taking the medicine they may increase in virtue day by day until by thy favour they come to the grace of baptism. Through our Lord . . .

O Lord we beseech thee, of thy goodness hear our prayers, and   20
protect these thine elect with the power of the Lord's Cross, with which we sign them, that from this first beginning of the worship of

thy majesty, being ever set about by thy commandments, they may attain to the glory of the second birth. Through . . .

21 God, who hast created the human race that thou mightest also restore it, look with mercy on thine adopted people, set the offspring of thy new race within thy new covenant, that what they could not attain by nature, the children of promise may joyfully receive by grace. Through our Lord . . .

XXXI

22
S. 5
A. 26

THE BLESSING OF THE SALT TO BE GIVEN TO THE CATECHUMENS

I exorcize thee, creature of salt, in the Name of God the Father Almighty, and in the love of our Lord Jesus Christ, and in the power of the Holy Spirit. I exorcize thee by the living God and by the true God, who has created thee to be a safeguard of the human race, and has commanded thee to be consecrated by his servants for those who come to faith. And therefore we ask thee, O Lord our God, that in the Name of the Trinity this creature of salt may be a saving sacrament to drive away the enemy: do thou, O Lord, sanctify it and bless it, that it may remain as perfect medicine in the bowels of all who receive it, in the Name of our Lord Jesus Christ who shall come to judge the quick and the dead and this world by fire.

23
A. 36

And after this prayer, you place salt in the mouth of the infant, and say:

N., receive the salt of wisdom, for a token of propitiation unto eternal life.

XXXII

24
A. 37

THE BLESSING AFTER THE SALT IS GIVEN

O God of our fathers, O God who dost establish all truth, we humbly beseech thee to look favourably upon this thy servant, and grant that he who has taken this first morsel of salt may hunger only until he be satisfied with heavenly food: until then, Lord, may he ever be *fervent in spirit, rejoicing in hope*, and alway *serving* [Rom. 12.11] thy Name. Lead him to the laver of the second birth that with thy faithful people he may be worthy to receive the eternal rewards of thy promises. Through the Lord . . .

XXXIII

25

THE EXORCISM OVER THE ELECT

The acolytes shall lay a hand upon them and say:

God of Abraham, God of Isaac, God of Jacob, God who appearedst to thy servant Moses upon Mount Sinai and didst lead the children of Israel out of the land of Egypt, sending to them the angel of thy goodness to guard them by day and by night, we beseech thee, O Lord, that thou wouldest send thy holy angel that likewise he may also guard these thy servants and lead them to the grace of thy baptism.

Therefore, accursed devil, remember thy sentence and give honour to God, the living and the true, give honour to Jesus Christ his Son, and to the Holy Spirit, and depart from these servants of God. For Jesus Christ our Lord and God is pleased to call them to himself and to give them his holy grace and blessing and the fount of baptism. This sign of the holy cross which we now make upon their brows do thou accursed devil never dare to violate. *26*

And over Females *27*

God of heaven, God of earth, God of angels, God of archangels, God of the prophets, God of the martyrs, God of all who live good lives, God whom *every tongue confesses, of things in heaven and things in earth, and things under the earth* [Phil. 2.10], I call upon thee, Lord, to watch over these thy servants and lead them to the grace of thy baptism.

Therefore, accursed *as above.*

And over Males *28*

Hearken, accursed Satan, adjured by the Name of the eternal God, and of our Saviour the Son of God: thou and thy envy art conquered, depart trembling and groaning. Let there be nothing between thee and the servants of God, who even now ponder heavenly things, who are to renounce thee and thy kingdom and make their way to blessed immortality. Give honour therefore to the Holy Spirit as he approaches, descending from the highest place of heaven, who shall confound thy deceits and at the divine fount shall cleanse and sanctify their breasts unto a temple and dwelling place of God: so that, being freed from all the inward hurts of past offences, as the servants of God they may always praise the everlasting God, and bless his holy Name throughout all ages. Through our Lord Jesus Christ who shall come to judge the quick and the dead and this world by fire.

And over Females *29*

God of Abraham, God of Isaac, God of Jacob, who didst admonish the tribes of Israel and didst free Susanna from false accusation, I humbly beseech thee, Lord, to free also these thy servants, and to lead them to the grace of thy baptism.

Therefore, accursed *as above.*

30 *And over Males*

I exorcize thee, unclean spirit, in the Name of the Father and of the Son and of the Holy Spirit, that thou mayest go away and depart from these servants of God. For he himself commands thee, accursed one, damned one, he who walked with his feet on the sea and stretched out his right hand to Peter as he sank.

Therefore, accursed *as above.*

31 *And over Females*

I exorcize thee, unclean spirit, through the Father and the Son and the Holy Spirit, that thou mayest go away and depart from these servants of God. For he himself commands thee, accursed one, damned one, who opened the eyes of the man born blind, and on the fourth day raised Lazarus from the tomb.

Therefore, accursed *as above.*

32
A. 32 *Then shall a priest* [sacerdos] *say the prayer following:*

O Lord, holy Father, everlasting God of light and truth, I call upon thy eternal and most just piety for these thy servants, that thou wouldest lighten them with the light of thy understanding. Cleanse and sanctify them. Give them true knowledge that they may come worthily to the grace of thy baptism. Let them hold a firm hope, right counsel, holy doctrine, that they may be fitted to receive thy grace. Through . . .

XXXIV

33
B. 174 ### THE EXPOSITION OF THE GOSPELS TO THE ELECT
AT THE OPENING OF THE EARS

First, four deacons come forth from the sacristry bearing the four gospels: they are preceded by two candles and censers. The gospels are placed at the four corners of the altar. Before they are read, a priest [presbyter] *first speaks in these words:*

Beloved children, we shall open to you now the gospels, that is, the story of the divine life. But first we must explain what the gospel is, and whence it comes, and whose words are written therein, and why they be four who wrote of this life, and who are the four who, as the prophet foretold, have been marked by the divine Spirit: lest haply without this explanation we should confuse your minds: and because it is for this that ye are come, that your ears should be opened and not that your senses should be blunted. The word gospel properly means good tidings, and such indeed are the tidings of Jesus Christ our Lord. The gospel comes to us that it might set forth and show that he, who spake by the prophets, came in the flesh, as it is written, *Lo, I who spake am here* [Isa. 52.6, Vulg.]. But to explain briefly what the gospel is, and who those four are who by the prophet were shown aforetime, let us now show how each name was disclosed by its own sign. The prophet Ezekiel says, *And the likeness of the face of them was as the face of a man and the face of a lion on the right side: and the face of an ox and the face of an eagle on the left side* [Ezek. 1.10]. There is no doubt that those four who had those faces are the four evangelists: but the names of those who wrote the gospels are these, Matthew, Mark, Luke, John.

Then the deacon says, Stand in silence and listen attentively.

And he begins and reads the beginning of the gospel according to Matthew, as far as: for he shall save his people from their sins [1.21].

Then the priest [presbyter] *explains in these words:*

Beloved children, lest we keep you too long, let us explain to you what reason and what symbol each embodies and why Matthew has the symbol of a man: it is because in his opening verses he speaks of nothing other than the birth of the Saviour and sets out the full order of his generation. For he begins thus: *The book of the generation of Jesus Christ the son of David the son of Abraham.* You see that it is not unsuitable that to this there should be assigned the person of a man, since it is from the birth of a man that it takes its beginning: it is not unsuitable, as we say, that to this mystery is assigned the person of Matthew.

Then the deacon says, Stand in silence and listen attentively.

And he shall read the beginning of the gospel according to Mark, as far as: I baptize you with water: he verily shall baptize you with the Holy Spirit [1.8].

Then the priest [presbyter] *continues in these words:*

The evangelist Mark, who has the symbol of a lion on account of its solitude, begins with *The voice of one crying in the wilderness* [1.3]: possibly because lions rule unconquered. Of this lion we find many

34
B. 175

35
B. 176

36
B. 177

37
B. 178

examples, so that that passage is not without significance which says *Judah, my son, thou art a lion's whelp, thou hast sprung up from my seed: he stooped down, he couched as a lion and as a lion's whelp: who shall rouse him up* [Gen. 49.9].

38
B. 179

And the deacon speaks as above. And he reads the beginning of the gospel according to Luke, as far as: To make ready for the Lord a perfect people [1.14].

39
B. 180

Then shall the priest [presbyter] *continue in these words:*

The evangelist Luke has the appearance of an ox, which is a type of our Saviour's sacrifice. For when Luke sets out to tell the gospel of Christ, he takes his beginning from Zacharias and Elisabeth, of whom John the Baptist was born in their extreme old age. And that is the reason why Luke is compared to an ox, because like tender things springing from hard ones he contained within himself two horns, that is two testaments, and four hooves, that is four gospels.

40
B. 181

The announcement is made by the deacon as above. And he reads the beginning of the gospel of John, as far as: full of grace and truth [1.14].

41
B. 182

Again the priest [presbyter] *continues in these words:*

John has the likeness of an eagle because he sought the greatest heights: for he says *In the beginning was the word, and the word was with God, and the word was God. This was in the beginning with God.* And David says of the person of Christ, *Thy youth shall be renewed as that of an eagle* [Ps. 103.5]: that is, of Jesus Christ our Lord who rose from the dead and ascended up into the heavens. And so now the Church, being pregnant by your conception, glories that amidst her festal worship she labours to bring forth new lives subject to the Christian law: so that when the day of the venerable Pascha shall come, being reborn in the laver of baptism, ye shall be found worthy like all the saints to receive the promised gift of infancy from Christ our Lord, who liveth and reigneth unto the ages of ages.

XXXV

42

THE INTRODUCTION OF THE CREED TO THE ELECT

That is, before you say the Creed, you proceed in these words:

Dearly beloved, who seek to receive the sacraments of baptism, and to be born unto a new creature of the Holy Spirit: lay hold with your whole heart upon the faith which ye shall receive to your justification: and setting your minds upon right paths turn to God who is the light of our minds and receive the sacrament of the gospel symbol; which is inspired by the Lord and instituted by the Apostles, of which the words indeed are few but the mystery great. For the Holy Spirit who spoke it to the masters of the Church instituted this saving confession with such eloquence and such brevity that the things which you are to believe and always profess can neither escape your understanding nor burden your memory. And so you must learn the Creed with attentive minds, and those things which we *deliver to you (as we have received them)* [I Cor. 15.3] you must write not on any corruptible material but on the pages of your heart. And so the confession of the faith which you have undertaken begins thus:

After this an acolyte takes one boy from the infants and holding him in his left arm places his hand upon his head. And the priest asks him: In what language do they confess our Lord Jesus Christ? R̷. In Greek. **43**

Again the priest says: Declare their faith according as they believe.

And the acolyte chants the Creed in Greek, holding his hand upon the infant's head, in these words:

I believe in one God, the Father Almighty, maker of heaven and earth, and of all things visible and invisible. And in one Lord Jesus Christ, the Only-Begotten Son of God; born of the Father before all worlds; light of light; very God of very God; born, not made, being of one substance with the Father; by whom all things were made; who for us men and for our salvation coming down from heaven; and being incarnate of the Holy Ghost and the Virgin Mary and being made human; crucified also for us under Pontius Pilate, suffering and being buried; rising again the third day according to the scriptures; and ascending into heaven and sitting at the right hand of the Father; to come again with glory to judge the quick and the dead; whose kingdom shall have no end. And in the Holy Spirit, the Lord, and giver of life; proceeding from the Father; who with the Father and the Son together is worshipped and glorified; who spake by the prophets. In one holy, catholic, and apostolic Church. I acknowledge one baptism unto the remission of sins. I hope for the resurrection of the dead and the life of the world to come. Amen.

[The MS. provides a Greek text for this Creed, transliterated into Roman characters, with a Latin interlinear translation.]

Beloved children, you have heard the Creed iɳ Greek, hear it also in Latin. *And you say:* In what language do they confess our Lord Jesus Christ?

R̷. In Latin.

Again the priest says: Declare their faith according as they believe.

Placing a hand upon the head of the infant, the acolyte chants the Creed in these words:

I believe in one God, etc.

[A Latin text of the same Creed is here provided.]

44   *Then the priest continues in these words:*

Dearly beloved, this is the sum of our belief, these are the words of the Creed, not contrived by art of human wisdom but set out by God's grace in a true order. There is no one who is not sufficient and fitted to understand and to observe these things. Here is affirmed the one equal power of God the Father and the Son. Here is shown the Only-Begotten Son of God, born of the Virgin Mary and the Holy Spirit according to the flesh. Here is set out his crucifixion, his burial, and his resurrection on the third day. Here is recognized his ascension above the heavens and his session at the right hand of his Father's majesty; here it is declared that he shall come to judge the quick and the dead. Here the Holy Spirit is shown to share an undivided Godhead with the Father and the Son. Here, lastly, is taught the Church's calling, the remission of sins and the resurrection of the flesh. And so, dearly beloved, we transform you from the *old man into the new* [cf. Eph. 4.22]: from *carnal* you begin to be *spiritual,* from *earthly* to be *heavenly* [cf. 1 Cor. 15.44ff]: with quiet and steadfast faith you must believe that the resurrection, which in Christ became a fact, must be completed in us all, that what started in *the Head shall follow in the whole body* [cf. Col. 1.18]. Moreover, the very sacrament of baptism which you are to receive expresses the form of this hope. For in it is celebrated a kind of death and resurrection. *The old man is put off and the new man put on* [cf. Eph. 4.22, 24]. A sinner goes into the waters and comes out justified. He is thrown out who draws you to death, and he is received who leads you back to life, through whose grace it is given you to become *sons of God,* not brought forth *by the will of the flesh* [John 1.13], but begotten by the power of the Holy Spirit. And therefore you must allow this brief abundance so to dwell in your minds that at all times you may use the defence of this confession. For the power of such weapons is always invincible, it is of service to every good soldier of Christ against all the snares of the enemy. The devil, who never ceases to tempt mankind, must always find you protected by this Creed: so that with the enemy whom you renounce cast down, and by the

protection of him whom you confess, you may preserve the grace of
the Lord pure and spotless unto the end, so that wherein you receive
remission of sins, you may also have the glory of the resurrection.
Therefore, dearly beloved, you have heard the symbol of the catholic
faith: you go now and receive entire instruction in what you have
heard. Powerful is the mercy of God, which is both able to lead you
who seek after the faith of baptism to the end of your search, and to
bring us who deliver these mysteries to you, together with you, to the
heavenly kingdom. Through the same Jesus Christ our Lord, who
liveth and reigneth unto the ages of ages.

XXXVI

THE INTRODUCTION OF THE LORD'S PRAYER

They are instructed by the deacon as above.

Our Lord and Saviour Jesus Christ, among the rest of his saving
precepts, when his disciples would learn in what manner they ought
to pray, taught them that form of prayer which you have now heard
read. Your love must now hear in what manner he teaches his disciples
to pray to God the Father Almighty: *But thou, when thou wilt pray,
enter into thy closet and when thou hast shut thy door pray to thy Father*
[Matt. 6.6]. When he says a closet, he does not mean some hidden
place, but reminds us that the secret places of our hearts should be open
to him alone. And that we should shut the door when we worship
God means this, that with a mystic key we should shut our breast to
evil thoughts and with closed lips and pure minds speak to God. For
God hears our faith, not our voice. Let therefore our breast be shut
with the key of faith against the snares of the adversary, and let it be
open to God alone whose temple we know it to be, that as he dwells
in our hearts so he may be an advocate in our prayers. Therefore the
Word of God and the Wisdom of God, Christ our Lord, taught us
this prayer, that we should pray thus.

After this you begin and say:

"Our Father, which art in heaven". This is the language of liberty
and entire trust. Therefore you must live after such a manner that you
may be able to be *sons of God and brothers of Christ* [cf. Rom. 8.17].
What impertinence it would be if a man called God his Father, and
then fell away from God's will. And so do you, dearly beloved, show
yourselves worthy of the divine adoption, since it is written, *As many*

45

46

as believed on him, to them gave he power to become the sons of God [John 1.12].

47   "Hallowed be thy Name". That is to say, not that God should be hallowed by our prayers, since he is always holy, but we desire that his Name should be hallowed in us, so that we who are sanctified in his baptism may persevere in that which we begin to be.

48   "Thy Kingdom come". You may ask when God is without a kingdom, especially since his kingdom is immortal. But when we say, *Thy kingdom come*, we desire the coming of our own kingdom, which God has promised us and which Christ sought with his Blood and Passion.

49   "Thy will be done". That is to say, thy will be done in such a way that what thou willest in heaven we on earth may irreproachably perform.

50   "Give us this day our daily bread". Here we are to understand our spiritual food. For Christ is our bread, who said, *I am the living bread who came down from heaven* [John 6.41]. We say *daily* because we ought always to seek freedom from sin, in such a manner that we may be worthy of heavenly nourishment.

51   "And forgive us our trespasses as we forgive them that trespass against us". Signifying by these words that we cannot deserve pardon for our sins unless we first show lenience to others who have hurt us: as the Lord says in the gospel: *Unless ye shall have forgiven men their sins, neither will your Father forgive your sins* [Matt. 6.15].

52   "And lead us not into temptation". That is, suffer us not to be led by him who tempts, the author of wickedness. For scripture says *God may threaten us with evil* [James 1.13, Vulg.]. But it is the devil who tempts: it is to encompass his downfall that the Lord says, *Watch and pray, that ye enter not into temptation* [Mark 14.38].

53   "But deliver us from evil". This it says for this reason, because the Apostle says, *Ye know not for what ye ought to pray* [cf. Rom. 8.26]. Our prayers must be made to the one Almighty God for this, that when human frailty is too weak to beware of and avoid anything, the power may of his favour be bestowed upon us by Jesus Christ our Lord, who liveth and reigneth, God in the unity of the Holy Spirit throughout all ages of ages.

54   *The deacon announces as above:* Stand in order and in silence, and listen attentively.

You have heard, dearly beloved, the holy mysteries of the Lord's Prayer. As you go now, keep them fresh in your hearts, so that you may be perfect in Christ to beseech and to receive the mercy of God. Powerful is our Lord God, who is able both to lead you who seek after the faith to the laver of the water of regeneration, and to bring us, who have delivered to you the mystery of the catholic faith, together with you to the heavenly kingdom. Who liveth and reigneth with God the Father in the unity of the Holy Spirit, throughout all ages of ages.

XXXVII

MASS FOR PALM SUNDAY AND THE THREE DAYS FOLLOWING

55

XXXVIII

MAUNDY THURSDAY. MASS AND PRAYERS AT THE RECONCILIATION OF PENITENTS

56

[The section which follows is numbered XL in the manuscript.]

XL

ALSO ON THE FIFTH FERIA

The Chrismal Mass

57

O Lord God, who in bringing new birth to thy people dost use the ministry of priests, grant that thy servants may persevere in thy will, so that in our time, by the gift of thy grace, thy holy people may be increased both in numbers and in righteousness. Through our Lord.

Bestow upon us, Almighty God, the remedy of our human condition, that we may offer to thee a pure worship and go forward upon the path of salvation. Through . . .

58

The Secret

59

O Lord we beseech thee, may the power of this sacrifice take away the years of our age, and bring us youth and salvation. Through . . .

[*The Preface*]

60

It is verily meet humbly to beseech thy clemency to confirm the creature of chrism unto its use in the sacrament of perfect salvation and life for those who are to be renewed in the baptism of the spiritual laver, so that when the unction is poured out to sanctify them and the corruption of their first birth is drawn out, each one may be thy holy temple and send up to thee the innocent savour of an acceptable life:

so that being imbued, as thy sacrament doth show, with royal and priestly and prophetic honour, they may be clothed with the garment of thy perfect gift. Through whom the [angels] praise thy majesty [etc.] [*Per quem majestatem*].

61　　　We beseech thee therefore, O Lord, graciously to receive [*placatus accipias*] this oblation of thy servants and maidservants [*hanc igitur oblationem*] which they offer unto thee in memory of the day in which our Lord Jesus Christ gave to his disciples to celebrate the mysteries of his Body and Blood: and of thy goodness grant that in health and safety for many years to come they may be deemed worthy to offer their gifts to thee, O Lord; and dispose our days [etc.] [*diesque nostros*].

62　　　　　　　　　*The Blessing of the Oil*

[*It is announced*] *to the people in these words*: The oil for anointing the sick. *But when you read*, And to us sinners thy servants [*nobis quoque peccatoribus*] *and the rest up to* through Christ our Lord, *then you begin*:

Send down, we beseech thee O Lord, the Holy Spirit the Paraclete from heaven upon this richness of oil, which thou hast provided from the green wood for the refreshment both of mind and body. And may thy holy blessing rest upon all who anoint, who taste, or touch, to be a safeguard of body, soul, and spirit, to take away all griefs, all illness, all sickness of mind and body: thy perfect chrism remaining in our bowels, wherewith thou hast anointed priests, kings, prophets, and martyrs; which thou O Lord hast blessed in the Name of our Lord Jesus Christ. Through whom O Lord thou dost create all things [etc.] [*Per quem haec omnia*].

63　　　*And when the Canon is ended you say*: Let us pray. Taught by the saving precepts. *The Lord's Prayer follows. And after that the other prayer*, Deliver us we beseech thee O Lord. *Then you break the gifts and cover them with the altar cloth and go up to the throne. And there other oil is offered by the deacon to be blessed, and you say*:

64　　　　　　　　　The Lord be with you.
　　　　　　　℞. And with thy spirit.

You say, Let us pray, *and begin*:

O God who dost bestow growth and advancement in spiritual things, who by the power of thy Holy Spirit dost perfect the early endeavours of simple minds, we pray thee O Lord that to those who shall come to the laver of blessed rebirth thou wouldest grant cleansing of mind and body by the working of this creature: so that every remnant of the enemy spirits which may cling to them may at the touch of this sanctified oil depart. May there be no place for spiritual wickedness: may no opportunity be left to the retreating powers of evil: may no leave to hide be granted to the evil ones which lie in wait: but to thy servants who come unto faith, who are to be cleansed by the operation of thy Holy Spirit, may this unction which we prepare avail unto salvation, which through the birth of a heavenly generation they are to attain in the sacrament of baptism. Through our Lord Jesus Christ, who shall come to judge this world by fire.

Again you say,   The Lord be with you.   *65*
        R̷. And with thy spirit.

        Lift up your hearts.
        R̷. We lift them up unto the Lord.

        Let us give thanks unto our Lord God.
        R̷. It is meet and right.

It is verily meet and right, befitting and salutary, that we should at all times, both here and in all places, give thanks unto thee O Lord holy, Father Almighty, everlasting God. For thou in the beginning, among other gifts of thy goodness and lovingkindness, didst command the earth to bring forth fruit-bearing trees. Thus were born the providers of this richest essence, the olive trees, that their fruit might be of use for this sacred chrism. For David, in prophetic spirit, foreseeing the sacraments of thy grace, sang that our *countenance* should be made *cheerful with oil* [Ps. 104.15]. And when in olden days the sins of the world were to be expiated by the outpouring of the flood, a dove displayed with the branch of an olive the likeness of a future gift, and announced that peace had been restored to earth: and so in these last days this has its clear fulfilment when, as the waters of baptism destroy the offences of all sins, this unction of oil makes our faces joyful and serene. Moreover to Moses thy servant thou didst give commandment that he should make Aaron his brother priest, first washing in water, then by the infusion of this anointing. Yet greater honour was granted to chrism when thy Son our Lord Jesus Christ had been washed at his own command in the waves of Jordan, when thy Holy Spirit had been sent from above in the likeness of a dove. Then thou didst show forth, and bear witness by the voice which was then heard, to thy *Only-Begotten Son, in whom thou wast well pleased* [Mark 1.11], and thus thou didst most evidently affirm that this was that of which David sang, that he should be *anointed with the oil of gladness above his fellows* [Ps. 45.7]. We therefore pray thee, O Lord holy, Father Almighty, everlasting God, through Jesus Christ thy Son our Lord, that thou wouldest deign with thy blessing to sanctify the richness of this creature and to infuse it with the power of the Holy Spirit, through the might of thy Christ, from whose holy Name chrism took its name, wherewith thou hast anointed priests, kings, prophets, and martyrs, that to those who shall be born again of water and the Holy Spirit it may be the chrism of salvation, that thou mayest bring them to partake of eternal life and to share in the glory of heaven. Through the same thy Son our Lord Jesus Christ.

66   *The Blessing* [Confectio] *of the Exorcized Oil*

At this point you mix the balsam with oil, and this exorcism follows:

I exorcize thee, creature of oil, in the Name of God the Father Almighty, and in the Name of Jesus Christ his Son, and of the Holy Spirit, that by this invocation of the threefold might and by the power of the Godhead, all the most evil powers of the adversary, all the inveterate malice of the devil, all clash of violence, every blind disordered phantom, may be rooted up, may depart and be put to flight by this creature of oil which thou hast made for man's use: that this unction, being purified by divine sacraments, may be for the adoption of body and spirit to all who shall be anointed with it, unto the remission of all their sins: may it effect in them a heart pure and sanctified unto all spiritual grace. Through the same Jesus Christ our Lord, who shall come in the Holy Spirit to judge the quick and the dead and this world by fire. Through our Lord.

67   It is verily meet, almighty, everlasting God, who to the eyes of Noah didst reveal the secrets of thy mysteries, and didst show him the branch carried in the mouth of the dove, that the dwellers in the ark might learn that by the Holy Spirit and the chrism of the olive the glory of liberation was soon to return to the world. Through our Lord Jesus Christ, who shall come to judge the quick and the dead and this world by fire.

68   *After this is done, you come before the altar, and place a part of the Host in the mouth of the chalice: you do not say* The peace of the Lord, *and they do not make the Pax; but they communicate and set aside some of the sacrifice from which to communicate next day.*

69   [Section XLI is concerned with the observances of Good Friday.]

XLII

[HOLY] SATURDAY

70
S. 10

Early in the morning the infants make their return of the Creed. First you catechize them, laying a hand on their heads, and saying:

Be not deceived, Satan: punishment threatens thee, torment threatens thee, the day of judgement threatens thee, the day of punishment, the day which shall come as a burning furnace, when everlasting destruction shall come upon thee and all thine angels. And therefore, accursed one, give honour to God, the living and the true, give honour to Jesus Christ his Son, and to the Holy Spirit, in whose Name and power I command thee. Come out and depart from this servant of God, whom this day our Lord Jesus Christ has deigned to call to the gift of his holy grace and of his blessing and the fount of baptism: that he may become his temple, through the water of regeneration unto the remission of sins, in the Name of our Lord Jesus Christ, who shall come to judge the quick and the dead and this world by fire.

71
LO. 4
A. 29
B. 241
s. 12
72

Then you touch his nostrils and ears with spittle, and speak into his ear:

Effeta, that is, be opened, unto the odour of sweetness. But thou, O devil, take flight, for the judgement of God has drawn near.

And after that you touch his breast and between the shoulder blades with exorcized oil, and to each one, addressing them by name, you say:

Dost thou renounce Satan?

R̷. I renounce.

And all his works?

R̷. I renounce.

And all his pomps?

R̷. I renounce.

And then you say the Creed, first laying a hand upon their heads.

73

After that the archdeacon says to them:

74

Pray, ye elect, and bow the knee. Complete your prayers together and say Amen.

And they all reply Amen.

Again they are admonished by the archdeacon, in these words:

Let the catechumens go. Let all the catechumens go outside.

And the deacon says:

75

Dearly beloved brethren, go back now to your homes, and await the hour when the grace of God in baptism shall be able to enfold you.

XLIII

76 THE PRAYERS AT EACH LESSON ON HOLY SATURDAY

God, who in this night especially dost bestow the gifts of thy mercy, look with favour upon the whole order of the priesthood: and by the perfect remission of our sins sanctify all ranks of us thy servants, so that by no offence may we be found unfit to administer thy regenerating grace. Through . . .

77 *The lesson follows:* In the beginning God created.

O God of unchangeable power and eternal light, look favourably on thy whole Church, that wonderful mystery, and by the tranquil operation of thy perpetual providence carry out the work of man's salvation, and let the whole world feel and see that things which were cast down are being raised up, that things which had grown old are being made new, and that all things are returning to perfection through him from whom they took their origin. Through . . .

78 *The next [lesson] is about Noah.*

Almighty everlasting God, who hast wonderfully ordained all thy works, grant to thy redeemed people to know that the creation of the world in the beginning was not more wonderful than the sacrifice in these last days of Christ our Passover. Through the same Lord.

79 *The third [lesson] is about Abraham.*

O God, sovereign Father of the faithful, who in all places of the world dost adopt thy children to multiply the sons of promise, and by the Paschal sacrament dost make thy servant Abraham the father of all nations, as thou hast sworn: grant unto thy people that they may worthily enter into the grace of thy calling. Through . . .

80 *The fourth [lesson] is from Exodus, with the canticle,* Let us sing unto the Lord.

O God, the light of whose ancient miracles shines yet upon these times, who once by the power of thy right hand didst bring freedom to thy people from the persecution of Egypt, and now by the water of regeneration dost bring the same freedom unto the salvation of the Gentiles: grant that all nations of the world may pass over to be the sons of Abraham and to share the glory of Israel. Through . . .

81 *The fifth [lesson] is from Isaiah.*

Almighty everlasting God, for the honour of thy Name fulfil the promises thou didst make to the fathers, and increase by thy sacred adoption the sons of promise: that what the saints of old time doubted not should come to pass, thy Church may now find in great measure accomplished. Through . . .

The sixth [lesson] is from Ezekiel.   82

God, who in the pages of each testament dost teach us to observe the Paschal sacrament, give us such a sense of thy mercies that we who receive thy present favours may have a firm hope of thy future blessings. Through . . .

The seventh [lesson] is from Isaiah, with the canticle, The vineyard of the   83
Lord.

O God, who through the mouth of thy holy prophets hast declared that thou art the sower of good seed in thy Church's children, that thou in every place of thy dominion dost raise up the choicest branches: grant to thy people whom thou dost call thy vineyards and thy corn that by cutting away the wretched thorns and briars they may be made worthy of fruit in plenty. Through . . .

The eighth [lesson] is from Exodus.   84

God, who hast made the diversity of all nations to be one in the confession of thy Name, grant us both the will and the power to do what thou commandest: that thy people who are called to eternity may have one faith in their hearts and one devotion inspiring all their works. Through . . .

The ninth [lesson] is from Deuteronomy, with the Canticle.   85

God, who dost lift up the humble and strengthen the just, who by thy holy servant Moses didst seek so to instruct thy people by the singing of this sacred canticle that the reading of the law might be for our guidance: raise up thy power upon all the fullness of the Gentiles whom thou hast justified, and grant them joy by taking away their terrors, that the sins of all men being blotted out by thy forgiveness thy threats of vengeance may turn to a promise of salvation. Through . . .

The tenth [lesson] is from Daniel.   86

Almighty everlasting God, the one hope of the world, who by the proclamation of the prophets didst declare the mysteries of these present times, graciously increase the devotion of thy people: forasmuch as in none of the faithful can any increase of virtue be found except by thy inspiration. Through . .

The prayer after Psalm 41.   87

Almighty everlasting God, look favourably on the devotion of thy people at their second birth, who *like as the hart* [Ps. 42.1] await the fountain of waters: and of thy favour grant that in the mystery of baptism their thirst for the faith may sanctify their souls and bodies. [Through . . .]

88   *Then they proceed to the fonts for baptism, while a litany is sung. When the baptism is ended, the infants are sealed by the bishop, while they receive the seven gifts of grace of the Holy Spirit, and he places chrism on their foreheads. Then the priest returns with all the Orders of clergy to the vestry: and after a little they begin the third litany: and they enter upon the Mass during the vigil, when the [first] star has appeared in the sky. And they should so order things that the number of litanies corresponds to the number in the Trinity.*

XLIV

89   *Then a litany is chanted while you go down to the font.*
S. 21
A. 15, 42   The Blessing of the Font

Almighty everlasting God, be present at the mysteries of thy great goodness, be present at thy sacraments, and for the creation of the new people which the fount of baptism brings forth to thee send down the *Spirit of adoption* [Rom. 8.5]: that those things which our lowly ministry performs may be perfected by the operation of thy power. Through . . .

90   The Consecration of the Font
S. 22, 23

God, who by thine invisible power dost wonderfully effect thy sacraments: although we are not worthy to perform so great mysteries, yet do thou not forsake the gifts of thy grace, but incline the ears of thy goodness to our prayers. God whose Spirit at the beginning of the world was *borne upon the waters* [Gen. 1.2], that even the nature of water might conceive the power of sanctification: God who by the outpouring of the flood didst signify a type of regeneration, when thou by water didst wash away the sins of a wicked world, so that by the mystery of one and the same element there should be both an end of sin and a beginning of virtue: look down, O Lord, upon thy Church and multiply in her thy generations, thou who dost *make glad thy city with the rush of the flood* [Ps. 46.5] of thy grace: open the fount of baptism for the renewal of all nations of the world, that by the command of thy majesty it may receive the grace of thy Only-Begotten by the Holy Spirit: let thy Holy Spirit by the secret admixture of his light give fecundity to this water prepared for man's regeneration, so that, sanctification being conceived therein, there may come forth from the unspotted womb of the divine font a heavenly offspring, reborn unto a new creature: that grace may be a mother to people of every age and sex, who are brought forth into a common infancy. Therefore, O Lord, at thy command let every unclean spirit depart far hence, let all the wickedness of the wiles of the devil stand far off, let him not fly about to lay his snares, let him not creep secretly in, let him not corrupt with his infection. May this holy and innocent creature be free from every assault of the enemy and purified by the departure of all wickedness. May the fount be alive, the water regenerating, the wave purifying, so that all who shall be washed in this saving laver by the operation of the Holy Spirit within them may be brought to the mercy of perfect cleansing.

Here you sign [the water].

91
S. 17, 18, 24
A. 18

Wherefore I bless thee, O creature of water, through God the living, through God the holy, through God who in the beginning did separate thee by his word from the dry land and commanded thee in four rivers to water the whole earth, who in the desert gave sweetness to thy bitterness that men might drink thee, and for a thirsty people brought thee forth from the rock. I bless thee also through Jesus Christ his only Son our Lord, who in Cana of Galilee by his power in a wonderful sign did change thee into wine, who walked upon thee with his feet, and was baptized in thee by John in Jordan, who shed thee forth from his side with his blood, and commanded his disciples that believers should be baptized in thee, saying Go, *teach all nations, baptizing them in the Name of the Father and of the Son and of the Holy Ghost* [Matt. 28.19].

Here you shall change your voice.

92
S. 25

O thou Almighty God, be present of thy favour among us as we observe thy commands: do thou graciously inspire us. Bless with thy mouth these simple waters, that besides their natural purity which fits them for the washing of men's bodies they may have the power to purify their minds. May the power of thy Holy Spirit descend into all the water of this font and make the whole substance of this water fruitful with regenerating power. Here may the stains of all sins be blotted out. Here may the nature which was founded upon thine image be restored to the honour of its origin and cleansed from the filth of age, that every man that enters this sacrament of regeneration may be reborn in a new infancy of true innocence. Through our Lord

Jesus Christ thy Son, who shall come in the Holy Spirit to judge the quick and the dead and this world by fire.

93
S. 26

Then when the font is blessed you baptize each one in order, and ask these questions:

Dost thou believe in God the Father Almighty? R̲7. I believe.

And dost thou believe in Jesus Christ his only Son our Lord, who was born and suffered? R̲7. I believe.

And dost thou believe in the Holy Spirit; the holy Church; the remission of sins; the resurrection of the flesh? R̲7. I believe.

Then by single turns you dip him three times in the water. [Deinde per singulas vices mergis eum tertio in aqua.]

94
S. 28
B. 249
A. 23, 47

Then when the infant has gone up from the font he is signed on the head with chrism by the presbyter, with these words:

The Almighty God, the Father of our Lord Jesus Christ, who has made thee to be regenerated *of water and the Holy Spirit* [John 3.5], and has given thee remission of all thy sins, himself anoints thee with the chrism of salvation in Christ Jesus unto eternal life. R̲7. Amen.

95

Then the sevenfold Spirit is given to them by the bishop. To seal them [ad consignandum], *he lays his hand upon them with these words:*

Almighty God, Father of our Lord Jesus Christ, who hast made thy servants to be regenerated *of water and the Holy Spirit* [John 3.5], and hast given them remission of all their sins, do thou, Lord, send upon them thy Holy Spirit the Paraclete, and give them the *spirit of wisdom and understanding, the spirit of counsel and might, the spirit of knowledge and godliness,* and fill *them with the spirit of fear* [Isa. 11.2f] of God, in the Name of our Lord Jesus Christ with whom thou livest and reignest ever God with the Holy Spirit, throughout all ages of ages. Amen.

96

Then he signs them on the forehead with chrism, saying:

The sign of Christ unto life eternal.
R̲7. Amen.
Peace be with you.
R̲7. And with thy spirit.

97

Then, while a litany is chanted, he goes up to his throne, and says:

Glory be to God on high.

XLV

COLLECTS AND PRAYERS AT MASS ON THE [PASCHAL] NIGHT

98
B. 257

Almighty everlasting God, who throughout all the world dost illumine this most holy night with the glory of the Lord's Resurrection, preserve in the new offspring of thy family the spirit of adoption which thou hast given them: that being renewed in body and mind they may ever show forth before thee a pure mind and a pure heart. Through the Lord . . .

99
B. 285

God, who dost illumine this most holy night with the glory of the Lord's Resurrection, preserve in the new offspring of thy family the spirit of adoption which thou hast given them: that being renewed in body and mind they may present themselves before thee in pure worship. Through the Lord . . .

The Secret

100

Receive, we beseech thee, O Lord, the offerings of thy people and of thy new-born servants, that being renewed by the confession of thy Name and by baptism they may attain unto everlasting blessedness. Through the Lord . . .

101

Receive, O Lord, the prayers of thy people and their offerings for sacrifice, and lead us who have shared in these Paschal mysteries unto eternal life. Through the Lord . . .

[The Preface]

102

It is verily meet and right, befitting and salutary. For the time has come which so much we have desired, the light of the long awaited night has come. For what greater or better thing could be found than to proclaim the power of the Rising Lord? For he broke the bonds of hell, raised up the banners of his resurrection, banners most glorious to us to-day, and returned to lift up mankind, cast down by the envy of the enemy, to lift him up among the wondering stars. O the mystic and venerable traffic of that night! O the great and everlasting benefits of the holy mother Church! He wishes not to have something to destroy, but to find something to redeem. Mary has rejoiced in her most holy childbirth. The Church rejoices in the type of the regeneration of her sons. Thus that blessed fount that flowed from the Lord's side carried away the burdens of our sins so that at these sacred altars the perpetual life of the new-born might gather living food. And therefore with angels and archangels.

It is verily meet at all times to praise thee, but far more gloriously upon this night when *Christ our passover was sacrificed for us* [1 Cor 5.7]. For he is the true *Lamb who has taken away the sins of the world* [John 1.29]: who by dying hath destroyed our death and by his rising again hath restored life. Therefore the whole terrestrial orb rejoices in unrestrained Paschal joy; therefore the virtues on high and the angel powers sing together, endlessly raising the hymn of thy glory.

103   *Within the Action*

Communicating and celebrating the most holy night of the resurrection of our Lord Jesus Christ according to the flesh.

104   *Also within the Action*

And therefore we beseech thee, Lord, graciously to receive this oblation of thy servants and of all thy family, which we offer unto thee for all whom thou hast deigned to regenerate by water and the Holy Spirit, granting unto them remission of all their sins that they may be found in Christ Jesus. In supplication we offer to thy majesty our prayers for them, that thou mayest command their names to be written in the book of life: and dispose our days.

105   *Postcommunion*

Grant, we beseech thee, Almighty God, that being full filled with the divine gift by thy sacred mysteries we may walk henceforth in newness of life. Through . . .

106   *And Another*

Grant, we beseech thee, Almighty God, that the Paschal reception of this sacrament may continue and abide in our minds. Through . . .
[Sections 46–65 provide propers from Easter to Ascension.]

LXVI

107   *On the eve* [sabbato] *of Pentecost, you shall celebrate baptism as on the night of the holy Pascha.*

The Imposition of Hands on a Sick Catechumen

Lord holy, Father Almighty, everlasting God, we beseech thee to show forth thy healing power, as Christ brought forth healing to human infirmity: raise up thy servant who is now cast down and weak with sickness: visit and support his every sense, that in the joy of health he may receive thy adoption. Pluck out all the darts of ill-health that in thy good time he may come to thy grace. Lift up thy servant whom thou dost condescend to redeem, that his warfare may end in baptism and not in death, that he may joyfully receive the glorious sign of thy cross. Through Christ our Lord who shall come to judge the quick and the dead.

LXVII

The Imposition of Hands upon a Catechumen
who is Possessed

108

Almighty, everlasting God, before whose face the heavens drop down water, the hills melt like wax, the earth trembles, before whom the depths open and hell doth quake, before whom the raging of the mind is stilled, O Lord that dost rule all things, I humbly beseech thee that by the invocation of thy Name the enemy may depart in confusion and cease to trouble this thy servant: that being freed from this possession he may return to the captain of his salvation and, washing away the filth of the devil, may perceive the sweet odour of the Holy Spirit and follow the author of his freedom. Through . . .

LXVIII

Another, for an Infant Possessed

109

O Lord holy, Father Almighty, everlasting God, with much groaning I implore thy power for this infant oppressed by the devil. O thou that dost protect those that are unjustly troubled, rise up for this infant borne down by warring powers and let him not long be bound: let not the sins of his parents come before thee, O thou that hast promised not to judge the father for the son nor the son for the father. Succour him that is troubled by the fury of the enemy, lest thou cause his mind without baptism to be taken over by the devil: but rather let his tender age go free from malign oppression and ever pay thee thanks. Through our Lord Jesus Christ who shall come to judge the quick and the dead and this world.

LXIX

A Prayer for a Sick Catechumen

110

O Lord, protect and watch over thy servant that comes to the grace of thy baptism, that by the sign of thy Name and by the mercies of the sacred font he may be released from the pains in which the devil has engaged him through the transgressions of original sin: and that stripping off the old man he may rise up arrayed in the robe of new life. Cast out from him all the poisons of the evil spirit, that he may receive thy gift and rejoice unto life eternal. Through the Lord.

LXX

111
S. 8, 9

If he was to have been baptized, the priest comes and says to him the Lord's Prayer and the Creed and catechizes him in these words following, having laid a hand upon his head: then he says over him the prayer: Be not deceived, Satan, *as it is provided for* [Holy] *Saturday.*

We humbly beseech thee, O Lord, that by thy holy visitation thou raise up this thy servant, that the adversary be not allowed to come and try his soul: set an end as thou didst with Job, lest the enemy begin to triumph over his soul without the redemption of baptism. O Lord, delay his death and prolong his days. Raise up thy servant whom thou dost lead to the sacrament of baptism, lest thou lay damage to the work of thy redemption. Take from the devil all occasion of triumph, and preserve him whom by the victory of Christ thou dost gain, that in full health he may be reborn in thy Church by the grace of baptism and do all things which we seek. Through . . .

LXXI

Again, when a Pagan is to be made a Catechumen

112
B. 232
LO. 2
A. 74

When you receive one of heathen upbringing, first you catechize him with divine words and teach him how he must live after he has come to the knowledge of the truth. Then you make him a catechumen: you blow into his face and make the sign of the cross upon his forehead: you lay a hand upon his head and say these words:

Receive the sign of the cross, as on thy brow, so on thy heart: take upon thee the faith of the heavenly commandments: live in such wise that ye may become the temple of God: enter the Church of God and joyfully acknowledge that thou hast cast off the toils of death. Let horror turn thee from idols, disgust from images: worship God the Father Almighty and Jesus Christ his Son, who liveth with the Father and the Holy Ghost throughout all ages.

113

This prayer follows:

I beseech thee, Lord holy, Father Almighty, everlasting God, command that this thy servant, who now wanders uncertain and doubtful in the darkness of this world, be shown the way of truth and of the knowledge of thee: that the eyes of his heart being opened he may acknowledge that thou art one God, the Father in the Son and the Son in the Father, and receive the fruit of this confession both here and in the world to come. Through . . .

Then, after he has tasted the medicine of salt, and signed himself, you bless him with these words:

114
S. 13
B. 231

Lord holy, Father Almighty, everlasting God, who art and who wast and remainest unto the end, whose beginning is not known and whose bounds no man can measure: we humbly beseech thee, Lord, for this thy servant whom thou hast delivered from the error of the Gentiles and their corrupt communications. Hear him who bows his head before thee: may he come to the fount of the laver that being reborn by water and the Holy Ghost he may strip off the *old man and put on the new, who is created after thee* [Eph. 4.24]: may he receive a pure and spotless robe, and be counted worthy to worship thee our Lord. Through . . .

LXXII

Again, a Brief Form for a Sick Catechumen

115

If he was to have been baptized, the priest comes and says over him the prayers which are written above: and he delivers to him the Creed and the Lord's Prayer; and he catechizes him in these words: Be not deceived, Satan, *and so on as it is provided above for the Holy Night. Then with his finger he touches his ears and nostrils with his own spittle, and says to him:*

Effeta, that is, be thou opened, unto the odour of sweetness. But thou, O devil, take flight, for the judgement of God has drawn near.

Then he touches his breast and between the shoulder-blades with exorcized oil while he questions him as follows:

116

Dost thou renounce Satan?
R̸. I renounce.
And all his works?
R̸. I renounce.
And all his pomps?
R̸. I renounce.

LXXIII

117   *When the sick man is undressed, he blesses the font.*

A Prayer

Hear us, Almighty God, and send down thy power upon this water, that he who is washed therein may at the same time receive both health and everlasting life. Through . . .

118   ### A Brief Form of Blessing the Water

I exorcize thee, creature of water, through God the living, through God the holy, through God who in the beginning did separate thee by his word from the dry land and dividing thee into four rivers did command thee to water the earth. I adjure thee through Jesus Christ his only Son our Lord that thou become in him who is to be baptized in thee a *well of water springing up unto eternal life* [John 4.14], and give him new birth unto God, the Father, the Son, and the Holy Ghost; who shall come to judge the quick and the dead and this world by fire.

LXXIV

119   ### Another Brief Form of Blessing

Be present, Lord, be present at thy gifts, that what we do may be perfected by thy help. Through the Lord . . .

120   *The blessing follows.*

O Lord holy, Father Almighty, everlasting God, that dost sanctify water unto spiritual ends, we humbly beseech thee to look down upon our lowly ministry, and upon these waters which are made ready to cleanse and give new life to men send down the spirit of holiness that when the sins of their former life are washed away and they are reborn, he may set up in them a pure dwelling for the Holy Spirit. Through our Lord . . .

LXXV

121
S. 20
B. 234   ### Another Blessing

I exorcize thee, creature of water, in the Name of God the Father Almighty, and in the Name of Jesus Christ his Son, and of the Holy Spirit, O all ye powers of the adversary, every assault of the devil, and every phantasm, be ye rooted out and put to flight from this creature of water, that it may become a *well springing up unto eternal life* [John 4.14], and that whoever shall be baptized therein may become a temple of the living God in the remission of sins. Through our Lord Jesus Christ thy Son who shall come to judge the quick and the dead and this world by fire.

And before you pour the water over him, you question him with the words   122
of the Creed, and say:

Dost thou believe in God the Father Almighty? R̷. I believe.

And dost thou believe in Jesus Christ his only Son our Lord, who was born and suffered? R̷. I believe.

And dost thou believe in the Holy Spirit; the Holy Church, the remission of sins, the resurrection of the flesh? R̷. I believe.

And while you ask the questions, you dip him three separate times in the   123
water. Afterwards, when he has come up from the water, the infant is signed
by a presbyter on his head with chrism, with these words:

May Almighty God, the Father of our Lord Jesus Christ, who has made thee to be born again of water and the Holy Ghost, and has given thee remission of all thy sins, himself anoint thee with the chrism of salvation in Christ Jesus unto life eternal. R̷. Amen.

Then, if offerings have been made, the Mass shall be performed and he   124
communicates: if not, you shall give him the sacraments of the body and blood
of Christ, saying:

The body of our Lord Jesus Christ: may it be to thee unto life eternal.

And you say this prayer over him: 125

Almighty, everlasting God, who hast made thy servant to be born again of water and the Holy Spirit, and hast given him remission of all his sins, give him continual health of mind, that he may acknowledge the truth of thy unity. Through our Lord . . .

Almighty and merciful God, we humbly beseech thy majesty to   126
look with kindness upon thy servant: and as thou hast given him the sacrament of baptism, give him health of mind for all his days.

Then he is sealed [consignatus] *by the bishop with these words:*   127

Almighty God, Father of our Lord Jesus Christ, who hast made thy servants to be born again of water and the Holy Ghost, and hast given them remission of all their sins, do thou, Lord, pour upon them thy Holy Spirit the Paraclete, and give them *the spirit of wisdom and under-standing, the spirit of counsel and might, the spirit of knowledge and godliness.* and fill them with *the spirit of the fear* [Isa. 11.2f] of God and of our

H

Lord Jesus Christ; and grant him to be sealed unto life eternal by the sign of the cross. Through thy Son Jesus Christ our Lord, with whom thou livest and reignest in the unity of the Holy Spirit.

128   *Then he signs him on the forehead with chrism, saying:*

The sign of Christ unto life eternal.
℞.   Amen.

The Lord be with you.
℞.   And with thy spirit.

LXXVI

129
A. 27

A Brief Form for the Blessing of the Exorcized Oil

I exorcize thee, creature of oil, by God the Father Almighty, who *made heaven and earth, the sea and all that in them is* [Ex. 20.11]. All ye powers of the adversary, thou whole army of the devil, every assault and every phantasm of Satan, be ye rooted out and put to flight from this creature of oil, that to all who are anointed therewith it may be unto the adoption of sons through the Holy Spirit. In the Name of God the Father Almighty and in the love of Jesus Christ our Lord, who shall come in the Holy Spirit to judge the quick and the dead and this world by fire.

ORDO ROMANUS XI

Text: Andrieu, *Les Ordines Romani du Haut Moyen-Age*, Vol. 2, Louvain, 1948.

Here begins the order for the scrutiny of the elect, and the announcement which is first made in the third week of Lent, on the second day of the week.

G. 17   1. *Dearly beloved brethren, take notice that the scrutiny is at hand, when the elect are instructed in divine things: with watchful devotion, therefore, let us meet on Wednesday next following at about the third hour, so that the heavenly mystery, when the devil with his retinue is destroyed and the door of the heavenly kingdom is opened, may by the Lord's help be perfectly performed.*

G. 18   2. When they have come to the church on the fourth day of the week at the third hour, as we have said, let the names of the infants and those who are to receive them from the font be written down by an acolyte: and the acolyte calls the infants into church by name in order as they are written, saying: *Such and such a boy*, and so the males are placed one by one by themselves on the right side: *Such and such a girl*, and so the females are placed one by one by themselves on the left side.

3. And then first of all let the presbyter make the sign of the cross upon the forehead of each one with his thumb saying: *In the Name of the Father and of the Son and of the Holy Ghost.*

4. And placing a hand over their heads he says: *Almighty everlasting God, Father of our Lord Jesus Christ.* And he does the same over the females.

G. 19

5. Afterwards he blesses salt, in this manner: *I exorcize thee, creature of salt.*

G. 22

6. And he places some of the salt in the mouth of the infants, one by one, saying: *Receive, such a one, the salt of wisdom, for a token of propitiation unto eternal life.*

G. 23

7. Then let them go out of church and await the hour when they shall be recalled.

8. Then a clerk begins the antiphon for the introit: *When I shall have been sanctified in you* [Ezek. 36.23].

9. When it is finished he says: *Let us pray. We beseech thee, O Lord, bestow upon these elect.*

G. 1

10. And after that he sits in his seat and the deacon says: *Let the catechumens come forward.* And the infants are called by an acolyte by name in order as they are written, and are placed as before.

11. And then they are admonished by the deacon: *Pray, ye elect. Bow the knee.* And when they have prayed, he says: *Rise up. Complete your prayer together, and say, Amen.* And all reply, *Amen.*

12. And the deacon says: *Sign them. Come forward for the blessing.* And let the godfathers and godmothers sign the infants on their foreheads with their thumbs, saying: *In the Name of the Father and of the Son and of the Holy Ghost.*

13. Then an acolyte comes, again making the sign of the cross on the forehead of each one, saying: *In the Name of the Father and of the Son and of the Holy Ghost.*

14. And he places a hand over them and says this prayer over them in a loud voice: *God of Abraham.*

G. 25

15. And he turns to the females and makes the sign of the cross on the forehead of each as above.

16. And he places a hand over the head of each, saying: *God of heaven, God of earth.*

G. 27

17. And the deacon says: *Pray, ye elect. Bow the knee*, and the rest. And the godfathers and godmothers make the sign of the cross as before.

G. 28   18. And another acolyte follows and makes the sign of the cross on the males as before, and placing a hand over them, he says: *Hearken, accursed Satan*.

G. 29   19. And likewise over the females he makes the sign of the cross and places his hand over them saying: *God of Abraham, God of Isaac*.

20. And the deacon bids the elect to pray, as before. And the godfathers and godmothers make the sign of the cross as before.

G. 30   21. Then a third acolyte makes the sign of the cross on the forehead of the boys, as before, and places a hand over their heads, saying: *I exorcize thee, unclean spirit*.

G. 31   22. Likewise over the females he makes the sign of the cross as before and places a hand over their heads, saying: *I exorcize thee, unclean spirit*.

23. And the deacon admonishes them: *Pray, ye elect*, and the rest as before. And the godfathers sign them as before.

G. 32   24. And then the presbyter comes, and makes the sign of the cross on the forehead of each as before, and places a hand over their heads, saying this prayer: *O Lord, holy Father, everlasting God of light and truth*.

25. And he does the same over the females, and says the same prayer.

26. When all this has been performed, again they are admonished by the deacon, *Pray, ye elect. Bow the knee*. And after a little, he says: *Rise up. Complete your prayer together and say, Amen*. And all reply, *Amen*.

27. Again he says: *Sign them. Stand in order and silence*. And the godfathers sign them as before.

28. The priest then returns to his seat. And the lesson of Ezekiel the prophet is read: *Thus saith the Lord, I will sprinkle clean water upon you*, to: *and I will save you from all your uncleannesses* [Ezek. 36.25–9]. The responsory follows: *I will have respect unto you and make you fruitful* [Lev. 26.9].

29. Then they are admonished by the deacon thus:
Let the catechumens retire.
Let anyone who is a catechumen retire.
Let all catechumens go outside.

30. And the elect go out and wait outside the doors until the solemnities of the Mass are finished.

31. Then is read the gospel according to St Matthew: *At that season Jesus answered and said, I thank thee O Father of heaven*, to: *for my yoke is easy and my burden is light* [Matt. 25–30].

32. And oblations are offered by their parents and by those who are to receive them from the font.

33. And let the priest place them on the altar and say this prayer in secret: *O God we beseech thee, bring thy servants in pity to thy mysteries.* G. 2

34. When he says: *Remember Lord thy servants, both men and women*, let the names be read of the men and women who are to receive the infants from the font. G. 3

35. Then, when *Hanc igitur* has been said, let the names of the elect be recited. And when they have been recited he says: *We pray thee Lord for these who are to be renewed in the font of baptism.* G. 4

36. When the solemnities of the Mass are finished, let all communicate, except the infants.

37. Then the presbyter announces that in the same week they are to return for a scrutiny, saying: *Come on Saturday, gather in due time at such and such a church.*

38. And when they come upon the day, as it was told them, they perform the scrutiny and the Mass in full order, as it is written above.

39. Again the presbyter announces upon what day he wishes them to come in the following week, which is the fourth from the beginning of Lent, saying: *Upon such a day, come and gather together at such a church*, whichever he has told them.

40. And when they have come to the church on the day on which they were told, let the deacon say: *Let the catechumens come forward.*

41. And an acolyte calls the infants by name, in order as before, and they perform the scrutiny exactly as they performed the two earlier ones, to the point where he says: *Sign them. Stand in order and silence.*

42. And then are read these two lessons for the opening of the ears: *The lesson of Isaiah the prophet: Thus saith the Lord, Listen and hearken unto me and eat ye that which is good*, to: *and to our God, for he will abundantly pardon* [Isa. 55.2–7]. The responsory follows: *Come, children.*

43. Then another lesson, to the Colossians: Brethren, *putting off the old man with his doings* [Col. 3.9], to: *Yea verily, their sound went out into all the earth and their words unto the ends of the world* [Rom. 10.18]. The responsory follows: *A blessed nation.*

44. Then four deacons come forth from the sacristy bearing the four books of the gospels. They are preceded by two candles, with censers and incense. They place the gospels at the four corners of the altar. G. 33

45. Before they are read, a presbyter speaks in these words: *Beloved children, we shall open to you now the gospels . . . Luke, John.*

46. And when that is done, the deacon says: *Stand in silence and listen attentively.*

47. Then one of the deacons takes the book of the gospel from the near corner of the altar on the left hand side and goes up to read, being preceded by two candles and censers.

48. And he reads: *The beginning of the holy gospel according to Matthew,* to: *for he shall save his people from their sins* [1.21].

49. And when he has read it, a subdeacon receives the book from him upon a cloth and takes it to the sacristy.

G. 35   50. And the presbyter speaks in these words: *Beloved children, lest we keep you too long . . . person of Matthew.*

51. And when that is done, the deacon says: *Stand in silence and listen attentively.*

52. Again the deacon takes another book of the gospel from the other corner on the left side of the altar, being preceded likewise.

53. Again he says: *The beginning of the holy gospel according to Mark,* to: *I baptize you in water, he shall baptize you in the Holy Ghost.* [1.8].

G. 37   54. Then the presbyter continues in these words: *The evangelist Mark, who has the symbol of a lion . . .*

55. When that is done, the deacon says: *Stand in silence and listen attentively.*

56. And the deacon takes the third book of the gospel, according to Luke, from the third corner of the altar on the right hand side. And he goes up to read and says: *The Lord be with you. And with thy spirit.* And he reads: *The beginning of the holy gospel according to Luke,* to: *to make ready for the Lord a perfect people* [1.14].

G. 39   57. And the presbyter speaks in these words: *The evangelist Luke has the appearance of an ox . . . four gospels.*

58. When that is done, the deacon makes his proclamation again as above.

59. And from the fourth corner on the right side of the altar the deacon takes the fourth book of the gospel, according to John, being preceded likewise. And he goes up to read and says: *The Lord be with you. And with thy spirit.* And he reads: *The beginning of the holy gospel according to John. In the beginning was the Word,* to: *full of grace and truth.*

G. 41   60. Again the presbyter continues, in these words: *John has the likeness of an eagle . . . throughout all ages.*

61. And he says the introduction to the Creed: *Dearly beloved, who*   G. 42
seek to receive the sacraments of baptism . . . begins thus:

62. When that is done, an acolyte holds one of the male infants in   G. 43
his left arm, and the presbyter asks him saying: *In what language do*
they confess. our Lord Jesus Christ? R7. *In Greek.—Declare their faith*
according as they believe. And the acolyte says the Creed in Greek,
chanting in these words: *Pisteuo eis ena theon.*

63. When this is done, he turns to the females and does likewise.

64. Again another acolyte takes one of the Latin infants in his left
arm, placing his right hand on his head, and the presbyter asks him:
In what language do they confess? as before. And he replies: *In Latin.* The
presbyter says to him: *Declare their faith according as they believe.* And he
chants the Creed:

65. *I believe in one God, the Father Almighty, maker of heaven and earth*
and of [all things] visible.

66. When this is done, he turns to the females and does likewise.

67. Then the presbyter continues in these words: *Dearly beloved, this*   G. 44
is the sum of our belief . . . throughout all ages.

68. When that is done, the deacon says: *Stand in silence and listen*
attentively.

69. Then the priest continues with this introduction to the Lord's   G 44–53
Prayer: *Our Lord and Saviour Jesus Christ . . . throughout all ages.*

70. When that is done, let them be admonished by the deacon:
Stand in silence and listen attentively.

71. And the presbyter says: *Ye have heard . . . throughout all ages.*

72. When that is done, the deacon proclaims:
Let the catechumens retire.
Let anyone who is a catechumen retire.
Let all catechumens go outside.

73. The parents go outside with their infants, and outside the doors
they give their children into somebody's keeping.

74. Then they go back into the church, the parents and those who
are to receive the infants from the font, with their offerings, and the
offerings are made for themselves, while the infants wait outside until
the solemnities of the Mass are completed.

75. When the Mass is done, let all communicate, except the infants
themselves.

76. Again the presbyter announces upon what day in the following
week, which is the fifth after the beginning of Lent, he wishes them to
return for the scrutiny.

77. And when they have come to celebrate the scrutiny, they observe the entire order in the same manner as the two earlier scrutinies before the opening of the ears.

78. And afterwards the presbyter announces that in the same week they are to return for the fifth scrutiny, and on what day and to which church he wishes them to come.

79. And when they have come, they observe the scrutiny in the same way as they did before.

80. When this is done, again he announces to them, as above, that they are to return for the sixth scrutiny, in the following week, the last before the Pascha, and on what day and to which church he wishes them to come. And they complete the scrutiny and the Mass, doing everything as before.

81. It is to be so ordered that from the first scrutiny which begins in the third week of Lent to the vigil of the Pascha on Holy Saturday there shall be seven scrutinies, corresponding to the seven gifts of the Holy Spirit, so that when the sevenfold number is completed there may be given to them the sevenfold grace of the Spirit.

82. And the presbyter announces that on Holy Saturday at the third hour they are to return to church and are then catechized and make return of the Creed and are baptized and their sevenfold oblations completed.

83. The order in which they are catechized is as follows.

After the third hour of the Sabbath, they go to the church and are arranged in the order in which their names are written down, males on the right side, females on the left.

G. 70   84. And the priest makes the sign of the cross on the forehead of each and places his hand on the head of each and says: *Be not deceived, Satan.*

G. 71   85. When that is done, the presbyter touches the nostrils and ears of each with spittle from his mouth and says in the ears of each one: *Effeta, that is be opened, unto the odour of sweetness,* and the rest.

G. 73   86. When this is done, he walks around them, placing a hand on their heads and chanting in a loud voice: *I believe in one God,* and the rest. He turns to the females and does likewise.

G. 74   87. Then the archdeacon says to them: *Pray, ye elect. Bow the knee. Complete your prayers together and say Amen.* And all reply *Amen.*

G. 74   88. Again they are admonished by the archdeacon in these words: *Let the catechumens go.*
If anyone is a catechumen, let him go.

Let all the catechumens go outside and await the hour when the grace of God shall be able to enfold you.

89. Then the blessing of the candle is performed. Then follow the lessons belonging to the day, each with its canticle.

G. 76–87

90. When this is done, the pontiff and all the priests go in procession from the church until they come to the fonts, singing the litany, that is *Kyrieleison*: the notaries go before the pontiff, holding on high two lighted candles the height of a man, with censers and incense, and they begin the litany which follows: *O Christ, hear us,* and the rest.

91. When the litany is finished, the whole clergy and people stand round about the font, and when silence has been made the pontiff says: *The Lord be with you.* And all the people reply: *And with thy spirit.*

92. And he says: *Let us pray,* and recites the blessing: *Almighty, everlasting God.*

G. 89

93. Another: *God, who by thine invisible power,* and the rest.

G. 90

94. When all this is done, he pours chrism from a golden vessel over the water into the fonts in the manner of a cross. With his hand he stirs the chrism and the water, and sprinkles all the font and the people standing about.

S. 26

95. When this is done, and before the children are baptized, everyone who wishes shall receive a blessing, each taking some of the water in his own vessel, for sprinkling in their houses or vineyards or fields or orchards.

S. 26

96. Then the pontiff baptizes one or two of the infants, or as many as he wishes, and the rest are baptized by a deacon whom he shall appoint.

97. Raising the infants in their hands, they offer them to one presbyter. The presbyter makes the sign of the cross with chrism upon the crown of their heads with his thumb, saying: *Almighty God, the Father of our Lord Jesus Christ,* and the rest.

G. 94

98. And those who are to receive them are ready with towels in their hands and accept them from the pontiff or the deacons who baptize them.

99. The pontiff goes from the font and sits in his throne which is placed ready in the church, wherever he wishes. And the infants are carried down before him and he gives to each a stole and overgarment [*stola, casula*] and chrismal cloth and ten coins, and they are robed.

100. And being vested, they are arranged in order as their names are written, in a circle, and the pontiff makes a prayer over them, con-

G. 95

firming them with an invocation of the sevenfold grace of the Holy
Spirit.

G. 96   101. When the prayer has been said, he makes the sign of the cross
with his thumb and chrism on the forehead of each one saying: *In
the Name of the Father and of the Son and of the Holy Ghost. Peace be to
thee.* And they reply: *Amen.*

102. Great care must be taken that this is not neglected, because it
is at that point that every baptism is confirmed and justification made
for the name of Christianity.

103. After this they go in to Mass and all the infants receive communion. Care is to be taken lest after they have been baptized they
receive any food or suckling before they communicate.

104. Afterwards let them come to Mass every day for the whole
week of the Pascha and let their parents make oblations for them.

105. This foregoing order of baptism is to be observed in just the
same way on the Sabbath of Pentecost as on the holy Sabbath of the
Pascha.

THE BOBBIO MISSAL

Text: E. A. Lowe, *The Bobbio Missal*, published by the Henry Bradshaw
Society, Vol. 58.

174
G. 33   ## AT THE CREED FOR THE OPENING OF THE
EARS OF THE ELECT

Dearly beloved, we shall open to you now the gospels, that is, the
divine joys. But first we must explain what the gospel is, and whence it
comes, and whose words are written therein, and why they be four
who wrote of this life, and who the four are who, as the prophet foretold, have been marked by the divine spirit: lest haply without this
explanation we should confuse your minds: and because it is for this
that ye are come, that your ears should be opened, and not that your
senses should be blunted. The word gospel truly means good tidings,
and such indeed are the tidings of Jesus Christ our Lord. The gospel
comes to us that it might set forth and show that he who spake by the
prophets is come in the flesh, as it is written, *Lo, I who spake am here*
[Isa. 52.6. Vulg.]. But to explain briefly what the gospel is, and who
those four are who by the prophet were shown aforetime, let us show
how each name was disclosed by its own sign. The prophet Ezekiel

says: *And the likeness of the face of them was as the face of a man, and the face of a lion on the right side: and the face of an ox, and the face of an eagle on the left side.* There is no doubt that those four who had those faces are the four evangelists: but the names of those who wrote the gospels are these: Matthew, Mark, Luke, John.

After this the deacon reads:

175
G. 34

The book of the generation of Jesus Christ the son of David, the son of Abraham: Abraham begat Isaac, and Isaac begat Jacob, and Jacob begat Judah and his brothers: now the birth of Jesus Christ was on this wise.

After this the presbyter explains:

176
G. 35

Beloved children, let us expound to you what symbol each [of the evangelists] embodies, and why Matthew has the symbol of a man: it is because in his opening verses he speaks of nothing other than the birth of the Saviour and sets forth the full order of his generation.

St Mark's Gospel begins

177
G. 36

The deacon reads: The beginning of the gospel of Jesus Christ the Son of God; as it is written in the prophet, Behold, I send my messenger before thy face which shall prepare thy way before thee. The voice of one crying in the wilderness, Prepare the way of the Lord, make his paths straight.

The presbyter explains: The evangelist Mark, who has the symbol of a lion, on account of its solitude, begins with, *The voice of one crying in the wilderness, Prepare ye the way of the Lord:* possibly because they rule unconquered. Of this lion we find many examples, so that that passage is not empty of meaning which says, *Judah, my son, thou art a lion's whelp, thou hast sprung up from my seed: thou hast stooped down and couched as a lion and as a lion's whelp: who shall rouse him up?*

178
G. 37

St Luke's Gospel begins

179
G. 38

The deacon reads: There was in the days of Herod, the king of Judah, a certain priest named Zacharias, of the course of Abia: and his wife was of the daughters of Aaron, and her name was Elisabeth.

The priest explains: The evangelist Luke has the appearance of an ox which is a type of our Saviour's sacrifice. And so Luke is compared to an ox because he contained two horns, that is two testaments, and four hooves, that is four gospels.

180
G. 39

181
G. 40

St John's Gospel begins

The deacon reads: In the beginning was the Word, and the Word was with God, and the Word was God. The same was in the beginning with God. All things were made through him, and without him nothing was made.

182
G. 41

The priest explains: John has the likeness of an eagle, because he sought the greatest heights. For David says of the person of Christ, *Thy youth shall be renewed as that of an eagle*: that is, of Jesus Christ our Lord, who rising from the dead ascended up into the heavens; and so now the Church, being pregnant by your conception, glories that she labours unto new beginnings of the Christian law.

183

THE EXPOSITION OF THE CREED

Dearly beloved brethren, the divine sacraments are not matters for discussion but rather for belief, and not only for belief but also for reverence: and no man can hold the discipline of the faith unless he has within him the foundation of the fear of the Lord; as Solomon says, *The fear of the Lord is the beginning of wisdom.* For he that fears the Lord in all things which are spoken by God is both wise and faithful. And so to-day you are to hear the Creed, without which it is not possible to preach Christ, to hold the faith, nor to celebrate the grace of baptism. The Creed is the token of the catholic faith, the sacrament of eternal devotion. You therefore who are *competentes* must prepare with great reverence to receive with all your faculties the Creed which the holy catholic Church with a mother's mouth to-day delivers to you.

184

I believe in God the Father Almighty, Maker of Heaven and Earth. I believe in Jesus Christ his Only-Begotten, everlasting Son, conceived of the Holy Spirit, born of the Virgin Mary, suffered under Pontius Pilate, was crucified, dead and buried, he descended into hell: the third day he rose again from the dead, he ascended into heaven, and sat down at the right hand of God the Father Almighty, from thence he shall come to judge the quick and the dead. I believe in the Holy Spirit, the Holy Catholic Church, the Communion of Saints, the remission of sins, the resurrection of the flesh, the life everlasting. Amen.

185

Dearly beloved, the words of this Creed must now be repeated to you in such a way that the words we say may better penetrate your mind. *I believe in God:* these words are said three times in the course of the Creed so that each time we may take up what follows with more faithful application. Observe that the word *Almighty* is added, and rightly: for you need not doubt God's promises but confidently await them, if you believe that he is almighty that promises. *And in Jesus Christ our only Lord*: this is the essential part of the faith, for unless you believe with all your mind in the Son of God, you cannot confess the Father; believe therefore in the Son of God, only-begotten from unbegotten, the living from the living, the true from the true. *Who was conceived of the Holy Spirit, born of the Virgin Mary*: you hear mention of the Holy Spirit as concerned in his birth, lest you doubt whether a virgin should have been able to conceive; for this is what the angel Gabriel said to Mary: *The Holy Spirit shall come upon thee and the power of the highest shall overshadow thee.* Why should you not believe that he took human form in the womb of the virgin, when you believe that man was made from the dust of the earth? And do not doubt that Mary remained a virgin after giving birth: for many ages before, the prophet Isaiah prophesied and said: *Behold, a virgin shall conceive in the womb and shall bring forth a son.* These things are to be believed upon the authority of God's word. *He suffered under Pontius Pilate, was crucified, dead and buried*: let not thy Lord's suffering overcome thee with trepidation, let not his cross and burial fill thee with fear, for it was not the weakness of fragility which redeemed thee, but the performance of love: his cross is thy kingdom, his death thy life. *He descended into hell, the third day he rose again from the dead, he ascended into heaven and sat down at the right hand of the Father Almighty*: if thy Lord's three days in the sephulchre disturb thee, his eternal resurrection strengthens thee the more. The weakness of Christ of which you may hear is a mystery: it is a marvellous thing that he to whom heaven belonged by right should bear the ignominy of the cross for thy sake. If you believe those things which you see, believe also the things of which the glory cannot be denied. *From thence he shall come to judge the quick and the dead:* observe that he who upon earth was judged by wicked men shall come from his heavenly throne in judgement. If you perceive his judgement, fear the judge. *You believe in the Holy Spirit*: if through faith you have believed in God the Father almighty and in his Only-Begotten Son, then you must also confess that the Holy Spirit is God. For this is the Holy Spirit who proceedeth from the Father, of whom the Saviour says to his blessed Apostles: *Go, baptize all nations in the Name of the Father and of the Son and of the Holy Spirit*: since their names cannot be separated, so neither can their power. *The holy catholic Church, the forgiveness of sins, the resurrection of the flesh, and the life everlasting*: unless you believe that the Church of God is holy, you cannot receive the gifts of God from the Church; for you confess that the Holy Spirit is God together with the Father and the Son in order that through the grace of baptism you may receive remission of sins. The resurrection of thy flesh restores thee to eternity; for unless you believe that your sins are forgiven you cannot be absolved, and unless you believe that in the resurrection of the flesh you are to be restored after death, you cannot come to the fruit of perpetual life. That is the end.

[There follows the propers for the Palm Sunday Mass (at which the Creed was delivered) and then the various formularies for the observance of Holy Week. Then:]

228 ## [Order] for Making a Christian ✠

O God of love, the strength and stay of all things, who hast created a death whereby we may escape the stains of the world: we pray and beseech thee to guard the soul of thy servant, N.: that the devil having been trodden underfoot thou wilt strengthen him, and when the darkness of his first birth is dispersed he may receive in faith the name of Christian.

229 ### Another [Collect]

O God who dost restore that which is lost and preserve that which is restored, God who hast ordained that the reproach of Gentile birth shall be taken away by the sign of thy Name, so that men may be accounted worthy to approach the fount of baptism . . . [text incomplete].

230 ### Another [Collect]

O Lord holy, Father Almighty, everlasting God, who hast made heaven and earth, the sea and all that in them is, receive my humble prayers for thy servant, N. Strengthen him by the invocation of thy Name, let the light of thy countenance shine upon him, bless and sanctify him as thou hast blessed the house of Abraham, Isaac, and Jacob, grant him the angel of peace, the angel of mercy, that he by the help of the Holy Spirit may lead him unto eternal life, and by the sign of Jesus Christ deliver him from the jaws of the enemy, that he may abide in the faith all the days of his life. Through.

231
G. 114
S. 13

O God who art and wast and shalt abide unto the end of the world, whose beginning is not known and whose bounds no man can measure, we pray and beseech thee to protect the soul of thy servant N. whom

thou hast delivered from the error of the Gentiles and their corrupt
communications: hear him who bows his head before thee, let him
approach the baptism of the fount of regeneration by water and the
Holy Spirit, who with the Father and the Son liveth and reigneth.

You make the sign of the cross ✠ *upon him and say the Creed.*   *232*
Receive the sign of the cross, as on thy brow so upon thy heart; be   G. 112
thou ever faithful; enter the temple of God; abandon idols; worship   A. 34
God the Father Almighty and Jesus Christ his Son, who shall come to   LO. 2
judge the quick and the dead and the world with fire with the Holy
Spirit unto the ages of ages.

After this you shall breathe into his mouth three times, and say,   *233*
N., receive the Holy Spirit, mayest thou guard him in thy heart.

The Order of Baptism   *234*
I exorcize thee, creature of water, in the Name of God the Father   G. 121
Almighty, and in the Name of our Lord Jesus Christ his Son, and of the   S. 20
Holy Spirit: all ye powers of the adversary, thou whole army of the
devil, every assault and every phantasm, be ye rooted out and put to
flight from this creature of water: that to all who shall go down into
it, it may be a fount of water giving health unto eternal life: that when
anyone shall have been baptized therein he may become a temple of
the living God in the remission of sins, in the Name of God the Father
Almighty and of Jesus Christ his Son and of the Holy Spirit, who shall
judge the world with fire, by this sign which remains unto all ages.

A Prayer   *235*
Almighty, everlasting God, be present at the mysteries of thy great   G. 89, 90
goodness, be present at these sacraments: and for the creation of a new   S. 21, 22,
people which the fount of baptism brings forth unto thee send forth   23
the spirit of adoption [Rom. 8.15], so that the mystery which we must   A. 15, 42
perform in our low estate may be completed by thy power. O God,
who by thine invisible power dost wonderfully effect thy sacraments;
though we are not worthy for the performance of so great mysteries,
yet do not thou forsake thy gifts of grace, but of thy goodness incline
thine ears to our prayers. God, whose spirit at the beginning of the
world *was borne upon the waters* [Gen. 1.2], so that even then the nature
of water should be endowed with sanctifying power . . .

[This] collect follows.   *236*
God, who by the outpouring of the flood didst signify a type of   G. 90, 91
regeneration, when thou by water didst wash away the sins of a   S. 23, 24

wicked world, deliver this water from every attack of the assailant, that being purged by the departure of all evil it may be a water of rebirth, a purifying wave, that in this laver all may attain salvation and the perfect gift of purification. Wherefore I bless thee, creature of water, through God the Living, through God the Holy, who in the beginning by his word did separate thee from the dry land, and did command thee to water the earth in four streams, who in the desert gave a sweetness to thy bitterness, that men might drink thee, and for a thirsty people did bring thee forth from a rock. I bless thee through Jesus Christ his only Son our Lord, who by his power in a wonderful sign at Cana of Galilee did change thee into wine, who walked upon thee with his feet, who was baptized by John in Jordan, who did shed thee from his side, mingled with blood, and commanded his disciples to baptize believers, in the Name of the Father and of the Son and of the Holy Spirit, who liveth and reigneth.

237   Lift up your hearts.

It is meet and right, Almighty God, who hast opened unto us a fount of eternal life and hast regenerated us by thy Holy Spirit, to whom thou hast committed this holy laver unto the remission of sins, that it might be a laver of water in the Holy Spirit through whom thou dost take from us every stain: thou dost deliver us from death and endue us with life, so that we who in this beginning receive power may stand about thee in glory and praise the Father for ever in the heavens, through our Lord Jesus Christ, through whom we pray thee, O God our Almighty Father, that thou wouldest send down the Holy Spirit upon this water, that whomsoever we shall baptize in thy Name and in the Name of thy Son our Lord Jesus Christ, and of the Holy Spirit, thou wilt purify and regenerate, and receive into the number of thy saints, and in thy Holy Spirit take them up into life everlasting unto all ages of ages.

238   *While the chrism pours down into the font, you make the sign of the cross ✠ and say,*

The infusion of the saving chrism of our Lord Jesus Christ, that it may be a fount of living water springing up for all them that draw near to eternal life.

239   *After this you say,*

Almighty God, we beseech thee admit thy family to the fount of eternal salvation, that of those whom thou hast commanded to return from darkness to light none may be deceived by the wiles of the enemy.

The Exorcism of a Man before he is Baptized

240
LO I
A. 33

I exorcize thee, unclean spirit, through God the Father Almighty, who made heaven and earth, the sea and all that in them is: all ye powers of the adversary, thou whole army of the devil, every assault and every phantasm, be ye rooted out and put to flight from this creature, that he may become a holy temple of God, in the Name of God the Father Almighty and of Jesus Christ his Son, who shall judge the world with fire in the Holy Spirit unto all ages.

You touch his nostrils and say, Effeta, the sacrifice is complete, unto the odour of sweetness.

241
S. 12

You anoint him with sanctified oil and say,

242
S. 30

I anoint thee with sanctified oil, as Samuel anointed David to be king and prophet.

You touch his nostrils, ears, and breast.

243
S. 31

Perform thy work, creature of oil, perform thy work that no unclean spirit may lurk here, neither in the limbs nor in the inward parts nor in the whole frame of the body: may the power of Christ, the Son of the most high God, and of the Holy Spirit, work in thee throughout all ages.

You ask his name, saying, What is he called?

244

Dost thou renounce Satan, his pomps, his luxuries, this present world?

He replies, May he renounce them. *You say this three times.*

You ask his name, What is he called?

245

Dost thou believe in God the Father Almighty, Maker of Heaven and Earth?

He replies, May he believe.

Does he believe in Jesus Christ his only Son our Lord, conceived of the Holy Spirit, born of the Virgin Mary, suffered under Pontius Pilate, crucified and buried: he descended into hell, the third day he rose again from the dead, he ascended into heaven and sitteth at the right hand of God the Father Almighty, from thence he shall come to judge the quick and the dead?

246

He replies, May he believe.

Does he believe in the Holy Spirit, the holy catholic Church, the communion of saints, the forgiveness of sins, the resurrection of the

247

flesh, and that he shall rise in the glory of Christ to have everlasting life after death?

He replies, May he believe.

248   *You baptize him and say,*

I baptize thee in the Name of the Father and of the Son and of the Holy Spirit, that have one substance, that thou mayest have a part with the saints in everlasting life.

249   *You pour chrism over his brow, saying,*
G. 94
A. 23, 47   May God the Father of our Lord Jesus Christ, who hath regenerated
S. 28   thee by water and the Holy Spirit, and who hath given thee remission of sins through the laver of regeneration and of blood, himself anoint thee with his holy chrism unto eternal life.

250   *You array him in a garment, saying,*
S. 33
Goth. 263   Receive this white garment, and bear it stainless before the judgement seat of Christ.

Collect at the Washing of the Feet

251   I wash thy feet, as our Lord Jesus Christ washed his disciples' feet.
Goth. 263   Do thou even so to pilgrims and strangers. Our Lord Jesus Christ
252   dried his disciples' feet with the towel wherewith he was girded: I do
S. 36   the same to thee: do thou even so to strangers, to pilgrims, and to the poor.

253   ### After the Baptism
S.39
Goth. 265   Dearly beloved brethren, let us offer praise and thanks to the Lord, that he has deigned to increase the congregation of his Church by our dear ones who now have been baptized. Therefore let us seek of the Lord's mercy that they may bear the holy baptism which they have received unharmed, inviolate, and stainless before the judgement seat of Christ.

254   ### Another

Lord God Almighty, who hast commanded that these thy servants shall be reborn of water and the Holy Spirit, preserve in them the holy baptism which they have received and perfect them in the hallowing of thy Name; that thy grace may always grow in them, and that what by thy gift they have received, by the purity of their life they may preserve.

MASS AT THE PASCHAL VIGIL

Almighty, everlasting God, who throughout all the world dost illuminate this most holy night with the glory of the Lord's resurrection, preserve in the new offspring of thy family the spirit of sanctification which thou hast given them, that being renewed in body and soul they may ever show before thee a pure mind and a pure heart.

Collect

O God, who dost illuminate this most holy night with the glory of the Lord's resurrection, preserve in the new offspring of thy family the spirit of adoption which thou hast given them, that in body and mind they may show before thee a pure service.

Post Nomina

O God, whose wondrous gifts are completed in the mysteries of baptism, grant to thy people that being cleansed at the most holy font from the error of man's first downfall they may enter thy promised land, where they may take the sweet nourishment of thy sacraments.

[The three collects above are the only propers in the Mass which refer to baptism.]

THE STOWE MISSAL

Text: G. F. Warner, *The Stowe Missal*, published by the Henry Bradshaw Society, Vol. 32.

NOTES ON THE STOWE MISSAL

1. Both the first and second prayers are headed with the title, "The Order of Baptism". The beginning was originally with the second prayer, which was written on the first page of a gathering. The first prayer with its heading was written on the back page of the previous gathering, which happened to be left blank, in a rather later hand.

2. The rubrics numbered 11 and 29 are written not in Latin but in Irish, and appear to belong to the original document.

The administration of salt at some distance from its blessing is peculiar. The reference to sacrifice in the Effeta which follows possibly supplies the explanation: the Gospel saying "Every sacrifice shall be salted with salt", may be the link which caused the writer to draw them together (Mark 9.49).

3. *Item 12*. Latin: *Effeta quod est apertio effeta est hostia in honorem suauitatis in nomine dei patris et filii et spiritus sancti*. The second *effeta* has been translated as

though it was *effecta*. Item 270 in *Missale Gothicum* provides an example where *effectus* appears for *effetus*: and the MS. of the Gelasian Sacramentary reads *effecta* where *effeta* is probably meant. Current pronunciation seems to have offered room for confusion.

The Order of Baptism begins here.

1
G.26   God, who didst make Adam of the dust of the earth, and he sinned in Paradise, and thou didst not reckon his sin unto death but deigned to make restoration by the blood of thine Only-begotten and dost bring us back rejoicing unto the holy Jerusalem. Wherefore accursed one remember thy sentence and give honour to God the living, and depart from this servant of God, forasmuch as my God and Lord is pleased to call him to his holy grace and the mercy of baptism through this sign of the cross, which sign do thou O devil never dare to cross out [*hoc signum crucis quod tu diabole nunquam audeas designare*. cp. LO 3, A. 34]. Through our Lord.

THE ORDER OF BAPTISM

2   O Lord holy, Father Almighty, everlasting God, drive out from this man the devil and his heathen condition, from his head, his hairs, his crown, his pate, his brow, his eyes, his ears, his nostrils, his mouth, his tongue, the string of his tongue, his throat, his jaws, his neck, his breast, his heart, his whole body within and without, his hands, his feet and all his limbs, his sinews, his thoughts, his words, his works, and all his ways, both now and in the future, through thee, Jesus Christ, who doth reign.

3   O God, who for the salvation of the human race hast ordained certain most powerful sacraments in the substance of the waters, be present of thy goodness as we call upon thee, and pour out thy blessing upon this element by which in many ways thou dost work our purification, that this creature, being obedient to the service of thy mystery, may receive the power of thy divine grace to cast out demons and drive out diseases, so that in the homes of the faithful whatever may be aspersed with this water may be cleansed and freed from stain. Let not the spirit of pestilence nor the breath of corruption abide there, let all the snares of the lurking enemy remove thence: and if there be anything which envies the peace and quiet of them that dwell therein, let it be put to flight by the aspersion of this water, that the health which we seek by the invocation of thy Name may be defended against every attack. Through our Lord.

The Consecration of Salt begins here.

O God, who for man's salvation [hast given us] a medicine in this   **4**
healthful salt, grant that the soul of this man may be converted and
rescued from the error of his heathen condition, that he may confess
the threefold [*trinum*] God and drive away the devil by means of
renunciation and the sign of the cross of our Lord Jesus Christ, who
reigneth with the Father and the Holy Spirit unto all ages of ages.

Another Prayer

I exorcize thee, creature of salt, in the Name of God the Father   **5**
Almighty, and in the love of our Lord Jesus Christ, and in the power of   G. 22
the Holy Spirit. I exorcize thee by the living God and by the true God,   A. 26
who has created thee to be a safeguard of the human race, and has
commanded thee to be consecrated by his servants for those who come
to faith. And therefore we ask thee, O Lord our God, that in the Name
of the Trinity this creature of salt may be a saving sacrament to drive
away the enemy: do thou, O Lord, sanctify it, and bless it, that it may
remain as perfect medicine in the bowels of all who receive it, in the
Name of our Lord Jesus Christ who shall come to judge the quick and
the dead and this world by fire.

Concerning the Renunciation

Dost thou renounce Satan?	*He replies,* I renounce.
And all his works?	*He replies,* I renounce.
And all his pomps?	*He replies,* I renounce.

6

Concerning the Confession

Dost thou believe in God the Father Almighty?
He replies, I believe.
And dost thou believe in Jesus Christ?
He replies, I believe.
And dost thou believe in the Holy Ghost?
He replies, I believe.

*You make an exsufflation and touch him: then you touch his breast and
back with oil and chrism, saying:* I anoint thee with sanctified oil, in the
Name of the Father and of the Son and of the Holy Ghost.

Dost thou renounce Satan?	*He replies,* I renounce.
And all his works?	*He replies,* I renounce.
And all his pomps?	*He replies,* I renounce.

7
G. 19

We beseech thee, O Lord holy, Father Almighty, everlasting God, to have mercy upon thy servant N., whom thou hast called to the elements of the faith. Drive from him all *blindness of heart* [Mark 3.5; Eph. 4.18]: loose the bonds of Satan with which he is bound: open to him, O Lord, the door of thy truth: that bearing the sign of thy wisdom he may turn from the squalor of fleshly lusts and delight in the sweet savour of thy commandments and joyfully serve thee in thy Church: that he may go forward day by day until by thy favour he comes to thy promised grace, in the Name of the Father and of the Son and of the Holy Ghost unto the ages of ages.

8
G. 111

We humbly beseech thee, O Lord holy, Father Almighty, everlasting God, who dost succour us in dangers and dost gently correct us, that by thy holy visitation thou raise up thy servant N. from his sickness: set an end, as thou didst with Job, lest the enemy begin to triumph over his soul without the redemption of baptism.

9
G. 111

O Lord, delay his death and prolong his days. Raise up thy servant whom thou dost lead to the sacrament of baptism, lest thou lay damage to thy work of redemption. Take from the devil all occasion of triumph, and preserve him whom by the victory of Christ thou dost gain, that in full health he may be reborn in thy Church by the grace of baptism and do all things which we seek. Through . . .

10
G. 70

Be not deceived, Satan: punishment threatens thee, hell threatens thee, the day of judgement, the day of everlasting punishment, the day which shall come as a burning furnace of fire, when everlasting destruction is prepared for thee and thine angels. And therefore for thy wickedness, accursed one, that deservedly ought to be accursed, give honour to God the living, give honour to Jesus Christ, give honour to the Holy Spirit the Paraclete, in whose power I command thee, whatever unclean spirit thou art, come out and depart from these servants of God: give back to their God these whom our Lord God Jesus Christ has deigned to call to his grace and blessing: that they may become his temple through the water of regeneration unto the remission of all sins, in the Name of our Lord Jesus Christ who shall come

11

to judge the quick and the dead and this world by fire.

12
B. 241

It is here that the salt is put into the mouth of the child.

Effeta, which is The Opening: the victim [*hostia*] is complete [*effeta*] unto the honour [*sic*] of sweetness in the Name of God, the Father, the Son, and the Holy Ghost.

13
G. 114
B. 231

O Lord holy, Father Almighty, everlasting God, *who art and who was and who art to come* [Rev. 1.8], who remainest unto the end, whose beginning is not known and whose bounds no man can measure: we humbly beseech thee Lord for this thy servant N., whom thou hast delivered from the error of the Gentiles and their corrupt communications. Hear him who bows his head before thee: may he come to the fount of baptism that being renewed by water and the Holy Ghost he may strip off the *old man and put on the new, who is created after thee* [Eph. 4.24]: may he receive a pure and spotless robe and be counted worthy to worship thee our Lord. Through.

O God, who for the salvation of the human race hast ordained   *14*
certain most powerful sacraments in the substance of the waters, be present of thy goodness as we call upon thee, and pour out thy blessing upon this element by which in many ways thou dost work our purification, that this creature being obedient to the service of thy mystery may receive the power of thy divine grace to cast out demons and drive out diseases, so that in the homes of the faithful whatever may be showered by this water may be cleansed and freed from stain. Let not the spirit of pestilence nor the breath of corruption abide there, let all the snares of the lurking enemy remove thence: and if there be anything which envies the peace and quiet of them that dwell therein, let it be put to flight by the aspersion of this water, that the health which we seek by the invocation of thy Name may be defended against all attack. Through our Lord.

Hear us, O Lord holy, Father Almighty, everlasting God, and send   *15*
thy holy angel from heaven that he may guard, watch over, protect, visit, and defend all that dwell in this dwelling of thy servant.

Up to this point he has been a catechumen. He now begins to be anointed   *16*
with oil and chrism upon the breast and between the shoulder blades, before
he is baptized. Then a litany is sung around the font. Then two psalms: My
soul thirsteth, *as far as:* living God (*from the psalm* Quemadmodum)
[Ps. 42]: *and from the psalm* Adferte [Ps. 29], *to:* The voice of the Lord
is over the waterfloods.

I exorcize thee, O creature of water, through God the living,   *17*
through God the holy, who in the beginning did separate thee   G. 91
by his word from the dry land, whose Spirit was borne upon thee, who commanded thee to flow from paradise and in four rivers to water the whole earth, who brought thee forth from the rock that he might water the people, weary with thirst, whom he had set free from Egypt, who sweetened thy great bitterness with wood.

I exorcize thee also through Jesus Christ his Son, who in Cana of   *18*
     G. 91

Galilee by his power in a wonderful sign did change thee into wine, who walked upon thee with his feet, and was baptized in thee by John in Jordan, who shed thee forth from his side with blood, and commanded his disciples saying, *Go, teach all nations, baptizing them in the Name of the Father, and of the Son, and of the Holy Ghost.*

19   I command thee therefore, every unclean spirit, every phantasm, every lie, be thou rooted out and take flight from this creature of water, that to him that goeth down therein it may be a *well of water springing up unto eternal life* [John 4.14]; may the water be holy and blessed, for the raising up of new sons unto God the Father Almighty, in the Name of our Lord Jesus Christ who shall come in the Holy Spirit to judge this world by fire.

20
G. 121
B. 234

    I exorcize thee, creature of water, in the Name of God the Father Almighty, and in the Name of Jesus Christ his Son, and of the Holy Spirit. O all ye powers of the adversary, every assault of the devil, and every phantasm, be ye rooted out and put to flight from this creature of water, that it may be a *well springing up unto eternal life* [John 4.14], and that whoever shall be baptized therein may become a temple of the living God unto the remission of sins. Through our Lord Jesus Christ who shall come to judge this world by fire.

21
G. 89
B. 235
A. 15, 42

    Almighty everlasting God, be present at the mysteries of thy goodness, be present at thy sacraments: and for the creation of the new people which the fount of baptism brings forth unto thee, send down the *Spirit of adoption* [Rom. 8.15]: that those things which our lowly ministry performs may be perfected by the operation of thy power. Through.

22
G. 90
B. 235

    God, who by thine invisible power dost wonderfully effect thy sacraments: although we are not worthy to perform so great mysteries, yet do not thou forsake the gifts of thy grace, but incline the ears of thy goodness to our prayers. Through.

23
G. 90
B. 235, 236

    God, whose Spirit at the beginning of the world was *borne upon the waters* [Gen. 1.2], that even the nature of water might conceive the power of sanctification: God, who by the outpouring of the flood didst signify a type of regeneration, when thou by water didst wash away the sins of a wicked world, so that by the mystery of one and the same element there should be both an end of sin and a beginning of virtue: look down, O Lord, upon thy Church and multiply in her thy generations, thou who dost *make glad thy city with the rush of the flood* [Ps. 46.5] of thy grace: open the fount of baptism for the renewal of all the nations of the world, that by the command of thy majesty it may receive the grace of thy Only-begotten by the Holy Spirit: let thy

Holy Spirit by the hidden admixture of his light give fecundity to this water prepared for man's regeneration, so that, sanctification being conceived therein, there may come forth from the unspotted womb of the divine font a heavenly offspring, reborn unto a new creature: that grace may be a mother to people of every age and sex, who are brought forth into a common infancy. Therefore, O Lord, at thy command let every unclean spirit depart far hence, let all the wickedness of the wiles of the devil stand far off, let not the enemy's power haunt this place, let him not fly about to lay his snares, let him not creep secretly in, let him not corrupt with his infection. May this holy and innocent creature be free from every assault of the enemy and purified by the departure of all wickedness. May the fount be alive, the water regenerating, the wave purifying, so that all who shall be washed in this saving laver by the operation of the Holy Spirit within them may be brought to the mercy of perfect cleansing.

Wherefore I bless thee, O creature of water, through God the living, through God the holy, through God who in the beginning did separate thee by his word from the dry land and commanded thee in four rivers to water the whole earth, who in the desert gave sweetness to thy bitterness that men might drink thee, and for a thirsty people brought thee forth from the rock, I bless thee also through Jesus Christ his only Son our Lord, who in Cana of Galilee by his power in a wonderful sign did change thee into wine, who walked upon thee with his feet, and was baptized in thee by John in Jordan, who shed thee forth from his side with his blood, and commanded his disciples that believers should be baptized in thee, saying, *Go, teach all nations, baptizing them in the Name of the Father and of the Son and of the Holy Ghost* [Matt. 28.19].

24
G. 91
B. 236
A. 18

O thou Almighty God, be present of thy favour among us as we observe thy commands: do thou graciously inspire us. Bless with thy mouth these simple waters, that besides their natural purity which fits them for the washing of men's bodies they may have the power to purify their minds. May the power of thy Holy Spirit descend into all the water of this font and make the whole substance of this water fruitful with regenerating power. Here may the stains of all sins be blotted out. Here may the nature which was founded upon thine image be restored to the honour of its origin and cleansed from the filth of age, that every man that enters this sacrament of regeneration may be reborn in the new infancy of true innocence. Through our Lord Jesus Christ.

25
G. 92

26
O. 94, 95
G. 93

Then when the blessing is finished the priest pours chrism crosswise into the font, and anyone that wishes fills a vessel with the water of blessing for consecrating his house, and the people that are present are sprinkled with blessed water. Question him through the deacon, whether he believes in the Father, the Son, and the Holy Ghost.

Dost thou believe in God the Father Almighty?

Let him reply, I believe.

Dost thou believe in Jesus Christ his only Son our Lord, who was born and suffered?

Let him reply, I believe.

Dost thou believe in the Holy Ghost, the catholic Church, the remission of sins, the resurrection of the flesh?

Let him reply, I believe.

27

He goes down into the font and is dipped or sprinkled thrice: after he has been baptized, let him be anointed with chrism on his head on his forehead; and the deacon puts the white robe over his head upon his forehead and·the presbyter says:

28
G. 94
A. 23, 47
B. 249

May Almighty God, the Father of our Lord Jesus Christ, who has made thee to be regenerated *of water and the Holy Ghost* [John 3.5], and has given thee remission of all thy sins, himself anoint thee with the chrism of salvation in Christ Jesus.

29

It is here that the anointing is done.

30
B. 241

I anoint thee with the oil and the chrism of salvation and sanctification in the Name of the Father and of the Son and of the Holy Ghost, now and throughout all ages of ages.

31
B. 243

Perform thy work, creature of oil, perform thy work, in the Name of God the Father Almighty, and of the Son, and of the Holy Ghost, that no unclean spirit may lurk here, neither in the limbs nor in the inward parts nor in the frame of the body: may the power of Christ the Son of the most high God and of the Holy Ghost work in thee throughout all ages of ages.

32

And the deacon puts a white robe over his head upon his brow, and while he is clothed in the white garment the presbyter says:

33
B. 250
Goth. 263

Receive this robe, white, holy, and stainless, and bear it before the judgement seat of our Lord Jesus Christ.

Let him reply, I receive it and will bear it.

34

And the presbyter says, Let the hand of the boy be opened, *and then he says:*

Receive the sign of the cross of Christ upon thy right hand, and may it preserve thee unto eternal life.

Let him reply, Amen.[1]

Then a towel is taken and his feet are washed.   35

Alleluia. *Thy word is a lantern unto my feet, O Lord* [Ps. 119.105].
Alleluia. *Help me, Lord, and I shall be safe* [Ps. 119.117].
Alleluia. *Visit us, Lord, with thy salvation* [Ps. 106.4].
Alleluia. *Thou hast charged that we shall diligently keep thy command-
            ments* [Ps. 119.4].
           Thou has commanded thy mercy. *Despise not the works of
           thine own hands* [Ps. 138.8].

*If I, your Lord and Master, have washed your feet, ye also ought to wash
one another's feet. For I have given you an example, that ye should do to
others as I have done to you* [John 13.14].

Our Lord and Saviour Jesus Christ, on the day before he suffered,   36
took a towel, splendid, holy, and immaculate, girded his loins, poured   B. 252
water into a basin, and washed his disciples' feet. After this example of Goth. 262
our Lord Jesus Christ, do thou also the same to pilgrims and strangers
that turn to thee.

The Body and Blood of our Lord Jesus Christ: may it avail to thee   37
unto eternal life.

Refreshed with spiritual meat, restored with the heavenly food of   38
the Body and Blood of the Lord, let us give due praise and thanks to
our Lord Jesus Christ, and beseech his unwearied mercy that we may
possess the sacrament of the divine gift unto the increase of faith and
the advancement of eternal salvation. Through.

Dearly beloved brethren, let us pray for our brother N., who has   39
attained to the grace of the Lord, that he may bear the baptism which   B.253
he has received stainless and entire before the judgement seat of our   Goth. 265
Lord Jesus Christ, who, *etc.*

O God, we raise to thee our thanks that by thine aid we have   40
celebrated these holy mysteries, and we ask of thee the gifts of holiness.
Through the Lord.

---

[1]The provision of replies in sections 26, 33, 34, and the full liturgical
provision for the *pedilavium* indicate a rite at a stage when the baptism of
adults was normal, and therefore suggests that the Gallican document on which
the compiler of Stowe has drawn was relatively early.

12. *Local Councils in the West*

Councils of bishops were held from time to time in various localities to discuss matters relating to Church order and discipline. The conclusions and decisions of these councils were summarized in a code of "Canons". The canons of local councils could only command obedience in the area which was represented by the bishops who attended the council.

In some cases the canons of a number of councils in the same area were collected and codified in one body: the Gallican collection known as the *Statuta Ecclesiae Antiqua* from which some canons are translated below, is an example of this.

The following translations are made from Bruns, *Canones Apostolorum et Conciliorum*, Berlin, 1839, with the exception of the letter of Pope Innocent to Decentius, which is translated from Migne, P.L., Vol. 56, col. 513.

AFRICA

The Third Council of Carthage

Canon 5. It was agreed that no sacrament should be given to catechumens, even during the most solemn Paschal season, except the usual salt: for if the faithful make no change in the sacrament during that season, it should not be changed for catechumens.

Canon 24. It was agreed that nothing more should be offered in the sacrament of the Body and Blood of the Lord than the Lord himself delivered, that is, bread and wine mixed with water. The first fruits, milk and honey, which at the mysteries on the one solemn day are accustomed to be offered for infants, although they are offered at the altar, have their own benediction, that they may be distinguished from the sacraments of the Body and Blood of the Lord.[1]

SPAIN

The Council of Elvira, 305

Canon 38. That in cases of necessity, even laymen [fideles] *may baptize.*

[It was agreed] that a faithful man, who has held fast to his baptism and is not bigamous may baptize a sick catechumen at sea, or where

---

[1] According to Bruns, this version of Canon 24 is attested in very ancient codices: but other editions of the canons attest a quite different canon at this point.

there is no church at hand: provided that if he survives he shall bring him to a bishop so that he may be confirmed [perfici] through the laying on of a hand.

Canon 39. Concerning heathen who seek to be baptized in time of danger.

It was agreed that, when heathen men fall sick and wish to have the hand laid on them, if their life is in any way upright the hand may be laid on them, and that they may become Christians.

Canon 42. Concerning the time when those who come to the faith may be baptized.

It was agreed that those who come to the beginning of faith, if they are of good behaviour, may be admitted to the grace of baptism after two years: except when under the compulsion of sickness reason requires earlier support for the man in danger or asking for grace.

Canon 45. Concerning catechumens who do not attend church.

If a man has been made a catechumen and yet for a long [*infinita*] time has not gone to church, if any of the clergy know him to be a Christian, or if there are any witnesses to him among the faithful, it is agreed that baptism shall not be denied him in so far as he appears to have put off the old man.

Canon 48. Concerning the baptized, that the clergy shall accept no [payment].

It was agreed to amend the custom which has grown up, so that those who are baptized shall not make any payment, lest the priest seem to make a charge for what he received freely. And their feet shall not be washed by priests or by clerks (*a sacerdotibus vel clericis*: but another reading is *a sacerdotibus sed clericis*, i.e., not by priests *but* by clerks).

Canon 77. Concerning baptized people who die before they have been confirmed.

It was agreed that when a deacon who has charge of faithful people [*regens plebem*] baptizes some of them in the absence of a bishop or presbyter, it shall be the duty of the bishop to confirm [*perficere*] them: but if any depart this life before confirmation, he will be justified by virtue of the faith in which he has believed.

The First Council of Toledo, 398

Canon 20. Although the custom is almost everywhere preserved, that none but the bishop blesses chrism, yet because in some places or provinces the presbyters are said to bless chrism, it was agreed that none but the bishop shall henceforth bless chrism: and he shall send it into his diocese in such fashion that deacons and sub-deacons shall be sent from each church to the bishop before Easter, so that the chrism which the bishop has blessed shall arrive in time for Easter. While the bishops have the undoubted right to bless chrism at any time, presbyters may do nothing without the knowledge of the bishop: it is decreed that the deacon may not give chrism but the presbyter may do so in the absence of the bishop, or in his presence if he commands.

THE FOURTH COUNCIL OF TOLEDO, 633

Canon 6. Concerning the sacrament of baptism, some priests in Spain baptize candidates with three immersions and some with one: wherefore some people suppose a state of schism to exist and the unity of the faith to be broken for while differing and as it were contrary customs prevail, some people maintain that others are not baptized. We are informed by precepts of the Apostolic See what we ought to do in this diversity, following not our own but our fathers' institution. Gregory of blessed memory, Bishop of the Roman Church, who enlightened with his teaching not only Italy but more distant Churches also, when the most holy bishop Leander asked him what should be done about this diversity in Spain, replied amongst other things in these terms: "Regarding triple immersion in baptism, as you perceive yourself (and I can add no more), differing customs within the one faith of the Church can do no harm. We ourselves immerse thrice and signify thereby the three days in the tomb, so that when the child is taken from the water for the third time the resurrection after three days is expressed. Yet though it might be supposed that our practice tended towards reverence for the Trinity on high, yet no difficulty can be raised if a candidate were immersed in the water but once, since in the three persons there is but one substance; no objection can be raised, whether a child is immersed three times or once, since in three immersions the Trinity of persons is indicated and in one immersion the Unity of the Godhead. But if hitherto the heretics have been baptizing by triple immersion, I do not think that you should do the same, lest in counting the immersions they divide the Godhead, lest while they continue to do what they were doing, they may boast that they have overcome your own practice . . .". And therefore let us observe single immersion . . .

THE SEVENTEENTH COUNCIL OF TOLEDO, 732

Canon 2. At the beginning of Lent the mystery of Baptism is universally restricted, and it is necessary as the Church's custom requires that the doors of the baptistry should then be shut by the bishop's hand and sealed with his ring, and under no circumstances opened until Maundy Thursday is celebrated: the reason is that it should be universally declared by the bishop's seal that during this season baptism and sanctification cannot be administered, except in the most serious cases of necessity; and again, when the bishop opens the door it may signify the mystery of the Lord's resurrection in which an entry upon life was made for man, that as he is dead and buried with Christ in baptism, so he may rise with him again in the glory of God. And because in some churches the bishops take very little trouble to perform and preserve this holy custom, therefore through this our statement we determine and decree that it shall be preserved by the bishops throughout all Spain and Gaul, so that on the aforesaid day, that is, at the beginning of Lent, the doors of the holy baptistery shall be shut at the end of Lauds and sealed by the bishops with their rings: and they shall not be opened until Maundy Thursday is celebrated, when according to custom the altar cloths are removed. For it is not fitting that the baptistery should be open to all men at a time when it is forbidden to baptize.

THE COUNCIL OF GERONA, 517

Canon 4. That baptism is to be given only at Easter and on the Nativity of the Lord.[1]

Concerning catechumens who are to be baptized, it was decreed that, inasmuch as they do not commonly come to baptism at the celebration of Easter and the Nativity of the Lord, when the occasion gives greater solemnity to the celebration: at other festivals (*solemnitatibus*) only the sick shall be baptized, to whom baptism ought not to be denied at any time.

THE FIRST COUNCIL OF BRAGA, 563

Canon 5. Concerning the Order of Baptism.

It was also agreed that none should disregard the Order for the

---

[1] Some versions of this canon read "Pentecost" for "the Nativity of the Lord", both in the title of the canon and in its text.

administration of baptism which both formerly was observed by the metropolitan church of Braga, and which for the removal of doubt was written and sent to bishop Profuturus from the see of the most blessed Apostle Peter.

The Letter of Pope Vigilius to Profuturus, 538

Text: Migne, P.L. Vol. 69, col. 19.
This is the letter to which reference was made at the first council of Braga. The following are the relevant extracts:

2. Now concerning the performance of baptism in the accustomed way, which apostolic authority has likewise sanctioned and observes, your charity will without difficulty acknowledge those things which are set out below.

However, in our judgment this is a novel error, that whereas at the end of the psalms the custom of all catholics is to say: *Glory be to the Father and to the Son and to the Holy Spirit*, some as you judge take away one conjunctive syllable, endeavour to diminish the perfect name of the Trinity, and say: *Glory be to the Father and to the Son, to the Holy Spirit*. Therefore, although reason itself teaches us clearly that by the removal of one syllable they declare in a manner of speaking that the person of the Son and of the Holy Spirit is one; yet the words of the Lord Jesus Christ are sufficient to convince them of their error, when he declared that the baptism of believers should be performed with the invocation of the Trinity: *Go, teach all nations, baptizing them in the name of the Father and of the Son and of the Holy Spirit*. Therefore since he did not say: *In the name of the Father and of the Son, of the Holy Spirit*, but commanded that the Father and the Son and the Holy Spirit should be named with equal distinction, it follows that people who seek to remove anything from this confession deviate completely from the teaching of the Lord. And if they continue in this error, they can have no association with us . . .

6. If any bishop or priest has not baptized as the Lord commanded, in the name of the Father and of the Son and of the Holy Spirit, but in one person of the Trinity, or in two, or three, Fathers, or in three Sons, or three Paracletes, let him be cast out of the Church of God.

THE SECOND COUNCIL OF BRAGA, 572

Canon 1. That the bishop is to perambulate his diocese and catechumens are to be taught the Creed twenty days before Easter.

It seemed proper to all the bishops, and was agreed, that the bishops in every church should perambulate their dioceses and first examine their clergy, in what manner they observe the order of Baptism and the Mass, and how they observe any other rites: if their findings are satisfactory, thanks be to God: if not, they shall teach the ignorant, and particularly they shall teach that catechumens (as the ancient canons command) shall come for the cleansing of exorcism twenty days before baptism, in which twenty days they shall especially be taught the Creed, which is: I believe in God the Father Almighty . . .

FRANCE

THE FIRST COUNCIL OF ARLES, 314

Canon 8. Concerning the baptism of those who are converted from heresy.

Concerning Africans, since they have their own regulations requiring rebaptism, it was agreed that if anyone come from heresy to the church, they shall put to him the symbol questions: and if they see clearly that he has been baptized in the name of the Father and of the Son and of the Holy Spirit, it shall be sufficient to lay the hand on him that he may receive the Holy Spirit. But if when he is questioned he does not affirm this Trinity, he must be baptised.

STATUTA ECCLESIAE ANTIQUA (late fifth century)

Canon 7 (95). When an exorcist is ordained, let him receive from the bishop's hand a book, in which are written the exorcisms; while the bishop says to him: Receive [these words] and commit [them to thy memory], and have the power of laying hands upon the possessed, whether baptised or catechumens.

Canon 12 (100). Let widows and nuns who are chosen for ministering to female candidates for baptism be so instructed in their duty that they may be able in clear and sensible language to teach the uneducated and rustic women at the time of their preparation for baptism how they are to reply to the questions of him that baptizes them, and in what manner they are to live when they have been baptized.

I

Canon 85 (23). Candidates for baptism must give in their names; and having been tested [*examinati*] by long abstinence from wine and meat, and by frequent imposition of the hand, let them receive baptism.

THE FIRST COUNCIL OF ORANGE, 441

Canon 2. That the blessing with [of] chrism must not be repeated.

No minister who has the office of baptizing shall begin without chrism: for that it was agreed among us that there shall be one chrismation [in baptism]. When anyone for any reason does not receive chrism in baptism, the bishop [*sacerdos*] shall be advised of this at the confirmation. For chrism can only confer its blessing once: and we say this not to any man's prejudice, but that the repetition of chrismation should not be thought necessary.

Canon 18. That catechumens are to hear the reading of the Gospel.

It was agreed that the Gospel shall be read to catechumens in all churches in our provinces.

Canon 19. That catechumens are not to enter baptisteries.

[It was agreed that] catechumens are never to be admitted to the baptistery.

THE COUNCIL OF AGDE, 506

Canon 13. That the Creed is to be declared to the competentes *eight days before Easter.*

It was agreed by all the churches that upon one day, that is, the eighth before the day of the Lord's resurrection, the Creed should be delivered to the *competentes* publicly in church.

THE COUNCIL OF AUXERRE, 578

Canon 18. That baptism is not to be administered outside the Paschal season except to the dying.

It is forbidden to baptize at any time except the Easter service, except in the case of those who are near to death and those whom they call bedridden. And if anyone living in another district shall after this interdict contumaciously bring his children to be baptized in our churches, let them not be received, and any presbyter who shall presume to receive them shall be banned from the communion of the Church for three months.

THE SECOND COUNCIL OF MACON, 585

Canon 3. Concerning baptism, that it is to be celebrated at Easter.

We learn from our brethren that Christian people, not observing the appointed day for baptism, baptize their children on other days, and on the festivals of martyrs, so that at the holy Pascha only two or three can be found to be regenerated by water and the Holy Ghost. And therefore it is our decision that none shall henceforth be permitted to do such things, except they are compelled by serious illness or approaching death to have their children baptized: and therefore we require all men, being recalled by this present admonition from their errors or ignorance, to attend church with their children from the first Sunday of Lent, that having received the imposition of hands on certain days, and being anointed with the holy oil, they may rejoice in the festivities of the appointed day, and be regenerated by holy baptism...

ROME

THE "CANONES AD GALLOS"[1]

Canon 8. Concerning the exorcized oil, whether it should be administered on a few days or many matters less than its meaning. For who shall be cleansed by the sufficiency of his faith? For if the chrism poured upon the head imparts its grace to the whole body, in the same way also if he who is scrutinized at the third scrutiny is touched with the oil only once and not many times, God [nevertheless] acts upon his [whole] life.

THE LETTER OF POPE INNOCENT TO DECENTIUS, 416

3. Concerning the consignation of infants, it is clear that this should not be done by any but the bishop. For presbyters, although they are priests, have not attained the highest rank of the pontificate. The right of bishops alone to seal and to deliver the Spirit the Paraclete is proved not only by the custom of the Church but also by that reading in the Acts of the Apostles which tells how Peter and John were directed to deliver the Holy Spirit to people who were already baptized. For it is

---

[1] These canons are the reply of a Roman synod, c. 400, to a request from certain French bishops for advice on particular matters: the terms of the request are not known.

permissible for presbyters, either in the absence of a bishop, or when they baptize in his presence, to anoint the baptized with chrism, but only with such as has been consecrated by the bishop: and even then they are not to sign the brow with that oil, for this is reserved to bishops alone when they deliver the Spirit the Paraclete.

13. The Sarum Rite [1]

We have here translated the text of the Order for the making of a Catechumen, the Blessing of the Font, Baptism and Confirmation, published by A. J. Collins in 1960 in his *Manuale ad usum percelebris ecclesiae Sarisburiensis* (Henry Bradshaw Society, XCIX). He says (p. xxi) that his text is based chiefly on the edition of the *Manual* printed in Rouen in 1543, the last edition to be published before the introduction of the first English Prayer Book in 1549. Hence the initiatory rite in this book is that which was in use in many parts of England on the eve of the Reformation, and it reflects the pastoral situation which Cranmer and his colleagues had known all their lives when they addressed themselves to the task of revising the offices of baptism and confirmation.

THE ORDER FOR THE MAKING OF A CATECHUMEN [2]

The order for the making of a catechumen.

First let the infant be brought to the doors of the church: and let the priest ask of the midwife whether the infant is a male or female. Then if the infant has been baptized at home: and by what name he is to be called.

Let a male be set on the right of the priest: but a female on his left. When these questions have been asked let him make the sign of the cross with his thumb on the forehead of the infant, saying this: The sign of our Saviour and Lord Jesus Christ I place upon thy forehead. *And afterwards on his breast, saying thus:* The sign of our Saviour and Lord Jesus Christ I place upon thy breast. [3]

---

[1] This section reproduces the text and notes of pp. 158-81 of J. D. C. Fisher's *Christian Initiation: Baptism in the Medieval West.*

[2] ed. cit., p. 25. [3] *Rituale* Romanum of 1487: not in the *Gelasianum.*

Then holding his right hand upon the head of the infant, let him say: The
Lord be with you. *And*

Let us pray.[1]

G.19 Almighty and everlasting God, the Father of our Lord Jesus Christ,
vouchsafe to look upon this thy servant (*or* this thine handmaid),
(*Here first let the priest ask the name of the infant: and let the godparents
reply.*) N., whom thou hast vouchsafed to call to the first beginnings of
faith: all blindness of heart drive from him (*or* her): break all the bonds
of Satan with which he (*or* she) was bound. Open to him (*or* her), O
Lord, the door of thy goodness, so that, wearing the sign of thy wisdom, he (*or* she) may be free from the defilements of all fleshly lusts:
and rejoicing in the sweet odour of thy commandments may serve
thee in thy Church, and may advance in goodness from day to day, so
that he (*or* she) may be made worthy to attain to the grace of thy
baptism having received thy medicine; through the same Christ our
Lord. Amen.

Then let this prayer be said without The Lord be with you: *but with*
Let us pray.

PRAYER[2]

G.20 We beseech thee, Lord, mercifully to hear our prayers: and this thine
elect (*Here let the godfathers and godmothers name the child*) N. do thou
guard with the power of the Lord's cross, with the imprint of which
(*Here let the priest make a cross on the forehead of the infant*) we sign him
(*or* her): so that preserving the first beginnings of the worship of thy
majesty, through the keeping of thy commandments he (*or* she) may
be found meet to enter the glory of the new birth. Through Christ our
Lord. Amen.

PRAYER[3]

Let us pray.

G.21 O God, who didst create the human race in such wise that thou
mightest also restore it, look in mercy upon thine adopted people:
and within the new covenant place the children of thy new race, so
that that which they could not obtain by nature the sons of promise
may rejoice that they have received through grace. Through our
Lord.

---

[1] *Gel.*, n. 285.   [2] *Gel.*, n. 286.   [3] *Gel.*, n. 287.

The exorcism of salt without Let us pray.[1]

I exorcize thee, creature of salt, in the name of God the Father almighty, and in the love of our Lord Jesus Christ, and in the power of the Holy Spirit. I exorcize thee by the living God, by the true God, by the holy God, by the God who created thee for the protection of the human race, and ordered thee to be consecrated by his servants for the people that comes to faith, so that thou mayest be made a saving sacrament for putting to flight the adversary. Therefore we ask thee, O Lord our God, that this creature of salt (*Here let the priest look at the salt*) thou wouldest sanctify ✠ and bless ✠, so that for all who receive it it may become a perfect medicine remaining in their bowels, in the power of the same our Lord Jesus Christ, who is to come to judge the quick and the dead and the world by fire.

G.22

R. Amen.

Afterwards let the priest ask the name of the child, and let some of the salt be placed in his (or her) mouth as he says:[2]

G.23

N. receive the salt of wisdom for a propitiation of God unto eternal life. Amen.

After the salt has been given, let the priest say over a male or a female: The Lord be with you. *And* Let us pray.

PRAYER[3]

O God of our fathers, God who hast established every creature, we thy suppliants beseech thee that thou wouldest vouchsafe to look favourably upon this thy servant (*or this* thine handmaid) N., and suffer him (*or her*) that tastes this first morsel of salt to hunger only until he is filled with heavenly food: wherefore may he be always, O Lord, fervent in spirit, rejoicing in hope, serving thy name; and lead him (*or her*) to the laver of new regeneration, so that with thy faithful people he (*or she*) may be found meet to receive the eternal rewards of thy promises. Through our Lord.

G.24

Let this prayer follow over a male only, without The Lord be with you, *but with* Let us pray. (*For a female child turn over.*)[4]

God of Abraham, God of Isaac, God of Jacob, God who didst appear to thy servant Moses on mount Sinai, and didst lead thy children Israel

G.25

---

[1] *Gel.*, n. 288.   [2] *Gel.*, n. 289.
[3] *Gel.*, n. 290.   [4] *Gel.*, n. 291.

out of the land of Egypt, appointing for them the angel of thy mercy, who should guard them by day and by night, we beseech thee, Lord, that thou wouldest vouchsafe to send thy holy angel from heaven, that he may likewise guard this thy servant N. and lead him to the grace of thy baptism.

Without Through Christ.

Adjuration over a male without The Lord be with you, *and without* Let us pray, *the priest saying thus:*[1]

G.26   Therefore, accursed devil, hearken to thy sentence, and give honour to the living and true God: give honour to Jesus Christ his Son and to the Holy Spirit, and depart from this servant of God N. because our God and Lord Jesus Christ has vouchsafed to call him to himself by the gift of the Holy Spirit to his holy grace and blessing and to the fount of baptism. And this sign of the holy cross, (*Here let the priest make the sign of the cross on the forehead of the infant with his thumb, saying thus:*) which we place upon his forehead, do thou, accursed devil, never dare to violate. Through him who is to come to judge the quick and the dead and the world by fire.

   R. Amen.

This following prayer is said over a male only without The Lord be with you, *and without* Let us pray.

O God, the immortal defence of all that beg, the deliverer of those that beseech, the peace of those that ask, the life of those that believe, the resurrection of the dead, I invoke thee upon this thy servant N. who, seeking the gift of thy baptism, desires to obtain eternal grace by spiritual regeneration. Receive him, Lord: and because thou hast vouchsafed to say, Ask and ye shall receive, seek and ye shall find, knock and it shall be opened unto you, grant a reward to him that asks, and open the door to him that knocks, so that having obtained the eternal blessing of the heavenly washing, he may receive the promised kingdom of thy bounty, who livest and reignest with God the Father in the unity of the Holy Spirit God, throughout all ages.

   R. Amen.

Adjuration over a male only, without The Lord be with you, *and without* Let us pray, *thus:*[2]

G.28   Hearken, accursed Satan, adjured by the name of the eternal God and

1 *Gel.*, n. 292.   2 *Gel.*, n. 294.

our Saviour his Son: with thy envy thou has been conquered: trembling and groaning depart: let there be nothing common to thee and to this servant of God N. who now ponders upon heavenly things, who is about to renounce thee and thy world, and is about to live in blessed immortality. Give honour therefore to the Holy Spirit as he draws near, who descending from the highest arch of heaven, having confounded thy deceits, will make his breast cleansed in the divine fount and sanctified into a temple and dwelling-place for God, so that, inwardly set free from all the hurts of his past sins, this servant of God may ever give thanks to the everlasting God, and bless his holy name throughout all ages. Amen.

Exorcism over a male only, without Let us pray.[1]

I exorcize thee, unclean spirit, in the name of God the Father, and of   G.30
the Son, and of the Holy Ghost, that thou come out and depart from this servant of God (*look upon him*) N. for he himself commands thee, accursed one, damned and to be damned, even he who walked on his feet on the sea, and stretched out his right hand to Peter as he was sinking.

Let this adjuration follow.

Therefore, accursed one, *as above.*

Let this prayer following be said over a female only, without The Lord be with you, *and without* Let us pray.[2]

God of heaven, God of earth, God of angels, God of archangels, God   G.27
of patriarchs, God of prophets, God of apostles, God of martyrs, God of confessors, God of virgins, God of all that live good lives, God whom every tongue confesses and before whom every knee bows, of things in heaven and things on earth and things under the earth, I invoke thee, Lord, upon this thine handmaid (*look upon her*) N. that thou mightest vouchsafe to lead her to the grace of thy baptism.

Let this adjuration follow over a female.

Therefore, accursed devil, hearken to thy sentence, and give honour   G.26
to the living and true God: give honour to Jesus Christ his Son and to the Holy Spirit, and depart from this handmaid of God N. because our God and Lord Jesus Christ has vouchsafed to call her to himself by the gift of the Holy Spirit to his holy grace and blessing and to the fount of baptism. And this sign of the holy ✠ cross, (*Here let the priest*

---

[1] *Gel.*, n. 296.   [2] *Gel.*, n. 293.

make the sign of the cross on the forehead of the infant with his thumb, saying) which we place upon her forehead, do thou, accursed devil, never dare to violate. Through him who is to come to judge the quick and the dead and the world by fire.

R. Amen.

The following prayer is said over a female only without The Lord be with you, *and without* Let us pray.[1]

G.29   God of Abraham, God of Isaac, God of Jacob, God who didst set free the tribes of Israel from bondage in Egypt, and through Moses thy servant didst admonish them in the desert to keep thy commandments, and didst free Susanna from a false accusation, I humbly beseech thee, O Lord, that thou wouldest also set free this thine handmaid N. (*look upon her*) and vouchsafe to lead her to the grace of thy baptism.

Let this adjuration follow.

Therefore, accursed, *as above.*

Exorcism over a female only, without The Lord be with you, *and without* Let us pray.

PRAYER[2]

G.31   I exorcize thee, unclean spirit, by the Father and the Son and the Holy Ghost, that thou come out and depart from this handmaid of God, (*look upon her*) N. for he himself commands thee, accursed one, damned and to be damned, who opened the eyes of the man that was born blind, and on the fourth day raised Lazarus from the tomb.

Let this adjuration follow. Therefore, accursed one, *as above.*

Then both over males and females let the following prayers be said, without The Lord be with you, *and without* Let us pray.

Here let the priest make a cross with his thumb on the forehead of the infant, and holding his hand upon his head let him say:[3]

G.32   I beseech thine eternal and most just goodness, O holy Lord, almighty Father, everlasting God, author of light and truth, look upon this thy servant (*or this thine handmaid*), (*look upon him*) N. that thou wouldest vouchsafe to illuminate him (*or her*) with the light of thine understanding. Cleanse and sanctify him (*or her*): give him (*or her*) true knowledge, so that he (*or she*) may be made meet to come to the

---

[1] *Gel.*, n. 295.   [2] *Gel.*, n. 297.   [3] *Gel.*, n. 298.

grace of thy baptism: let him (*or* her) keep a firm hope, a right counsel, a holy doctrine, so that he (*or* she) may be fit to receive the grace of thy baptism. Through Christ our Lord.

Without Let us pray.

Let this prayer follow.[1]

Be not deceived, Satan, punishment threatens thee: torments threaten thee: the day of judgement threatens thee, that day of eternal punishment, that day which is about to come as a fiery furnace, in which eternal death will overtake thee and all thine angels. And therefore for thy wickedness, thou that art damned and to be damned, give honour to the living and true God: give honour to Jesus Christ his Son: give honour to the Holy Spirit the Paraclete, in whose name and power I command thee, whoever thou art, to come out and depart from this servant of God (*or* from this handmaid of God), (*look upon him*) N. whom to-day the same God and our Lord Jesus Christ has vouchsafed to call to his holy grace and blessing and to the fount of baptism, so that he (*or* she) may become his temple through the water of regeneration, unto the remission of all his (*or* her) sins. In the name of the same our Lord Jesus Christ, who is to come to judge the quick and the dead and the world by fire.

R. Amen.

G.70

When these things have been said, let the priest say:

The Lord be with you. And with thy spirit.

THE GOSPEL ACCORDING TO MATTHEW

At that time little children were presented to Jesus . . . And when he had laid his hand upon them, he departed thence.

Then let the priest spit in his left hand, and let him touch the ears and nose of the infant with his right thumb with saliva saying in his right ear,[2] Effeta, which is Be opened. *On his nose.* Unto the odour of sweetness. *In his left ear.* Be thou put to flight, O devil, for the judgement of God is at hand.

G.71

Afterwards let the priest say to the godfathers and godmothers together with all that stand about, that they themselves must say in order, Our Father, *and* Hail Mary, *and* I believe in God.

[1] *Gel.,* n. 419.   [2] *Gel.,* n. 420.

*Which also let the priest himself say with all listening reverently and distinctly
thus:*

Our Father who art in heaven, hallowed be thy name: thy kingdom
come: thy will be done on earth as it is in heaven: give us this day our
daily bread: and forgive us our trespasses as we forgive them that trespass
against us: and lead us not into temptation: but deliver us from evil. Amen.

Hail Mary, full of grace, the Lord is with thee: blessed art thou among
women, and blessed is the fruit of thy womb Jesus. Amen.

I believe in God the Father almighty, maker of heaven and earth, and
in Jesus Christ, his only Son, our Lord, who was conceived by the
Holy Ghost, born of the virgin Mary, suffered under Pontius Pilate,
was crucified, dead and buried: he descended into hell: the third day
he rose from the dead: he ascended into heaven, sitteth on the right
hand of God the Father almighty: thence he shall come to judge the
quick and the dead. I believe in the Holy Ghost, the holy catholic
Church, the communion of saints, the forgiveness of sins, the resurrection of the flesh, the life everlasting. Amen.

*When these have been said let the priest make the sign of the cross on the
right hand of the infant, having asked his name, saying thus:*[1]

S 34   N. I give thee the sign of our Lord Jesus Christ on thy right hand, that
thou mayest sign thyself and keep thyself from adversity and remain in
the catholic faith and have eternal life and life for ever and ever.
R. Amen.

Next let the priest say in blessing the infant thus:

The blessing of God the Father almighty and of the Son and of the
Holy Ghost descend upon thee, and remain with thee always.
R. Amen.

*Next let him introduce the catechumen by the right hand into the church,
having asked his (or her) name, saying:*

N. enter into the temple of God, that thou mayest have eternal life,
and live for ever and ever. Amen.

THE BLESSING OF THE FONT

*When the font is to be cleansed and renewed with fresh water, (which often
ought to be done because water grows stale) then let the following litany be*

[1] cf. *Stowe Missal*, ed. Warner, p. 32.

said: and let the font be blessed in the following manner. And note that the water of baptism must not be changed in deference to somebody of distinction, unless it has become stale.

Note that the consecrated water of the fonts at the vigil of Easter and of Pentecost is not to be sprinkled in the church, but other water blessed in the customary manner as on other Sundays.

It must be borne in mind that holy water is to be sprinkled round the fonts, but not the water of the fonts, whether it has been consecrated with chrism or not. For in the original decrees of the holy Fathers, Popes Clement and Paschasius, it is found that the water of the fonts is not water for sprinkling, but for baptism and purification. Wherefore let every priest take care that with that water he only touches those whom he baptizes, because there is no need for those who have been baptized to be baptized again. Therefore let the foolish and presumptuous sprinkling both at the vigil of Easter and of Pentecost cease, and on all other days, because through the Roman Church it is forbidden to all Christians under the pain of the greater excommunication.

Here the litany begins in this manner.[1]

Goodfaders and goodmoders and all that be here about, say in the worshyppe of god and our ladye and of the xii apostellys an *Our Father*, and *Hail Mary*, and *I believe in God*, that we may so mynyster thys blessed sacrament, that yt may be to the pleasure of almyghty god, and confusyon of our gostly enmy, and salvacyon of te sowle of thys chylde.

God faders and godmodyrs of thys chylde whe charge you that ye charge the foder and te moder to kepe it from fyer and water and other perels to the age of vii yere, and that he lerne or se yt be lerned the *Our Father*, *Hail Mary*, and *I believe*, after the lawe of all holy churche and in all goodly haste to be confermed of my lorde of the dyocise or of hys depute and that the moder brynge ayen the crysom at hyr puryfcation and washe your hande or ye departe the chyrche.

The Litanies follow.

Lord, have mercy.

Christ, have mercy.

Christ, hear us.

O God the Father, of heaven, have mercy upon us.

G.88
G.89

---

[1] In view of this rubric it is evident that this following section in the vernacular is a later interpolation.

O God the Son, redeemer of the world, have mercy upon us.

O God the Holy Ghost, have mercy upon us.

O Holy Trinity, one God, have mercy upon us.

Holy Mary, pray for us.

Holy Mother of God, pray.

Holy virgin of virgins, pray.

Holy Michael, pray.

Holy Gabriel, pray.

Holy Raphael, pray.

All ye holy angels and archangels of God, pray for us.

All the holy orders of blessed spirits, pray for us.

Holy John Baptist, pray for us.

All the holy patriarchs and prophets, pray.

Holy Peter, pray.

Holy Paul, pray.

Holy Andrew, pray.

Holy John, pray.

Holy James, pray.

Holy Thomas, pray.

Holy Philip, pray.

Holy James, pray.

Holy Matthew, pray.

Holy Bartholomew, pray.

Holy Simon, pray.

Holy Thaddaeus, pray.

Holy Matthias, pray.

Holy Barnabas, pray.

Holy Mark, pray.

Holy Luke, pray.

All the holy apostles and evangelists, pray.

All the holy disciples and innocents, pray.

Holy Stephen, pray.

Holy Linus, pray.

Holy Cletus, pray.

Holy Clement, pray.

Holy Fabian, pray.

Holy Sebastian, pray.

Holy Cosmas, pray.

Holy Damian, pray.

Holy Primus, pray.

Holy Felician, pray.

Holy Dionysius with thy companions, pray.

Holy Victor with thy companions, pray.

All the holy martyrs, pray for us.

Holy Silvester, pray.

Holy Leo, pray.

Holy Jerome, pray.

Holy Augustine, pray.

Holy Isidore, pray.

Holy Julian, pray.

Holy Gildard, pray.

Holy Medard, pray.

Holy Albinus, pray.

Holy Eusebius, pray.

Holy Swithun, pray.

Holy Birinus, pray.

All the holy confessors, pray.

All the holy monks and hermits, pray.

Holy Mary Magdalene, pray.

Holy Mary of Egypt, pray.

Holy Margaret, pray.

Holy Scholastica, pray.

Holy Petronella, pray.

Holy Genoveve, pray.

Holy Praxedis, pray.

Holy Sotheris, pray.

Holy Prisca, pray.

Holy Thecla, pray.

Holy Affra, pray.

Holy Edith, pray.

All the holy virgins, pray.

All the saints, pray.

So when these litanies have been finished, let the priest come to the consecration of the fonts, which is always said without chant, save only at the vigil of Easter and of Pentecost, for then a second litany having been sung, let the priest begin at this place and sing in a moderate voice thus:

> The Lord be with you
> And with thy spirit.
> Let us pray.[1]

G.89 Almighty and everlasting God, be present at the mysteries of thy great goodness: be present at these sacraments, and for the recreation of the new people whom the fount of baptism brings forth for thee, send forth the Spirit of adoption, so that what is performed by our humble mystery [ministration?] may be completed by the working of thy power. Through our Lord Jesus Christ thy Son, who with thee liveth and reigneth in the unity of the Holy Spirit God. (*Here he changes his voice after the manner of a preface, thus:*) For ever and ever. Amen.

> The Lord be with you.
> And with thy spirit.
>
> Lift up your hearts.
> We lift them up unto the Lord.
>
> Let us give thanks unto our Lord God.
> It is meet and right.

G.90 It is very meet, right, just and salutary, that we should at all times and in all places give thanks unto thee, O holy Lord, almighty Father, everlasting God,[2] who by thine invisible power dost wonderfully bring to pass the effect of thy sacraments. And although we are unworthy to perform such great mysteries, yet do thou, not forsaking

---

[1] *Gel.*, n. 444.   [2] *Gel.*, n. 445.

the gifts of thy grace, incline the ears of thy goodness even to our prayers. God, whose Spirit was borne upon the waters at the very beginning of the world so that even now the nature of water might conceive the power of sanctification, God, who washing away the sins of a guilty world by water didst signify a type of regeneration by the outpouring of the flood, so that by the mystery of one and the same element there might be both an end of vices and a beginning of virtues, look, we beseech thee, Lord, upon the face of thy Church, and multiply in her thy regeneration, thou who dost make glad thy city with the rush of the flood of thy grace, and openest the fount of baptism for the renewing of all the nations in the whole world so that by the command of thy majesty it may receive the grace of thine only-begotten by the Holy Spirit. (*Here let the priest divide the water with his right hand in the form of a cross thus*:) May the same Holy Spirit make fruitful this water prepared for the regeneration of men by the secret admixture of his light, so that sanctification having been conceived in it from the immaculate womb of the divine font a heavenly offspring may come forth reborn unto a new creature, and that all those who are different either in sex or in age grace may bring forth as a mother unto the same infancy. At thy command, therefore, O Lord, let every unclean spirit depart far from hence: let all the wickedness of the devil's deceit be removed away. Let the adverse power have no part here, nor fly around to ensnare, nor secretly creep in, nor corrupt with its infection. Be this holy and innocent creature free from every onset of the enemy and purged by the departure of all wickedness. Be this fount living, this water regenerating, this wave purifying, so that all who are to be washed in this saving laver by the operation of the Holy Spirit in them, may obtain the favour of a perfect cleansing.[1] Therefore I bless thee ✠ , creature of water, through the living ✠ God, through the true ✠ God, through the holy ✠ God, through the God who in the beginning separated thee by his word from the dry land, whose Spirit was borne upon thee, who made thee to flow from paradise, and commanded thee to water the whole earth in four rivers, (*Here let the priest cast some water from the font in four directions with his right hand in the form of a cross.*) who in the desert giving sweetness to thy bitterness made thee good to drink, and for a thirsting people brought thee forth from a rock. I bless thee ✠ through Jesus Christ his only Son our Lord, who in Cana of Galilee in a wonderful sign by his own power

G.91

---

[1] *Gel.*, n. 446.

turned thee into wine, who with his feet walked upon thee and was baptized in thee by John in the Jordan, who shed thee together with blood from his side, and gave command to his disciples that those who believed should be baptized in thee saying, Go, teach all nations baptizing them in the name of the ✠ Father and of the ✠ Son and of the Holy ✠ Ghost. (*Here let the priest change his voice as if reading and say thus:*) With us as we observe these commandments do thou, O God almighty, mercifully be present, do thou favourably inspire us. (*Here let the priest breathe three times into the font in the form of a cross: then let him say as if reading thus:*) Do thou with thy mouth bless these simple waters, so that besides the natural cleansing which they can impart for the washing of men's bodies they may be also able to purify their minds. (*Here let the priest drop wax from a candle in the font in the form of a cross: next let him say as if reading a preface:*) May there descend into the fullness of this font the virtue of the Holy Spirit,[1] and may it make the whole substance of this water fruitful with the power to regenerate. (*Here let the priest divide the water with the candle in the form of a cross saying:*) Here be the stains of all sins blotted out. Here may the nature created in thine image and restored to the honour of its beginning be cleansed from every filth of age, (*Here let the priest lift the candle from the water: and let him deliver it to a cleric by whom it shall be held before the fonts until the whole preface is finished.*) so that every man who enters into this sacrament of regeneration may be reborn in a new infancy of true innocence. (*Here let him change his voice as if reading.*) Through our Lord Jesus Christ, thy Son, who with thee liveth and reigneth in the unity of the same Spirit God for ever and ever. Amen.

At the vigils of Easter and Pentecost this office should not be continued further, unless there were somebody to be baptized, as will be shown later.

Note that at the vigil of Easter and of Pentecost when the fonts have been consecrated neither oil nor chrism shall be poured into them, unless there be present some who are to be baptized: but let them be covered with a clean cloth, and kept until the end of the Paschal or Pentecostal season, so that, if it happen that during those days someone comes to be baptized, then the fonts may be made fruitful and sanctified by the infusion of oil and chrism, and he may be baptized.

[1] *Gel.,* n. 448.

After this let the priest pour holy oil with the rod[1] *which is in its vessel into the water, making the sign of the cross and saying:*

The admixture of the oil of unction and the water of baptism. In the name of the Father and of the Son and of the Holy Ghost. Amen.

In like manner let him put chrism in the water saying:[2]

Be this font made fruitful and sanctified with this saving chrism of salvation. In the name of the Father, *etc.*

Next let him put in together oil and chrism in the aforesaid manner, saying:

The admixture of the chrism of sanctification and the oil of unction and the water of baptism. In the name of the Father, *etc.*

CONCERNING BAPTISM

Then let the infant be carried to the fonts by those who are to receive him at baptism, they themselves holding the child in their hands over the fonts: and let the priest place his right hand over him: and his name being asked, let those who hold him reply, N. So let the priest say:

N. dost thou renounce Satan?[3]   G.72

Let the godfathers and godmothers reply:

I renounce.

Again the priest asks:

And all his works?

R. I renounce.

[1] "cum ipsa billione quae est in vase ejus." H. A. Wilson (*Officium Ecclesiasticum Abbatum secundum usum Eveshamensis Monasterii*, H. Bradshaw Soc., VI, London, 1896, p. 201) says that the *billio* was a small metal rod, kept in a *vas* or *ampulla*; it was used, it seems, to remove the oil from the *vas* into the font. The author is indebted to Dr F. J. E. Raby and Professor E. C. Ratcliff for this information concerning the meaning of the word *billio*.

[2] The evidence of the Evesham book, to which we have just referred, suggests that another *billio* was used at this point. Wilson gives no authority for his statement that the *billio* was a small metal rod; a small spoon with a long handle would, it seems, have served better. It is not clear whether the use of a *billio* is prescribed merely for practical convenience or out of reverence for the holy oils so that the priest should not have to touch them with his fingers. However this may be, in an earlier age *Ordo Romanus XI* (n. 94, ed. Andrieu, op. cit., II, p. 445) shows no such scruple, the pope, in consecrating the font, being ordered to mix the chrism with the water with his hand.

[3] *Gel.*, n. 421.

Again the priest:

And all his pomps?

R. I renounce.

Next let the priest touch the breast of the infant and between his shoulders with holy oil making the cross with his thumb saying:

N. I also anoint thee *upon the breast* with the oil of salvation, *between the shoulders*, in Christ Jesus our Lord that thou mayest have eternal life and live for ever and ever. Amen.

Then his name being asked let them reply N. Again the priest:

G.93　N. dost thou believe in God the Father almighty maker of heaven and earth?[1]

Let them reply: I believe.

Again the priest:

Dost thou believe also in Jesus Christ his only Son our Lord, who was born and suffered?

Let them reply:

I believe.

Again the priest:

Dost thou believe also in the Holy Ghost, the holy catholic Church, the communion of saints, the remission of sins, the resurrection of the flesh and eternal life after death?

Let them reply:

I believe.

Then let the priest ask the name of the infant saying:

What seekest thou?

Let them reply:

Baptism.

Again the priest:

Dost thou wish to be baptized?

Let them reply:

I wish.

[1] *Gel.*, n. 449.

Then let the priest receive the infant sideways in his hands: and having asked his name let him baptize him with a threefold dipping invoking the Holy Trinity once saying thus:

N. I also baptize thee in the name of the Father (*and let him dip him once with his face turned towards the north and his head towards the east*) and of the Son (*and again let him dip him once with his face turned towards the south*) and of the Holy Ghost. Amen (*and let him dip him the third time with his face towards the water*).

Then let the godparents re ceiving the infant from the hands of the priest raise him from the font. But when he has come up from the font let the priest take some chrism with his thumb, saying:

> The Lord be with you, *and*
> Let us pray.

PRAYER[1]

Almighty God, the Father of our Lord Jesus Christ, who hath regene-   G.94
rated thee by water and the Holy Ghost, and who hath given thee
remission of all thy sins (*here let him anoint the infant with the chrism with
his thumb on the head in the form of a cross, saying*) himself anoints thee
with the chrism of salvation in the same his Son our Lord Jesus Christ
unto eternal life.

Next let the infant be clad in his chrismal robe, the priest asking his name and saying thus:[2]

N. receive a white robe, holy and unstained, which thou must bring   Goth.263
before the tribunal of our Lord Jesus Christ, that thou mayest have   B.250
eternal life and live for ever and ever. Amen.   S.73

It is permitted to anoint the chrismal cloth with chrism a second time, and place it upon another baptized person: but the cloth must not be put to common uses, but brought back to the church, and kept for the uses of the church.

Then having asked the name let him place a burning candle in the hand of the infant, saying:

N. receive a lamp burning and without fault: guard thy baptism: keep the commandments, so that when the Lord comes to the wedding thou mayest meet him together with the saints in the heavenly hall, that thou mayest have eternal life, and live for ever and ever. Amen.

If a bishop is present he must immediately be confirmed and next communi-cated, if his age require it, the priest saying:

[1] *Gel.*, n. 450.   [2] *Rit. Rom.*, 1487.

The body of our Lord Jesus Christ preserve thy body and thy soul unto eternal life. Amen.

If he be an infant let the father and mother be enjoined to preserve their child from fire and water and all other dangers until the age of seven years: and if they do it not, the godfathers and godmothers are held responsible. Likewise the godmothers should be enjoined to teach the infant the Our Father, *and* Hail Mary, *and* I believe in God, *or cause them to be taught them, and to see that the chrismal be brought back to the church, and that the infant be confirmed as soon as the bishop comes within a distance of seven miles.*

Then let the following gospel be said over the infant if it seems good, because according to doctors it is a good protection against falling sickness.[1]

The Lord be with you.
R. And with thy spirit.

THE CONTINUATION OF THE HOLY GOSPEL
ACCORDING TO MARK

R. Glory be to thee, O Lord.

At that time replying one of the crowd said to Jesus, Master, I have brought my son to thee ... This kind can in no wise come out but by prayer and fasting.   (Mark 9.17–29)

And next let this gospel following be said in the aforesaid form namely, According to John.

In the beginning was the Word ... And we beheld his glory, the glory as of the only begotten of the Father, full of grace and truth. (John 1.1–14)

It must be noted that every parish priest must frequently on Sundays explain to his parishioners the form of baptizing in pure, natural and fresh water, and in no other liquid, so that if necessity arise they may know how to baptize infants according to the form of the Church, using the form of words of baptism in their mother tongue distinctly and openly and in an even voice in no wise repeating those words that are properly said once or similar words in addition to the same, but without any addition, subtraction, interpolation, alteration, corruption or transposition saying thus: I cristene the N, in the name of the fadir and of the sone and of the holy gost. Amen: *or in the Latin tongue thus*, Ego baptizo te N. in nomine patris et filii et spiritus sancti.

----

[1] i.e., epilepsy.

Amen. *Sprinkling water upon the infant or dipping him in the water three times or at least once.*

And if a child has been baptized according to that form, let everybody take care that he do not baptize him again: but if infants of this sort recover, let them be taken to church, and let there be said over them the exorcisms and catechisms with the unctions and all other things aforesaid except the dipping in water and the form of baptism which are on all account to be omitted, namely: What seekest thou? and from there to that point where the priest has to anoint the infant with chrism.

And therefore if a lay person has baptized a child before he is brought to the church let the priest ask carefully what he said and what he did: and if he finds that the layman has baptized discreetly and in the required manner and used completely the form of words of baptism as above in his own language, let him approve of what has been done, and not rebaptize him. But if the priest is in reasonable doubt whether an infant presented to him for baptism has already been baptized in the required form or not, he must do everything with that child as with another who is known not to have been baptized, except that he must use the essential sacramental words conditionally saying thus: N. if thou art baptized I do not rebaptize thee: but if thou art not yet baptized, I baptize thee in the Name of the Father and of the Son and of the Holy Ghost. Amen, *with aspersion or dipping as above.* And it is to be observed in regard both to baptism and confirmation that whenever there is doubt they be conferred without hesitation, because that is not said to be repeated which is not known to have been conferred: and therefore exposed infants whose baptism is in reasonable doubt should be baptized according to the aforesaid form, whether they be found with salt or without salt.[1]

It is to be noted also that if an infant be in danger of death, then first he should be brought to the font, and then baptized beginning at this place: "What seekest thou?" and if he lives after baptism he should have all the remainder of the service aforesaid.

Moreover this should be observed in every sacrament that whenever danger seems to threaten, a beginning should be made at the substance of that sacrament and afterwards the remainder should be completed if possible.

It is not lawful to baptize someone in a hall or apartment or some other private place, but only in churches in which there are fonts specially appointed for this purpose, unless it be the child of a king or prince, or such necessity have arisen that it is not possible to come to church without risk.

---

[1] Salt found beside a foundling was a sign that the child had been baptized; see Collins, op. cit., pp. 39f.

Moreover if possible let a presbyter have always a font of stone whole and decent for baptizing: but if he cannot, let him have a vessel suitable for baptism which may on no account be put to other uses nor taken outside the church.

Solemn baptism is customarily celebrated on the Saturday before Easter and at the vigil of Pentecost: and therefore children born within eight days of Easter or within eight days of Pentecost must be reserved for baptism on Easter Eve or on the vigil of Pentecost, if conveniently and without risk they can be reserved, in such wise that during the interval between the birth of the children and their baptism they receive the complete catechism: and on the aforesaid days when the fonts have been consecrated only the dipping is to be done.

Others however who happen to be born at other times of the year, when they have been born weak, on account of the mortal peril which often hangs over children unforeseen, should be baptized.

But on Easter Eve and the vigil of Pentecost when the consecration of the fonts is performed neither oil nor chrism shall be poured in, nor may the office of baptism be proceeded with further, unless someone happen to be present to be baptized: but they should be covered with a clean cloth and reserved until the end of the season of Easter or Pentecost, so that if during those days someone come to be baptized the fonts may be made fruitful and consecrated with the infusion of oil and chrism, and he may be baptized.

And note that the people should never be sprinkled with the water consecrated in the baptismal font on Easter Eve or the vigil of Pentecost either after the chrismation of the water or before.

It is not lawful for a layman or a woman to baptize someone, save in the constraint of necessity. But if a man and a woman should be present when the need to baptize a child became urgent, and no other minister more suitable for this task were present, let the man baptize and not the woman, unless the woman happened to know well the sacramental words and not the man, or there were some other impediment.

Likewise the father or the mother must not raise their own child from the sacred font, nor baptize him, save in the constraint of extreme necessity: for then they can well baptize him without prejudice to their conjugal bond, unless there was someone else who knew how to do this and was willing.

Further a man and wife must not together raise the child of another person from the sacred font. No religious may be admitted as godfathers, which prohibition is also to be observed in the case of nuns.

Men and women who receive children at baptism are appointed their sureties before God, and therefore must frequently admonish them when they are grown or capable of discipline, that they guard their chastity, love justice, hold to charity, and above all things are bound to teach them the Lord's Prayer and angelic salutation, the symbol of the faith and how to sign themselves with the sign of the cross.

Wherefore persons are not to be received nor admitted as godparents except those who know the aforesaid things, because godparents must instruct their spiritual children in the faith, which they cannot do unless they themselves have first been instructed in the faith.

If a person to be baptized cannot speak either because he is an infant, or because he is dumb, or because he is sick or for any other cause incapable, then the godparents must reply for him to all the questions in baptism. If however he can speak, then let him reply on his own behalf to each of the questions except only those about his name, to which always his godparents reply for him.

Those who raise children from the font must not present them before the bishop in confirmation unless need compel. Not more than one man and one woman must come to receive an infant from the sacred font: wherefore if more come together for this purpose, they err in acting contrary to the prohibition in the canon unless another custom has been approved: but more than three persons for this should on no account be accepted.

The laity are also to be warned that their infant children having been confirmed should on the third day after their confirmation be brought to church, and their foreheads should be washed in the baptistery by the hands of the priest out of reverence for the chrism, and their linen bands should then be burned with fire.

Also no one must be admitted to the sacrament of the body and blood of Christ save in danger of death, unless he has been confirmed or has been reasonably prevented from receiving the sacrament of confirmation.

A parish priest must not be without chrism: but every parish priest must every year before Easter fetch the chrism from his own bishop, and not from another, in person or through another priest, deacon or subdeacon.

A priest who anoints a baptized person with old chrism (save in case of necessity) is to be deposed: and therefore every day of the Lord's Supper[1] new chrism must be consecrated by the bishop and the old removed and burned.

Also both the holy oil and the chrism must be kept carefully under lock and key, lest a sacrilegious hand be able to reach them to do wicked things.

Note that in the time of a general interdict baptism and confirmation can

---

[1] i.e., Maundy Thursday.

lawfully be conferred both to adults and to infants,[1] *but not with the ringing of bells nor in a loud voice.*

Towards the end of the *Sarum Manual* is a section headed Blessings by bishops and suffragans, the first of these being entitled "The Confirmation of Children". In a manual intended for the use of parish priests one would not expect to find Confirmation included. Collins[2] cites an opinion that the episcopal blessings were included in the book in order to save the expense of printing a separate Pontifical for the use of bishops. Maskell, however,[3] argued that these blessings could with special permission be given by priests, and so were not out of place in a priest's book.

THE CONFIRMATION OF CHILDREN[4]

First let the bishop say:

> Our help.
> Let the name of the Lord, *etc.*
> The Lord be with you.
> And with thy spirit.

> Let us pray.[5]

G.95   Almighty and everlasting God who has vouchsafed to regenerate these thy servants (*or* these thine handmaids) by water and the Holy Ghost, and hast given unto them remission of all their sins, send upon them the sevenfold Holy Ghost, the Paraclete, from heaven. Amen.

The Spirit of wisdom and understanding. Amen.

The Spirit of knowledge and piety. Amen.

The Spirit of counsel and fortitude. ✠ Amen.

And fill them with the Spirit of the fear of the Lord. Amen.

And sign them with the sign of the holy cross ✠ and confirm them with the chrism of salvation unto life eternal. Amen.

G.96   *And then let the bishop ask the name and anoint his thumb with chrism: and*

---

[1] The minimum age for confirmation was now seven years in actual practice; but children of seven could still be called *parvuli*. (The *Manual* passes next to the Purification of Women, the order of Confirmation appearing, as we shall see, at a much later point in the book.)

[2] op. cit., p. 166n.   [3] *Monumenta Ritualia*, I, pp. cccvi–cccviii.
[4] Collins, op. cit., p. 167.   [5] *Gel.*, n. 451.

let him make on the forehead of the child a cross saying:

I sign thee N. with the sign of the cross ✠ and I confirm thee with the chrism of salvation, in the name of the Father ✠ and of the Son ✠ and of the Holy Ghost. ✠ Amen.

Peace be to thee.

Let us pray.

PRAYER

God who to thine apostles didst give the Holy Spirit and who didst wish him to be given through them to their successors and to the rest of the faithful people, look mercifully upon our humble family, and grant that the hearts of those whose foreheads we have anointed with holy chrism and signed with the sign of the holy cross the same Holy Spirit may come and make into a temple of his glory by vouchsafing to dwell therein. Through our Lord. In the unity of the same.

Behold, thus shall be blessed every man that feareth the Lord.

The Lord bless you out of Sion, that you may see the good things of Jerusalem all your days.

Almighty God bless you, the Father ✠ and the Son ✠ and the Holy Ghost. ✠ Amen.

Glossary

AGALLIELAION: a Greek word, meaning "oil of rejoicing". A similar term is *"hagielaion"*, meaning "holy oil". In the Coptic rite, the expressions are equivalent.

AGNILE: the meaning of this word in the *Liber Ordinum* is not clear. However, each baptistery had its own peculiarities of construction and design, and it is clear from the context that the *agnile* was the name given at Toledo to the place where the candidates were assembled before descending into the font.

AMBO: a raised platform from which the scriptures were read and other public parts of a service conducted.

CATECHUMEN: a person who had been admitted to the outer circle of the church, either formally by a rite of admission to the catechumenate (see for example The Rite of St Augustine) or informally. The Mass of the Catechumens was the first part of the Mass, to which catechumens were admitted: they were debarred from attending the Eucharist proper, which was reserved for baptized people only. Catechumens were known also as "hearers".

CHRISM: oil enriched with perfume, notably balsam. An equivalent Greek term is *muron*. The use of chrism tended to be reserved for more important occasions, particularly for Confirmation, that of oil for the less important occasions. But it will be noted that some writers appear to regard the two terms as equivalent.

CHRISMATION: generally, any application of chrism: particularly, the application of chrism in Confirmation: see "Consignation".

CHRISMON: the monogram of the name of Christ, consisting of the Greek letters *Chi Rho*. It was in this design that ashes were scattered upon a goatskin for the exorcisms in the scrutines at Milan, according to Beroldus.

COMPETENTES: catechumens who had put their names down at the beginning of Lent, requesting to be prepared for baptism at Easter, were known as *competentes*. By a local peculiarity, the term used at Rome was not *competentes*, but *electi*, elect.

CONSIGNATION: in the West, a term for Confirmation, administered by marking the sign of the cross in chrism (q.v.) on the candidate's forehead.

DIAKONIKA: those things in the Eastern rites which pertain to the part of the deacon: e.g., diaconal litanies.

EFFETA: in Spain, *Effetatio*. A form of the Hebrew *Ephphatha*, "Be thou opened". This term is used to refer to a rite, based on Mark 7.31ff, found in some Western rites.

ELECT, ELECTI: see *Competentes*.

EXSUFFLATION: a ceremony whereby the minister blew into the face of a candidate. This was understood as a mark of contempt for the devil. The term "insufflation" is sometimes used for the same thing. But insufflation can also denote a more gentle breathing into the face of the candidate, to symbolize the gift of the Holy Spirit (Bobbio 233).

GRADUS: a step, particularly of the ambo (q.v.) or at the altar.

MURON: see Chrism.

RETURN (of the Creed, Lord's Prayer): Latin, *Redditio Symboli*, etc. The ceremony at which the words of the Creed or Lord's Prayer were formally recited (returned) by the candidate.

SACRAMENT: this term is commonly used in a loose sense to denote any solemn action which was used in the preparation of candidates for baptism: e.g., "the sacrament of salt" was the common expression in Africa for the regular giving of salt to catechumens (q.v.).

SCRUTINY: originally this term referred especially to occasions in the final preparation of candidates for baptism when they were expected to endure severe exorcisms, in circumstances of some humiliation. There were three such occasions in the earlier Roman usage, less in some other places. John the Deacon however appears to suggest that advantage was taken of these occasions to scrutinize the extent to which candidates had profited by the instruction which they had received. At a later date again, the word tended to be used to refer to any assembly in preparation for baptism.

SYMBOL: Creed.

TRADITION (of the Creed, Lord's Prayer): Latin, *Traditio Symboli*, etc. The ceremony at which the words of the Creed (Symbol) or Lord's Prayer were formally made known to candidates.